THE SEEKER'S GUIDE TO HARRY POTTER

THE UNAUTHORIZED COURSE

First published by O Books, 2008
O Books is an imprint of John Hunt Publishing Ltd., The Bothy, Deershot Lodge, Park Lane, Ropley,
Hants, SO24 0BE, UK
office1@o-books.net
www.o-books.net

Distribution in:

UK and Europe
Orca Book Services
orders@orcabookservices.co.uk
Tel: 01202 665432 Fax: 01202 666219
Int. code (44)

USA and Canada
NBN
custserv@nbnbooks.com
Tel: 1 800 462 6420 Fax: 1 800 338 4550

Australia and New Zealand
Brumby Books
sales@brumbybooks.com.au
Tel: 61 3 9761 5535 Fax: 61 3 9761 7095

Far East (offices in Singapore, Thailand,
Hong Kong, Taiwan)
Pansing Distribution Pte Ltd
kemal@pansing.com
Tel: 65 6319 9939 Fax: 65 6462 5761

South Africa
Alternative Books
altbook@peterhyde.co.za
Tel: 021 555 4027 Fax: 021 447 1430

Text copyright Geo Athena Trevarthen 2008

Design: Stuart Davies

ISBN: 978 1 84694 093 4

A CIP catalogue record for this book is available
from the British Library.

Printed in the US by Maple Vail

O Books operates a distinctive and ethical publishing philosophy in
all areas of its business, from its global network of authors to
production and worldwide distribution.
No trees were cut down to print this particular book. The paper is
100% recycled, with 50% of that being post-consumer. It's processed
chlorine-free, and has no fibre from ancient or endangered forests.
This production method on this print run saved approximately
thirteen trees, 4,000 gallons of water, 600 pounds of solid waste,
990 pounds of greenhouse gases and 8 million BTU of energy. On its
publication a tree was planted in a new forest that O Books is
sponsoring at The Village www.thefourgates.com

THE SEEKER'S GUIDE TO HARRY POTTER

THE UNAUTHORIZED COURSE

GEO ATHENA TREVARTHEN, PHD

BOOKS

Winchester, UK
Washington, USA

*Dr. Geo Trevarthen has produced what I have to call a magical work —
scholarly but not boring, spiritual but not restricting, enlightening
without being stuffy; in short, a rewarding read for anyone who may have
wondered what was behind the Harry Potter phenomenon and why it
reaches so deeply into our core beings. I urge you to shout, "Accio The
Seeker's Guide to Harry Potter" ... I guarantee you a mind and heart
opening experience awaits.* **Roy Bauer,** DD, CSC, founder and
director: The Circle of the Sacred Earth

*Written with fluency and vigour, this represents a very interesting and
unusual way of relating J. K. Rowling's work to wider issues concerning
the nature of magic, the lived imagination and the experience of alternative states of consciousness.* **Ronald J Hutton,** Professor of History
at the University of Bristol, UK

CONTENTS

TO FOUR LADIES WHO BRING MAGIC INTO

MY LIFE

MY MOTHER ATHENA

MY SISTER KATY

AND MY DAUGHTERS TEA AND AURORA

AND TO A LADY WHO'S BROUGHT

MORE MAGIC INTO ALL OUR LIVES

JK ROWLING

I

ACKNOWLEDGEMENTS

he solitary occupation of writing is made much easier and more pleasant with others' help. I'll try to give thanks in some kind of order. First, I want to thank JK Rowling for writing such inspiring and engaging books. They were a great comfort to me at a difficult time and have also obviously given me a lot of food for thought.

Next, I'd like to thank Graham Venters, whose enthusiasm for *Harry Potter* and confidence in my approach led to this rather unorthodox class being taught at the University of Edinburgh's Office of Lifelong Learning. Next, to Jim Mooney who took over as my programmer there. A great big thanks to all my students for many stimulating discussions, including the post *Hallows* debriefing at the Spiegeltent. Special thanks to Sarah Kalnay, Shani MacInnes, Leanne Mattu, Susie McBay and Andy Shepherd. I also want to thank all my other students for their interest and support over the years and for waiting with patience, yet enthusiasm, for a book from me! Particular thanks go to Christine Thomas and Nadine Pettry for being great students and friends.

I'm extremely grateful to my publisher John Hunt for his instant enthusiasm for this book and patience in seeing the final product—not to mention for giving me a positive experience of the publishing industry! Thanks are also due to Trevor Greenfield, who alchemically distilled a rather large lump of *prima materia* into a manageable book.

I'd also like to thank everyone who read and commented on this book as a work in progress and later. Many thanks to Ronald

Hutton for dedicating some of his lunch hours to giving me insightful, well informed and supportive commentary. Thanks to Roy Bauer for his enthusiasm as a Harry fan, shaman, minister and friend. Thanks to David Lorimer for his interest and support, as well as for past inspiration. My gratitude to Neil Douglas-Klotz for the concept of 'caravan time' and insights into Christian mysticism that have inspired me for ages. Many thanks also to Lon Milo Duquette for corresponding with me at a very busy time and for offering insights into magical theory and practice in his books that inspired some of my thoughts on Harry in this book. Thanks also to Genevieve Chilvers for her inspiring presence and input on my writing. Thanks to Ronald Black for sending helpful references and to him and Professor William Gillies for mentoring me through my last little writing project.

Thanks to Aisling Willow Grey for her friendship and work on my web site. Gratitude to Rudy and Sharon Bauer for being great mentors in spiritual and psychological realms. Thanks to John Douglass for helping me develop my writing skills and to Bill Newman and Scip Barnhart for artistic mentoring. Thanks to Bill Dutterer for creatively supporting me, for his artwork and for his work helping children in Afghanistan. I also want to thank the Princess Grace Foundation for early support that still encourages me in my writing today.

Last but not least, of course, I want to thank my family, first my two grandmothers, Erszébet and Lavinia, who, each in their own way, gave me access to a world of magic and creativity. My Dad, Professor George Mueller, gave me insights into the broadest possible scientific world-view. They've never left me. Love and thanks to my Aunt Susan, for being an inspiration in so many ways. Deepest love and gratitude to my mum, Athena, who's made everything possible. Thanks to Katy for unfailing love and support—and last minute *Harry Potter* American edition page references! Thanks also to my two little ones, Téa and Aurora, who inspired me on trips to the park and slept next to me while I typed with my laptop on a plant stand next to the bed at five in the morning. Thanks to my husband David for finding the plant stand, for providing a morning thermos of coffee to aid awareness and for all his other help.

WHILE THERE IS CONSIDERABLE GLAMOUR ATTACHED TO THE POSITION OF SEEKER, FOR THEY ARE TRADITIONALLY THE BEST FLYERS ON THE PITCH, THEY ARE USUALLY THE PLAYERS WHO RECEIVE THE WORST INJURIES.

KENNILWORTHY WHISP

THE THIRSTY SEEK WATER, BUT WATER ALSO SEEKS THE THIRSTY.

JALAL AL-DIN AL-RUMI

SEEK AND YE SHALL FIND.

MATTHEW 7.7

V

INTRODUCTION

ovels are of the place they're written, in one way or another. The students at the University of Edinburgh class I taught on Harry Potter had the fun of discussing Harry and his magical world in the city, and even the cafés, where JK Rowling wrote his story. It was easy to think of Hogwarts as we looked out at Edinburgh Castle and the spires of Heriot's very grand school from the Elephant House Café.

Broomsticks and magical animals aside, Harry and his friends could equip and dress themselves nearly as well in Edinburgh as at Diagon Alley. Robe-makers Ede and Ravenscroft, whose web site proclaims "300 years of ceremonial dress," sell to royalty, academics and others. The Old Town's hilly, cobbled streets have sellers of Goth, antique and 'wyrd' and wonderful magical goods. Huge art and seasonal festivals mean you may come out of a Harry Potter film to see a parade of giant illuminated owls and dragons, led by a Gypsy band who could have walked out of Hogsmeade in top hats and brocades.

Robert Louis Stevenson wrote a description in 1879 that's still recognizable. He said that, "This profusion of eccentricities, this dream in masonry and living rock, is not a drop-scene in a theatre, but a city in the world of every-day reality."[1] A plaque by Edinburgh castle in memory of those executed there for witch-craft made it an especially appropriate locale for the penultimate Harry Potter book release event. A local historian even thinks that the castle hill was a site for goddess worship and Arthurian myth in ancient times.[2] We came full circle with an event celebrating a myth-making lady's work!

The Harry Potter books do serve as myths for many of us, on all the levels at which myth functions. They're wonderfully entertaining, they give us models for behavior and they speak of the deeper meanings in life that all seekers are looking for.

This book is based on the course I taught at the University of Edinburgh and draws from many different sources to bring you new insights into our favorite hero and his world. When I first began reading *Harry Potter*, I found that the novels echoed ideas I grew up with in a family tradition of Scottish and Irish shamanism, as well as themes that came up in my PhD research at Edinburgh. I'll refer to some hard to find sources, like the writings of actual wizards and alchemists that the books refer to, such as Flamel and Paracelsus.

However, this is a 'Seeker's Guide' not a 'Scholar's Guide!' I've focussed on layers of meaning in the books that give us the deepest applicable insights into life. I've tried to do this in a way that's suitable for seekers of any or no particular spiritual persuasion and requires no previous knowledge. We'll look at what JK Rowling says that she put into the books, as well as what we may take out of them. Because they resonate with so many mythic and spiritual themes we'll each have our own responses.

A MARAUDER'S MAP TO THIS BOOK

To give you a taste of what some of these themes may be, here's a brief chapter outline. I'll say up front that, as I'll be looking at all seven books, there will be 'spoilers.' If you haven't finished them all I encourage you to do so before reading further.

In what follows, I'll generally use *Harry Potter*, italicized, to refer to the book series as a whole, and 'Harry' to refer to him as a character. I'll use single words to refer to books in the series: *Stone* for the first book, *Chamber* for the second, *Azkaban* for the third, *Goblet* for the fourth, *Phoenix*, *Prince*, and *Hallows*, for the final books, all italicized.

I. BEGINNING: A LETTER IN GREEN INK

Harry's adventure really began with his Hogwarts letter, and ours began with reading his story. We'll start by looking at the books as literature and at the phenomenon, as well as discussing some of the basic ideas about magic and spirituality that frame this book.

II. BETWIXT AND BETWEEN AT PLATFORM 9 ¾

One of these ideas is that we can enter different realities, as Harry enters the wizarding world at Diagon Alley and platform 9 ¾. Here we'll look at how the 'Three Hallows' relate to three kinds of consciousness that we can experience: happiness, sorrow and the state of spiritual awareness that can help us deal with the first two most constructively.

III. FOUR HOUSES, FOUR ELEMENTS

This chapter explores the elemental associations of the Hogwarts houses and traditional esoteric precepts. To Know (Ravenclaw, air), to Will (Slytherin, water), to Dare (Gryffindor, fire), and to keep Silent, (Hufflepuff, earth.). We'll reflect on how these qualities operate in our own lives and what our own allocated House might be.

IV. THROUGH THE MAZE: HEROIC JOURNEYS

Just as the four Hogwarts houses validate different abilities, various characters' stories explore the different types of heroism. We'll see where mothers, fathers and redeemed villains go on their journeys, as well as prominent seekers in the novels like Draco, Cedric, Ginny, Regulus and Harry. We'll also have a look at the symbolism of Quidditch.

V. THE ART

Hermione is named for Hermes, patron deity of the 'Hermetic Arts' that include alchemy and magic. JK Rowling admitted to studying vast amounts of alchemy early on. We'll see how the principles of 'natural magic' in the books apply to life and how alchemical stages tell us a lot about our inner lives.

VI. THE TERRIBLE AND THE GREAT

From the patronus to the Dementors, from Harry's goodness to the bit of badness lodged within him, from the terrible power of love, to the great love inherent in terrible sacrifices, JK Rowling confronts us with many 'terrible greats' and 'great terribles.' So does life. Here we'll look at how we can begin to understand and cope with them.

VII. USING THE PHILOSOPHER'S STONE

The myriad debates about how the series would, and ultimately did, end, raises the larger question of what makes a good ending in art or life? Here we discuss what attaining the philosopher's stone (the ultimate spiritual goal, as expressed in alchemy) might actually mean. (It was re-named the 'sorcerer's stone' in the American edition of the first book.)

The chapters are followed by endnotes containing references and notes numbered by each chapter, a bibliography with full details of all the sources I refer to and a section on further resources, including suggested readings, books and web sites.

Well, there you have it. As you can see, there's more to the *Harry Potter* novels than meets the eye. Harry reminds us of legends of long ago. We need him, and other shared myths and symbols, but Harry doesn't simply echo them, he revitalizes them, as he does at the end of *Hallows*. Using the ring concealed in the golden snitch, he raises the benevolent spirits of ancestors and teachers, reviving ancient symbols to live anew.

The snitch itself is an easy example. You 'read' the golden snitch on this book's cover with a wealth of narrative associations from *Harry Potter*. Yet the associations don't stop with him, but re-invoke older symbols and ideas. I sculpted the 'golden snitch' pictured on the cover over fifteen years ago. You'll see it in a more traditional form on the epigram page at the start of this book. It symbolized the Egyptian deity, Horus, the young son of the widowed mother goddess, Isis, who also defeated his father's murderer. Other traditions saw it as the symbol of a perfected soul, or of the choice to live a righteous life.

Harry's story can tell us a lot about making choices and about much more besides. We all play the seeker in the game we're given. We seek love, wisdom, spiritual experience, survival, safety, excitement and fun. Harry's story can guide us on the quest.

GEO ATHENA TREVARTHEN
SCOTLAND, 7TH JULY 2007

I

BEGINNING: A LETTER IN GREEN INK

He looked out over the ocean and felt closer, this dawn, than ever before, closer to the heart of it all.
JK Rowling

The spirit has its homeland, which is the realm of the meaning of things.
Antoine de Saint Exupéry

arry's adventures in the world of wizards began with words on a page, his invitation to Hogwarts. This is also, of course, where *we* began with Harry! Harry didn't know that he was a wizard until he got his letter in green ink from Hogwarts. He only knew that every once in a while, something unusual happened to him. If we're honest, most of us can say the same. There are experiences in life that point us to a bigger reality, or at least make us wonder if one exists.

Others may think we're crazy for doing so. They don't want us to open that letter under any circumstances. The Dursleys would have had a nasty turn just looking at the green ink, even before they realized the letter was from Hogwarts. It's well known as the color 'loonies' use to write to newspapers! Blue black on ivory only please.

Whatever color their ink, words on paper open us to bigger realities. Great books don't just pass the time; they bring a greater sense of meaning to our lives. They tell us things about the world and ourselves.

The *Harry Potter* phenomenon has a lot to teach seekers of all kinds, even before we get to the books. The phenomenon itself tells us much about what many of us lack and the books say a lot about how to fill our cultural and personal voids, how we can enter a realm of greater magic and meaning.

In his book on fairy tales, *The Uses of Enchantment*, the child psychologist Bruno Bettelheim said that children wouldn't need special help if they were raised so that life was meaningful to them. Children find meaning through relationships, through their culture and through literature, especially if the first two don't provide what they need.[1] Literature also works for the rest of us! Fairy tales are a type of story, or genre, that tells us a lot about our inner problems and their solutions.[2] *Harry Potter* updates the fairy tale and fantasy, anchoring it in the real world.

JK Rowling uses many engaging literary devices to draw us in, fusing the boarding school story with the fantasy, and blending together two literary genres. Harry is a complex character, both loner and leader, outlaw and redeemer. There is the camaraderie of the group, the loyal war band promoting the ethics of virtue, courage, passion, friendship and humor. There is the eternal struggle and eventual triumph of good over evil, the battles that are lost and the war that is won.

Yet there's far more to it than that, because the play and the players that strut Rowling's stage do so against a greater social backdrop of a sense of loss, disenchantment and insecurity. In truth, Harry Potter has been so successful because our lives often seem empty and meaningless. We feel lost. In fact we have done for centuries, having lost our deep connections with the family, community, tribe and the natural world. We've lost our values of loyalty and integrity and lost our overall relationship with myth, magic and meaning. The *Harry Potter* books celebrate those lost values, but, more than that, they offer ways of recovering them.

From the death of his parents when he was a baby to his ten

years of loveless exile in suburbia living with his aunt and uncle, Harry is the very archetype of loss. Even after his initial rescue and time spent at Hogwarts he still returns to live with them during vacations, experiencing boredom, frustration and emotional neglect. However, despite, or perhaps because of, all his setbacks, Harry finds everything we often lack in our own existences: love, courage and a passionate engagement with life. This comes from his parents' transcendent love, his friends' tangible love, his own efforts and a magical world-view that implicitly acknowledges creation's wholeness. All these things bring Harry enough comfort and meaning to carry on, to play the seeker in the game he's been given.

If the *Harry Potter* series' only good point was showing us something of how to fill our cultural and personal voids, it would be enough and it would make them worthy of deeper reading, by fans and scholars alike. Yet some critics still march to the beat of an elitist drum... high and popular culture are two different animals and scholars are expected to steer clear of *Harry Potter* because popular culture isn't proper culture and doesn't deserve a second glance, let alone serious contemplation. Giselle Anatol made a good response to this when introducing Reading *Harry Potter*, a collection of critical essays. "I would argue", she contended "that it is exactly because the series has become so wildly popular that it is both critically significant and should be taken quite seriously."[3]

Ostensibly children's fiction, the books have transcended the barriers of age, appealing to young children, teenagers and adults. The Harry Potter novels were the first children's books to be offered with 'adult' covers, so grown-ups could read them on the train without embarrassment. Yet adult fans needn't be embarrassed. On one level, the books are simply great reads. Books exist to entertain as well as enrich us. Yet these books also have deeper symbolic levels that resonate with us in many ways.

Like pebbles thrown into a stream The Harry Potter novels have created immediate impacts followed by ripples of influence radiating out. The ripples intersect in various ways with each other, and with the flow of the stream.

The magic of Harry, like all deep magic, is about wholeness. It's about the flow of being, mystery and meaning, where ripples of influence cross each other, in Harry's world and ours. As I'll discuss throughout this book, the novels unite mythic themes from the past with diverse literary genres of the present and aspirations for right action in the future. They contain symbols and situations that echo those found in a host of ancient traditions.

We can read symbols in different ways at different times. Many spiritual traditions use symbols in their art and myths in multi-layered ways. The novice begins with one level of meaning, perhaps the moral of the tale. In time, they get another level of meaning, maybe more psychological, moving on to magical, mystical, devotional and cosmological levels; and these levels have levels of their own. That's one reason why myths bear repeated retellings. For many people the Harry Potter stories function as contemporary myths with their focus seeming to shift as our own perspectives change. So it is when we look at their deeper layers of meaning, we find a modern mythos where the whole is much more than the sum of its parts.

Many themes in the novels appear in Pagan, Christian, and other spiritual traditions. They're part of the perennial wisdom, a thread of knowledge that grows anew in many ages and traditions. One aspect of these traditions that I'll discuss in detail is magic. Most traditional cultures that practice magic see it as morally neutral, similar to using like fire or electricity. This is just how it appears in the Harry Potter novels. The books depict no gods or devils, just young wizards and witches of different cultures who may be of any religious persuasion or none, learning to use a natural force.

Many books have catalogued and explored specific symbols and mythic and magical themes in the novels.[4] Religious books have tended to be vehemently for or against Harry. Most either claim Harry as a Christian hero or revile him as the devil's poster boy.[5] I hope to do a bit of bridge building, recognizing Harry's broader spiritual resonance while acknowledging the religious elements in the tales. I intend to show that the lines between high magic and religion can be quite blurry in the novels, as in the real world.

Let's step away from the spiritual side for a moment to look at Harry's impact in the Muggle world. Anecdotal reports and studies have shown the series' effect on children's reading habits. *The Kids and Family Reading Report* (in conjunction with Scholastic, the books' American publisher) released a survey finding that 51% of Harry Potter readers between the ages of five to seventeen said that they did not read books for fun before they started reading Harry Potter. The study further reported that according to 65% of children and 76% of parents, the children's performance in school had improved since they started reading the series.[6]

Prince sold just shy of seven million copies in America on the first day. *Hallows* had a record first print run of twelve million in America alone, and sold there at a rate of five thousand copies a minute in the first few days of its release. Before this final book, the other six in the series had collectively sold more than three hundred and twenty-five million copies, and had been translated into more than sixty languages. JK Rowling is now the richest author in history.[7] Why do the books appeal to such a wide range of ages and nationalities? JK Rowling has responded that it's for others to say, and people have come up with a variety of answers.[8]

Andrew Blake, the Head of Cultural Studies at King Alfred's College and critic for the *Independent* newspaper, looked at the novels in the context of late 90s Britain. He also examined some of the broader issues the novels raise in the areas of literary criticism, sociology and commercialization. In *The Irresistible Rise of Harry Potter*, he wrote that J. K. Rowling's creation hit the spot "by addressing many of the anxieties in our changing political and cultural world." The first book came out in 1997, the year Tony Blair was elected as Prime Minister of the United Kingdom. The same year, the think tank, Demos, argued that Britain was too stuck in the past.[9]

On the surface, a book about a boarding school founded in the 11th century for wizards could be seen as going against the flow of 'cool Britannia,' a widely embraced catch phrase of the time. However, it ended up being much 'cooler' and more popular than other cultural exports of the time.

So why was this series universally popular at the close of the 20th century and the start of the 21st? The idea that it's down to hype is an easy answer. The first book had no hype and a five hundred copy initial print run. Unusually for today, the Harry Potter phenomenon isn't a product of commercial hype but of communication between child and adult fans via word of mouth and web sites. Anyone going to *The Leaky Cauldron, Mugglenet, The Pensieve, The Harry Potter Lexicon* or the encyclopedic *Accio-Quote* web sites, among others, will appreciate the vast amounts of work and time the web masters and fans put into discussing and promoting the Boy Who Lived. An article in *Advertising Age* reported that:

> Two-thirds of kids eight to eighteen have read at least one in author JK Rowling's series of Potter books, properties that initially arrived with little of the fanfare we've come to associate with new book titles. A generation that has been marketed to its entire life birthed its own buzz, took ownership of the Potter brand and declared it genuine... Harry grew organically, and it is the purity of these origins that created real equity for the brand.[10]

It's worth noting that JK Rowling dislikes the term 'property.'[11] It's also worth noting that despite the 'gushy' tone of the piece in describing the non-commercial growth of the phenomenon, it can't avoid using terms like 'brand' and 'equity.' The difficulty our culture now has describing anything without using monetary terms is a big issue very much in the foreground of the Harry Potter phenomenon. 'Social capital' used to be a natural part of family or neighborly life, like taking care of granny, or getting some cat food for old Mrs. Figg. Caring for each other was once such a part of life that it wasn't specifically named as a thing in its own right. Now it's couched in monetary terms and we scarcely know how to speak of it otherwise. This is part of what I mean by saying that the *Harry Potter* phenomenon draws attention to our cultural voids.

JK Rowling is deeply concerned with social justice. She worked for Amnesty International before she found herself living with a small child at the pointy end of inequality. She spoke about her experience in her introduction to the book *One City*. This was a collection of stories to benefit the Edinburgh charity of the same name, which works to lessen social and economic divisions.

She arrived in Edinburgh in 1993 to spend Christmas at her sister's home after her marriage ended in Portugal. She had gone to Portugal in part to get over her mother's early death from multiple sclerosis, and a later burglary in which she'd lost everything her mother had left her. This succession of traumas makes it easy to see why loss is such a big theme in the books. She ended up staying in Edinburgh. She'd follow along behind her daughter, toddling around the nourishing beauty of Princes Street Gardens and the grand museums. She wrote in cafés while her baby napped. Edinburgh is so beautiful that it's possible to forget you're poor for a while when sitting in a café, writing, even if you're nursing a cold cup of coffee.

Some of the series' popularity lies in the fact that a story which she wrote partly for her own escapist comfort gives the same comfort to others. When Scholastic bought the book in America, Arthur Levine paid the unusually large sum of $100,000 for it. He later said that what he loved most about the story was "The idea of growing up unappreciated, feeling outcast and then this great satisfaction of being discovered."[12]

Of course, JK Rowling is now no stranger to this experience. She secured an agent, Christopher Little, chosen because she liked the name. He said that this magical boarding school novel was perceived as not very politically correct, which made it a hard book to sell. She endured rejection, and finally sold the first book to Bloomsbury.

Initial reviews praised *Stone* highly, saying, "Rowling's ability to put a fantastic spin on sports, student rivalry and eccentric faculty contributes to the humor, charm and delight of her utterly captivating story."[13] *Stone* won the Nestle Smarties Book Prize, the Federation of Children's Books Group Award and the British Book Awards Children's Book of the Year.

Lots of people would like to have written a book. Few actually write one, or go through the often-frustrating experience of getting it in print. JK Rowling's success goes well beyond what hard work brings most of us, yet, if she hadn't put in the work, Harry would still only be in her head. As the old saying goes, we can do more than achieve success; we can be worthy of it.

There is, of course, much more to the novels than wish fulfillment fantasies. In a 2007 article, *Chicago Tribune* critic Judith Keller said that *Hallows* was less about clever plotting than about engaging the reader in a contemplation of life's big questions. She asked us to consider "the touchstones of the beginning and ending of the series, and all that lies between:" The first book came out in the year of Princess Diana's death in 1997. The decade between the first and last books saw major terrorist attacks and divisiveness caused by the invasions of Afghanistan and Iraq. The negative implications of globalization and global warming became much clearer. In short, "the books' life-span corresponds with an ominous and unsettling swath of world history, a time of confusion and unrest and instability." Paradoxically, the books gave us escapist relief from the darkness of the times even while enabling us to face their challenges.

One writer described their "glittering mystery and nail-biting suspense, compelling language and colorful imagery, magical feats juxtaposed with real-life concerns."[14] Another reason for the books' success is that "the books operate on many levels, with many layers of meaning."[15] Some critics, by contrast, ascribe a very specific and limited range of meaning to the novels. They say that Rowling has written a formulaic fairy story or simple morality tale. Others say that there are sinister subtexts lurking, encouraging children to practice witchcraft or (heaven forbid!) question authority.

There are definitely subtexts and direct messages to be found. Yet, while JK Rowling has said that Dumbledore often speaks for her, the books are nothing as boring as morality driven tomes. She doesn't drum in lessons. Rather, "her books get their depth from a combination of allegory and genuine human interactions that haven't been pre-chewed. She lets her characters learn from their mistakes (or fail to do so)."[16] Ms. Rowling has said she writes for the enjoyment of storytelling, not to deliver messages.[17]

Most of the layers of meaning we'll encounter throughout this book aren't the overt ones, but the deeper levels. The books, like myths, resonate on symbolic levels that have built in constellations of meaning. You can't pepper books with unicorns, three headed dogs, alchemical symbols and archetypes without invoking all their associated meanings.

The psychologist Carl Gustav Jung defined archetypes as "definite forms in the psyche which seem to be present always and everywhere."[18] We experience various figures in our lives as archetypes. A father, for example, is both a personal father and symbolically represents the universal positive and negative qualities of father figures. Harry's parents, and others in the book, work as archetypes as well as characters. As the *New Yorker* critic, Joan Acocella said, "Rowling's books are chock-a-block with archetypes, and she doesn't just use them; she glories in them, post-modernly."[19]

A clear example of JK Rowling's conscious use of symbolism is the way she uses prime numbers. These numbers, only divisible by themselves and one, were held to have spiritual significance in ancient times because of their indestructible quality. JK Rowling divided her narrative into seven, a number deemed sacred from the Sumerians forward. She's said that she used the number seven for its symbolic significance. Ginny is the Weasley's seventh child and only daughter. Various folk traditions believe that the seventh child (sometimes the seventh child of a seventh child) has particular spiritual abilities. There are seven players on a Quidditch team. Of particular importance is the fact that some alchemists believed that making the philosopher's stone was a seven-stage process.

The symbol of seven was built into pyramids, a square base with triangular sides. Some say that this represents the union of matter represented by the square on the ground, with spirit represented by the triangles of the sides pointing to the heavens. It was also built into Sumerian seven level ziggurats and held in the idea of the mystical seven pillars of wisdom. The sacred seven hasn't gone away. We arrange weeks into seven days, which brings up an important point. Seven, like other sacred numbers, wasn't just assigned sanctity, but was felt to be sacred because of how it appeared in the natural world. The ancients saw seven visible planets in the solar system, including the sun and moon, which give us the days of the week.

There are many other examples of the use of prime numbers in the novels. Philip Nel discusses the way that the use of prime numbers subtly introduce "the novel's themes of magic and the supernatural," in his *Reader's Guide* to the books.[20] For example, the wizard's monetary system relies on primes, seventeen silver sickles to a galleon and twenty-nine knuts to a sickle. Harry's wand is eleven inches, as was his fathers, and he pays seven galleons for it. He goes to Hogwarts aged eleven.

While JK Rowling's use of prime numbers is deliberate, it's hard to say how much of her other symbolism is. Some obviously comes from research but some may have arisen from instinct and inspiration; symbols take on a life of their own. This can manifest through what the Jung termed synchronicity, or meaningful 'coincidence.'

Rowling gives us an example of synchronicity when she describes assigning wands to her characters on her web site. She says that she chose holly and yew as symbolically appropriate wand woods for Harry and Voldemort. Holly is said to repel evil. In Celtic tradition holly can represent the warrior's quality of flexible strength. People used to make bow shafts from it.[21] There are also its Christian associations with the crown of thorns and the blood of Christ. The holly berries are out at Christmas, and so it has to do with the midwinter child hero of the new sun. There were a number of these heroes before Christ. The Roman deity Mithras was also born on December 25th.

Yews predominate in churchyards and are probably the oldest living beings in Europe, up to six thousand years old. There's a very ancient yew tree in Fortingall not too far from Edinburgh. Because of how they grow they never actually need to die. They grow out from a central trunk, sending shoots down from their branches. When that central trunk dies, the outer growth stays alive. Ultimately they form a huge circular 'grove' which is actually one tree. It's easy to see the horcrux symbolism in this 'one who is many' tree. It would be hard to put a better wand in the hands of someone who seeks physical immortality than yew and phoenix feather.[22]

Some time after JK Rowling assigned these wands, she found a description of a Celtic tree calendar.[23] Rowling says she found that "Entirely by coincidence, I had assigned Harry the 'correct' wood for his day of birth. I therefore decided to give Ron and Hermione Celtic wand woods, too."[24] Ron ended up with ash and Hermione, vine.

Of course, insights and archetypes aren't enough. A novelist must craft their inspirations and images into a story. JK Rowling is a master craftswoman. Like Jane Austen, who Rowling admires, she's not a show off. You don't notice her writing, but, as the books draw you in, you find that she has served her story so well that you don't notice it's a story. As Philip Nel observes, "The greatness of both Austen and Rowling lies in the subtlety and dexterity with which they set their plots in motion. Their novels reward the careful reader and encourage rereading: apparently minor details frequently turn out to have larger significance."[25]

Yet Rowling's craft isn't simply a matter of clever plotting. Returning for a moment to the Jane Austen comparison, the well-known author, Virginia Woolf said that Austen is a mistress of "much deeper emotion than appears on the surface. What she offers is, apparently, a trifle, yet it is composed of something that expands in the reader's mind and endows with the most enduring form of life scenes which are outwardly trivial."[26]

JK Rowling is likewise a master craftsman of much deeper layers of emotion and meaning than appears on the surface. There are obvious strands of meaning that relate to the perennial wisdom of many spiritual traditions and she draws also from more obscure hermetic sources, that is, sources that reflect the wisdom of Hermione's namesake, Hermes, the patron of magic and alchemy. In a 1998 interview she said:

"I've never wanted to be a witch, but an alchemist, now that's a different matter. To invent this wizard world, I've learned a ridiculous amount about alchemy. Perhaps much of it I'll never use in the books, but I have to know in detail what magic can and cannot do in order to set the parameters and establish the stories' internal logic."[27]

Symbols, archetypes and mythic themes teach by resonance. They affect us on deep levels. That's why myths bear repeated retellings and maybe that's why so many feel compelled to reread Harry Potter, yet feel at a loss to explain precisely why.

JK Rowling has created her own myth. Her life has become the kind of Cinderella story she wrote and her efforts to bring happy endings for others from her own success through charitable works make it a vastly larger achievement. She's waved a wand and brought all sorts of things into being, for herself and others.

She said that entering the Great Hall on the set of the first film felt like walking into her own head. She went on to describe being shown the chamber where Quirrell faces Harry at the end. She said, "There was a spooky, spooky moment when I was stood in front of the Mirror of Erised seeing myself, of course, exactly as I am, and you know what that means in the book. And so I was seeing myself as a successful, published author. Wow, so that was a very, almost embarrassingly symbolic moment, you can imagine."[28]

It's hard not to see magic here. We don't need to *practice* magic to *work* magic, to will something that we want to happen through less than obvious means. To declare, and mysteriously fill, a void. We may term it an answered prayer, a miracle, a synchronicity, or a coincidence, but we've all had at least one experience of this sort.

Harry Potter's popularity is partly about wish fulfillment, but even here there's a deeper truth. We all hope that we're more than we think we are, and we all hope that this will become apparent one day. The first statement is true, the second can be. It's mostly up to us, and firstly, to our perceptions of reality.

II

BETWIXT AND BETWEEN AT PLATFORM 9 ¾

Of course it is happening inside your head, Harry, but why on earth should it mean that it is not real?
Dumbledore

It was not my rational consciousness that brought me to an understanding of the fundamental laws of the universe.
Albert Einstein

wanted to cheer when I read Dumbledore's words in *Hallows*. Of course, they're actually JK Rowling's words, but I can't help but think of them as Dumbledore's. Great characters tend to take on a life of their own, for the author and for the readers. JRR Tolkien, author of *Lord of the Rings*, said that he was as surprised as Frodo to meet Strider at the Inn, and had no idea who he was at first. Only later did he realize that he was actually Aragorn, a central figure in the fellowship of the ring and heir to Gondor's throne. Similarly, Lothlorien and the Mines of Moria were just names until he came there. The 'sacred seven' featured in Tolkien's imaginings as well as Rowling's. The "seven stars, seven stones and one white tree" of Gondor had run through his mind long before he knew what they were.[1]

This is very much how JK Rowling describes discovering Harry. He just "made his appearance". She'd never felt such excitement.

I didn't know then that it was going to be a book for children.

I just knew that I had this boy, Harry. During that journey I also discovered Ron, Nearly Headless Nick, Hagrid and Peeves... It was a question of discovering why Harry was where he was, why his parents were dead. I was inventing it but it felt like research.[2]

This brings up the whole question of what is real. Our reality isn't the same when dreaming as it is when reading *Harry Potter*, or having a walk or a quarrel. Falling in love creates an alternate reality where we see the world, as well as our beloved, as especially delightful through the eyes of love. Ms. Rowling evokes the state well when Harry falls for Cho, then Ginny.

Harry Potter treats alternate realities in various ways. The first is simply the classic fantasy genre approach of making the alternate physically real. All the unicorns, giants and acromantulas are physical creatures. There are, however, alternates within this alternate reality. Harry often enters the alternate reality of dreams, like we all do. He dreams of Voldemort, beginning with childhood dreams of flashes of green light and flying motorcycles, moving to vague dreams involving Quirrell's turban, to the revelatory or disastrously deceptive visions in the later books. He also sees visions of Voldemort's activities during waking hours.

His use of his father's invisibility cloak is a more symbolic treatment of alternate realities. It alters other people's reality by making him invisible to them. It's also symbolic of entering alternate realities to gain knowledge, as shamans do. Its relationship to the other two Deathly Hallows tells us some very interesting things about the use of alternate states.

I prefer the terms 'alternate realities' and 'alternate states' to 'altered' because 'altered' implies that there is one normal state of consciousness and all others are deviations from it.[3] But there are many possible and equally 'normal' states of consciousness. On a basic level, the *Harry Potter* novels illustrate the very real truth that the person sitting next to us on the train may have an entirely different belief system, may in fact, live in a very 'different world' from our own. Most Western countries now even have large alternate 'wizarding' communities of various sorts, from Wiccans to shamans, ritual magicians and even practicing alchemists.

Other world-views don't need to have anything to do with the supernatural, of course. Social and political conflicts around the world often come from a basic failure to imagine how others might think differently. Dominant cultures tend to frame everything from their own point of reference. They may think that the 'other' would only attack them because they are 'jealous' of that culture's way of life. The 'other' may, in fact, want nothing to do with it, and attack because it is being foisted upon them. They may be no more jealous than wizards are of Muggles, or than the Dursleys are of wizards. The poverty of imagination that characterizes such exchanges often has disastrous results.

World-views also change with age, with mental state, even with the time of day. From *Goblet* on, Harry's innocence is gone. Harry becomes capable of dealing with more as he grows, but also goes through phases of fury, denial and sorrow. Think about how your own world-view has changed over your life, or even how it changes each day. How differently do you view a challenge at your personal best or worst time of day? Are you all doom and gloom before the first cup of coffee? Do problems seem bigger late at night? It's good to remember that there are always alternate ways to view anything—if you can 'put yourself in someone else's shoes' and imagine their point of view for a moment. For example, have you ever seen anything that you'd count as evidence for UFO's *if you believed* that we are being visited by beings from other planets? Many people have. Our beliefs don't just frame our realities. They create them.[4] The 'placebo effect,' the way that sugar pills cure a certain percentage of people in clinical trials, is a case in point. It demonstrates the

magical principle that mind can affect matter.

Discussion of alternate realities inevitably brings us to shamanism, the oldest branch of magic we know of. Shamanism is an ancient body of techniques for bringing the self into connection with sacred and magical realms of experience. Harry's shamanic ancestors relied on alternate approaches to reality. In fact, all of our ancestors relied on them. All cultures seem to have practicing shamans if you go back far enough.

Experience of alternate realities brings knowledge. The very words witch and wizard connote a sense of personal knowledge that we can call shamanic. This can be knowledge of the sacred, or knowledge of the day to day. Shamanic cultures tend to draw far fewer distinctions between these realms. They sanctify daily activities like fire lighting with prayer and ritual, and bring an earthy practicality to their spirituality, much as Dumbledore does. One quality that Harry shares with shamans is his reliance on insight and instinct rather than on rote learning. You are your own best 'expert' on consciousness. We can all experience a kind of 'betwixt and between' reality that isn't real like a brick, but doesn't feel like a delusion either.

Our memories of teachers, loved ones, and even much loved fictional characters in stories can act like the Hogwarts headmasters' portraits do, as a kind of faint imprint of their personalities or archetypes. It's akin to what Dumbledore tells Harry in *Azkaban* when the figure he thinks is his father turns out to be him. Harry found his dad within himself. Archetypes exist in us as well as in the outside world and in myth and fiction. Asking ourselves what Harry would do in a given circumstance, for example, isn't treating archetypes as physically real. It's called 'personifying' and on one level, it allows us to access parts of our own minds or psyches, the heroic and the wise parts.

As Dumbledore tells Harry, those we have shared love with never really leave us. Luna, like Harry, draws comfort from this idea when she feels sad about her mother's death. But even those who've missed out on physical reality love can experience it.

Ritual magician Ramsey Dukes tells us that "there is no more powerful technique for handling our environment" than personification.

> This is far from being a reversion to outmoded and primitive behavior. Look for conscious intelligence in phenomena and you awaken the greatest power of the human brain to assist your exploration or mastery. Whereas those who insist on hoarding 'conscious will' inside themselves, and seeing only mechanical processes outside themselves, are closing down most of their brain connections.[5]

Shamanic cultures experience alternate realities as real, but like the wizards in *Harry Potter*, they have little difficulty distinguishing one reality from another, or sane from crazy. In traditional cultures it's not crazy to see spirits, but to consistently lose control. Some of those confined to St Mungo's, like Gilderoy Lockhart and Neville's parents, have lost control of their state of consciousness. They're also no longer able to be as useful as they once were to their society. (Though I suppose Gilderoy's use was a bit debatable in the first place!)

Most indigenous cultures agree that where a crazy person may speak with spirits and enter alternate states, they have little control over it, and little ability to make their spiritual experience practically useful. Shamans, by contrast, typically demonstrate exquisite control of their state of consciousness, their movements in deep trance, and their drumming, singing and ritual behaviors.

The eccentrics in the novels, like Luna and her dad, aren't exactly 'loony,' but they demonstrate a problem that can arise in alternate pursuits: credulity. It's very important not to believe any old thing that comes along. You can end up with a uselessly baroque belief system and mistletoe full of nargles. The shamanic way is to believe what proves useful in your own experience of physical as well as spiritual realities. It's also the wizarding way. Both Dumbledore and McGonagall aren't very keen on divination because it's imprecise and of debatable use.

GETTING THROUGH THE BARRIER: ENTERING ALTERNATE REALITIES

JK Rowling depicts one entrance to the wizarding world as an apparently solid concrete barrier. The 'barrier of the concrete' is actually one of the main obstacles that stands in the way of experiencing any sort of alternate reality. Some say that the concrete, the physical, is all that exists and that there's only one way of looking at it. To get on to platform 9 ¾ and embark on the journey to Hogwarts, the prospective seeker, the student, must walk through a wall. "All you have to do is walk straight at the barrier between platforms nine and ten. Don't stop, and don't be scared you'll crash into it, that's very important. Best to do it at a bit of a run if you're nervous," as Molly Weasley says.[6] Walking through walls is impossible, but if you try in the right place, you learn that the wall isn't as solid as you thought.

Quantum physics is a friend to the wizard because it's found some physical evidence for ideas like that of the mind's effect on matter. As a practical branch of physics it's given us the laser, the superconductor and the electron microscope, among other things. Researchers at St Andrews University in Scotland have even begun to find ways that Harry's invisibility cloak and levitation spells could work.[7] Invisibility could be achieved by making light waves flow around an object, just as a river flows around a smooth rock. They can levitate objects by reversing the Casimir force, which normally causes objects to stick together, so that it repels instead of attracts. The Casimir force is a consequence of quantum mechanics, the theory that describes the world of atoms and subatomic particles, that is not only the most successful theory of physics but also the most baffling. The force is due to neither electrical charge nor gravity, for example, but to fluctuations in all-pervasive energy fields in the intervening empty space between the objects. It's one reason atoms stick together.

As a body of theories (some confirmed by experiments) quantum mechanics reveals amazing things about reality. Study of quantum 'micro-worlds' — that is, the worlds of matter and energy on atomic and subatomic levels — inform us about the 'macro-world' we experience. As the ancient magical text *The Emerald Tablet* says, "The superior agrees with the inferior, and the inferior with the superior, to effect that one truly wonderful work."[8] That is, microcosm and macrocosm reflect each other. For example, at a quantum level, physics tells us that 99% of that barrier between platforms nine and ten is empty space. Everything is actually mostly made of nothing. There are various kinds of invisible fields and forces holding all this nearly nothing together, like the Casimir force. The physical world we see is full of forces we can't see, like magnetism and gravity. So we have lots of nearly nothing, bound into apparent something by invisible forces. Next, all this nearly nothing changes all the time, like the 142 moving staircases at Hogwarts. Even our own 'architecture' isn't stable.

The physical body you're using to read this book is actually not the same one you used to pick it up. That's because when you take one deep breath "you inhale 10^{22} atoms from the universe." That's 10 with 22 zeroes after it. When you exhale, the same number of atoms that came from your body goes out into the universe. It's possible to make calculations that will show that "*beyond a shadow of a doubt*...you have in your physical body at least a million atoms that were once in the body of Christ, or the Buddha."[9] You also have atoms from Ramses the Great, Blackbeard the Pirate, and all the 'goodies' and 'baddies' currently on the world stage. In Harry's universe, he isn't the only one who shares parts of Voldemort. On an atomic level, everyone would, Muggle and magical alike. They'd also share atoms that had been in Dumbledore, Ollivander and everyone else. This is another counter to Voldemort's isolated way of being. None of us is truly separate.

Magical levels of reality may be seen as just another level of subtle reality, less dense than the physical, less dense than light. In the sea cave in *Prince* Dumbledore knows they're in the right place simply because he can feel "It has known magic."[10] Harry senses it too. They sense 'magic' in the same way they'd also sense that the cave was humid. You often can't see water vapor hanging in the air, but you can feel it. You might have difficulty describing exactly how you know it's humid, but you do know it, just as Harry and Dumbledore know magic. What takes us still deeper into the magical realm is that we affect all the constantly changing nearly nothing that is reality just by observing it.

The 'double slit' physics experiment showed that photons, 'particles' of light, passing through one of two slits in a barrier, behaved either as particles or as waves, depending upon whether or not the experimenter chose to look. Even stranger, the decision could be made *after* the photon had made its journey, implying that the observer could effect the past. This goes well beyond the placebo effect, because the matter in question isn't even attached to our bodies. There's no rational way it could work if our mind's influence was physically limited to the brain. The physicist Werner Heisenberg said, "The common division of the world into subject and object, inner and outer world, body and soul is no longer adequate."[11] Not that the wizarding world ever thought it was.

There are many different ways of sensing reality, even amongst the animal and plant species we know of. For example, when pests attack some trees, the plants send chemical warnings on the breeze to other trees, telling them to shore up their chemical defenses against the pest. What is it like to send or receive a message this way? Different animals have different modes of seeing. A honeybee will see a flower on that tree in ultraviolet wavelengths of light. A bat would experience the flower as sonar echoes as it flies by the tree at night. Which of us sees the real flower?

When we get to the brain we find that it's the biggest magician around. In *The Science of Harry Potter*, Roger Highfield makes the point that the brain takes "tiny, distorted, upside down images in your eyes and translates them into patterns of nerve cell activity that create an experience based on your surroundings." The brain also fills in a fairly large blind spot from the area of your retina where the optic nerve sends information to the brain.[12] This is the equipment we're trusting to accurately 'read' reality?

The whole question of where consciousness is located pops up in various ways in children's stories. The Scarecrow in *The Wizard of Oz* wants a brain so he can think, but that's not what he gets. In the film he gets a diploma, and he can suddenly think. It turns out that he needed only the idea of a brain! Location of consciousness issues come up in *Harry Potter* in Arthur Weasley's statement to Ginny, after she's hoodwinked by Riddle's diary, "Never trust anything that can think for itself *if you can't see where it keeps its brain*."[13] The biggest example is, of course, the Sorting Hat. The four founders of Hogwarts created it to place children into their Houses after they were gone. In *Goblet*, it sings:

> 'Twas Gryffindor who found the way,
> He whipped me off his head
> The founders put some brains in me
> So I could choose instead.
> Now slip me snug about your ears,
> I've never yet been wrong,

I'll have a look inside your mind
And tell where you belong![14]

Obviously the founders didn't put their *actual* physical brains in the hat, which would create a rather disagreeable Sorting Ceremony. The hat also couldn't look into the minds of students physically, but must be able to look in a subtler way.

Snape tells Harry he has no subtlety when Harry describes legilimency as 'mind reading'. Snape responds, "Only Muggles talk of 'mind reading.' The mind is not a book, to be opened at will and examined at leisure. Thoughts are not etched on the inside of skulls, to be perused by any invader. The mind is a complex and many-layered thing, Potter—or at least, most minds are."[15]

Some scientists and scholars feel that 'mind' has a non-physical aspect in reality, just as it does in Harry's world. A group of them formed the Scientific and Medical Network. They have an annual conference called 'Beyond the Brain,' where scholars and researchers from a variety of disciplines ranging from neuro-science to physics to theology discuss broader ideas about reality.[16]

At the heart of many discussions of consciousness is the question of who and what can be said to be conscious. Plants turn to the sun. That's a kind of consciousness. The whomping willow and mandrakes are particularly conscious plants in the novels, though this doesn't stop Professor Sprout chopping the latter to bits to make a restorative potion! Degree and location of consciousness also appears in a slightly creepy way in Harry's transfiguration classes, when, for example, an improperly trans-figured hedgehog became a pin-cushion that curled up in fright when approached with a pin. This brings up a point about how magical cultures understand consciousness, and attribute it to non-human persons, even to things that Muggles would call inanimate. It also brings us to three of the most important objects in the books.

THREE HALLOWS AND THREE ASPECTS OF CONSCIOUSNESS

Magical cultures tend to be animists, that is, they believe that everything has some kind of consciousness that we may think of as 'mind' or 'spirit.' In this reality, there are no truly inanimate objects. Everything has a degree of consciousness. A totem animal or ancestral spirit might have more than, say, a magical weapon like Gryffindor's sword, which in turn might have more than a hammer, but they all have some sort of consciousness and must be treated with awareness and respect.

Three such objects are the Deathly Hallows, which also give us an insight into how wizards perceive alternate realities. You'll be familiar with the story of *The Tale of the Three Brothers* from *Hallows*, so I'll just precis it here for reference.[17] Three brothers outwit Death by building a magic bridge to cross a river "too deep to wade through and too dangerous to swim across." Death, cheated of their lives, is displeased but offers them three boons as a trick. The eldest requests an unbeatable wand. The middle brother asks for a stone to raise the dead. The youngest, the humblest and wisest, asks for a gift to allow him to leave in safety without being "followed by death" so Death reluctantly gives him his own invisibility cloak. The eldest and middle brothers soon meet untimely ends. Only the youngest lives out his years and departs with Death as an equal when he removes the cloak to pass it on to his son.

If we approach this tale within a tale as we might a traditional folk tale, we see that JK Rowling has used a classic opening situation. There are many stories about rivers and the super-natural. In Scottish tradition, evil forces are not supposed to be able to cross running water. Some variants say that witches and wizards of any sort can't cross running water. This may not be the case in the world of the novels, but the author notes that the brothers show their power by creating a bridge to cross what can't be crossed. Death meets them halfway across.

The raging river can symbolize the watery element of our emotions and thoughts. It is too deep to wade through. We can't use our 'land based' rational skills, we're out of our depth, and there's nothing to stand on. The subconscious emotions and urges are too deep. It's too dangerous to swim.

In the story, death meets them 'halfway.' It usually does. Some time around life's mid-point many of us experience Death's reality in a visceral way. We might have a health scare, or see a loved one die, or have children who make us so keen to remain alive that we reflexively fear the opposite.

JK Rowling has drawn from classic fairy tale themes. Three brothers (or sisters) in stories often represent facets of the self. They can illustrate three ways of responding to a situation. The first two usually choose wrong solutions that tend to be opposites in some way. The youngest child usually chooses the correct response, which resolves these polar opposites or is simply the common sense choice.

The eldest brother acts from aggression, which in turn comes from fear. If we look at fear, we see that, in essence, it's always fear of loss and the sorrow that loss brings. We think we're going to lose something ranging from our dignity to our life, and tend to make ourselves small, curled up, hedgehog-like, to protect ourselves. Aggression is an explosive defense from fear. We attack to prevent loss and sorrow, but attacking brings loss and sorrow to others and ourselves. So, the first brother's choice relates to loss and sorrow.

The choice of the stone is a bit more complex. The second brother chooses the stone from arrogance, the desire to humiliate death still further. Desire is another bugbear on the spiritual path, but what does the brother really desire? Well, what shows up when he uses the stone is the figure of a girl he'd wanted to marry before her untimely death. His desire is really a desire for union. Most desires are. We want to unite with another person, a cherished goal, a vault full of galleons or a Firebolt racing broom because we think that these things will make us happy.

So the two brothers choose boons from Death that represent loss and sorrow in the form of the Deathstick on the one hand, and union and happiness in the form of the resurrection stone on the other: two boons, two opposites or 'polarities.'

The youngest brother is rewarded for making a 'modest' choice. All he wants is to leave the encounter unscathed. The modest choice is often rewarded in fairy tales, giving us the simple lesson: be reasonable. The seeker who does so may even be rewarded in unexpected ways.

The same lesson pops up in *Beauty and the Beast*. Her two elder sisters ask for extravagant gifts, where Beauty, the youngest, asks for a rose, a symbol of the divine feminine. Her father picks the rose from the Beast's enchanted garden, and at first, it looks as though Beauty made a bad choice, because the Beast demands her as the price of the rose. However, when the Beast turns out to be a handsome prince, it's clear that her choice was the best.

The 'modest' choice here also represents a point 'betwixt and between' the two polarities of the elder brothers' choices, a point between union and loss, happiness and sorrow. The symbol of the Deathly Hallows underscores the idea that Death's cloak represents what I'll call 'awareness,' a state of consciousness that transcends all polarities in life. It's described as silvery in appearance and watery in feeling. This calls to mind mercury or quicksilver, which often symbolizes the union of opposites in alchemy, as I'll discuss later.

In this case, I'm not sure that JK Rowling intended all the symbolism I'll speak of below. However, I'm reading the novels more from the perspective of what we can take out of them than what we know for sure went into them. The Three Hallows' symbol relates perfectly to ideas about alternate states and their purpose that we find in Celtic traditions and wizardry.

The symbol of the Deathly Hallows is a triangle representing the cloak surrounding a circle representing the stone with a vertical line representing the elder wand passing through the circle. Put together, they look a bit like an eye in a triangle, the Masonic symbol representing the all-seeing eye of God, an alternate kind of perception if ever there was one! We can trace this eye in the pyramid symbol back to Horus, the young son of the Egyptian pantheon, heroic avenger of his father's murder by the deity Set.

If we look at the circle, line and triangle individually, we realize that such simple symbols can be read in many ways. For example, the circle can be the feminine principle, the line can be the masculine, and the triangle can represent the trinity of father, mother and child that comes into being when the first two unite. The triangle can also obviously be read as a symbol of the Christian Trinity.

On the most basic possible level, a circle generally represents union, and the happiness it can bring. The line can symbolize division, and so, loss and sorrow. The Death Stick is a very obvious agent of conflict, division and loss, causing repeated mayhem as people vie for it.

We all experience union / happiness and loss / sorrow throughout our lives. One follows the other in a kind of oscillation. Some alchemists said that part of the process of making the philosopher's stone was an 'oscillation,' a repeated pendulum-like movement, between what they called the *nigredo*, a stage of terrible darkness and sense of loss, and the *coniunctio*, blissful union. Even the most blessed lives include deaths and departures, and lives like Harry's (at least before the *Hallows* epilogue) seem heavily weighted to the loss side.

How does one bear it? The transcendent triangle gives the answer. The triangle of death's cloak encompasses both the circle and the line. As an upward pointing triangle, it's figuratively 'based' on earth but pointing to heaven. It represents a state of consciousness that isn't based in sorrow or happiness, that isn't entirely physical but isn't a delusion.

THE TRANSCENDENT TRIANGLE

Ancient Celtic tradition spoke of a trinity of happiness, sorrow and a third kind of consciousness that's quite hard to translate from the Old Irish. I'll simply call it 'awareness' here. Hindu scriptures, ritual magic and other traditions agree that it's best defined by what it's not. It's not fear or desire-based consciousness. It's not most people's day to day personal consciousness. It's an expanded state in which the seeker becomes more than he usually thinks he is.

The nice thing about the term 'awareness' is that it leaves the level of the experience entirely up to the individual. It doesn't demand belief in spirit, but it also doesn't rule it out. It's a psychological reality that everyone can experience. What else it may be is up to each person to decide. They may experience it as an expansion into an absolutely real spiritual realm, or as entirely inside their heads, or, as Dumbledore suggests, both.

Harry is in just such an awareness state at King's Cross when Dumbledore tells him this. The 'near death experience' is a well-known type of encounter with alternate reality. But Harry also enters a kind of awareness beneath his cloak. Others are real to him; he isn't real to most of them. He gains real, applicable knowledge, just as people's experiences in awareness can bear fruits in physical reality.

Initially, awareness brings a sense of spaciousness and freedom. When Harry first dons the cloak, he feels exhilarated.

"The whole of Hogwarts was open to him in this cloak."[18] He had access to all its rooms, all its knowledge. There's a great sense of expanded power and possibility in awareness.

A seeker may see this sense of expansion as union with something bigger like God. The Chinese Taoist sages saw it as expanding into the natural world, the cosmos, feeling themselves to be part of everything. People sometimes experience it when playing sports.

The Quidditch Seeker can't simply be aware of what's happening in a 'regular' way. He has to be aware in a heightened way. He has to look for the snitch and be aware of the score so he doesn't catch it at the wrong moment and lose the game. He has to evade bludgers and hostile opponents. He also needs to keep an eye on the other Seeker, the weather and watch out for the unexpected, like Dementors on the Quidditch pitch. Doing so, he forgets personal problems. It's not 'situational' happiness, like you'd get from winning the Daily Prophet prize-draw, but it's a joyous, freeing sensation. The Seeker rises above it all, to a transcendent state where anything personal gets smaller in comparison with the 'bigger' self experienced in awareness.

Harry attained the same sort of awareness when performing the first task in *Goblet*. Standing before the dragon, he summoned his broom, jumped on it and kicked off. As he soared upwards, he realized that he'd "left not only the ground behind, but also his fear." This was just another Quidditch match and the dragon was just another opposing team.[19]

Awareness is a kind of 'basic' alternate state of consciousness, which, like the cloak, holds all the others. Harry's use of the cloak throughout the seven books affirms the idea that it can represent awareness. He uses it to acquire many kinds of knowledge and have many experiences. Likewise, people first need to experience awareness to enter deeply into meditation, to work magic, to do specific kinds of visualization or take a spirit journey.

Dumbledore gives him the cloak at Christmas, a time when many traditions celebrate light coming from darkness, symbolically and actually, as the days grow longer after the winter solstice. Albus means 'white' and stands for the alchemical *albus* stage, the 'whitening,' or purification borne of the oscillation of union and loss. Dumbledore and the cloak can represent similar qualities of awareness. Dumbledore is the only person who can see through it without a magical eye like Moody's.

Harry uses the cloak like a shaman uses spiritual awareness to journey into realms that stand for the Otherworld in the novels. These are realms that are even more 'other' than the wizarding world as a whole. They include the subterranean series of rooms that guard the philosopher's stone in the first novel. The trap door to these rooms is even guarded by Fluffy, a clear stand-in for the three headed Cerberus, canine guardian of the Underworld, in Greek mythology.

Harry repeatedly uses the cloak to gain knowledge that he otherwise wouldn't have access to, such as when he uses it to see the dragons for the first task of the tournament in *Goblet*. The knowledge gained through entering awareness states is not always expected, but it always confronts us with the dual specters of fear and desire, at one time or another.

JK Rowling hits us with these two up front the first time Harry uses his cloak to look for information on Flamel in the restricted section of the library. The first book Harry opens screams, frightening him. Then Filch comes and Harry flees in fear to find himself immediately confronted with his deepest desire in the Mirror of Erised. Desire, the other obstacle on the spiritual path, comes hot on the heels of fear. His first use of the cloak raises the twin specters that any seeker who practices meditation will tell you try to intrude into awareness.

DESIRE BEYOND THE MIRROR OF ERISED

Dealing with the mirror of desire is one of our biggest challenges. As Dumbledore says of the Mirror of Erised, "This mirror will give us neither knowledge or truth. Men have wasted away before it, entranced by what they have seen, or been driven mad, not knowing if what it shows is real or even possible."[20] Even though the mirror deceives, we can use its surface reflection as the starting point for an examination of what we truly want.

Desire is most often actually the desire for union of one sort or another, as I've mentioned above. Why do I say this? Let's look at the examples that encounters with the Mirror of Erised give us. Harry first sees his parents and loving relatives. Quirrell sees himself giving the philosopher's stone to his master, Voldemort, cementing their union even beyond Voldemort being stuck on the back of Quirrell's head. Ron sees himself as Head Boy, Quidditch Captain and winner of the House Cup and Quidditch Cup. Wait a minute, you may ask, how does that relate to union? Let's see.

I once learned a wonderful technique for a person to discover their 'root desire' from the teacher, Duncan MacIntosh, who draws from Sufi traditions. A person can do it with another asking prompting questions or on their own. They begin by asking themselves (or by being asked) what they want. It could be anything, a treacle tart, to win a Quidditch match, to punch their potions teacher in the nose or to get the person they fancy to notice them.

Then they ask themselves what it is about that thing that they want even more than the thing itself. It's like taking a step beyond the image in the Mirror of Erised to see the underlying aspects of the desire. If we take what Ron sees as an example, he might ask himself, "What is it about winning every possible Hogwarts distinction that I desire more than winning every possible Hogwarts distinction?"

Dumbledore has given us a clue about what his response

would be. Having always been overshadowed and preceded by his older brothers, he sees himself "standing alone, the best of all of them." So, Ron might respond, "A feeling that I am the best of all my brothers."

But we can go further. The next question would be "What is it about being the best of all my brothers that I desire even more than feeling that I'm the best of all my brothers?"

The answer might be "A feeling of triumph."

He'd then ask, "What is it about the feeling of triumph that I desire even more than the feeling of triumph?"

"A sense that I am powerful."

"What is it about a sense of power that I desire even more than that sense?"

"A feeling of safety and peace."

"What is it about a feeling of safety and peace that I desire even more than that feeling?"

"A sense that it's safe to connect with someone else."

"What is it about the ability to connect with someone that I desire even more than that ability?"

"The actual connection itself."

"And what is it about that?"

"The feeling of love and belonging."

"And...?"

"Well, just that, really, a sense of being one with someone or something, of mattering to them. Unity."

You can see how far the actual desire is from simple superiority. What's funny is that in rooms full of people, however divergent their desires are at first, most of them end up in exactly this sort of place.

There are two final questions to ask. First, "How does this change my feelings about the original desire? Do I even still want it?" Ron might realize that he actually wants a sense of connection with his family and with others, like Harry and

SEEKER'S GUIDE TO HARRY POTTER

Hermione, much more than he wants superiority over them. He's plagued by jealousy of Harry as well as of his older brothers, so this realization could have saved him a lot of trouble!

The final question to ask is "How can I experience something of this final desire right now?" Ron would realize that he already has deep and wonderful connections with his family and friends. His deeper desires, in this case, have been met. The desire for superiority that the Mirror of Erised reflects is just a phantom standing in the way of his true desire – *which he already has.*

Funny how often that's true for the rest of us. We're often not truly present with what we have. We don't pay attention. Entering awareness and journeying into other realms of consciousness and being must always draw us into fuller appreciation of this one. The ability that enables us to enter awareness is actually the same one that brings us the most enjoyment of life in physical reality. We begin by paying attention. Many Muggles don't.

NOTICING THE KNIGHT BUS: EXPERIENCING OTHER REALITIES

In *Azkaban*, Harry asks Stan Shunpike why Muggles don't notice the violently purple triple-decker Knight Bus appearing and disappearing with loud bangs and careening along at top speeds. "Them," said Stan contemptuously. "Don' listen properly, do they? Don' look properly either. Never notice nuffink, they don'."[21] Stan isn't depicted as the sharpest wand in the box, but even he recognizes a very basic difference between wizard and Muggle consciousness. Wizards look and listen properly. They pay attention.

I once heard the well-known hereditary witch and author, Paddy Slade, give a talk at a Pagan Federation conference. She spent a full hour saying that, anyone who wanted to become a witch should spend a lot of time out in nature just observing. Not

46

just on 'nice' days either, but in summer and winter, starlight and storm. She went on describe a few of the things you might encounter in each season. Indigenous Amazonian peoples are very much more in touch with both physical and spiritual realities than we are in our more technologically advanced settings. Awareness deepens perception of both realities. The 'root' idea is to be as profoundly in touch with all levels of reality as possible.

All spiritual work in awareness depends upon our ability to pay attention, and we cultivate that ability each moment, by paying attention to what is. If you can't be fully present where you are, then there's no way you can be sure of getting anywhere else. What's more, paying attention is a primary skill needed to enjoy physical life. The unobserved life flies by in a riot of the urgent. A life lived in awareness progresses more like a pageant of the important.

Lots of people experience life slowing down, along with a dramatic upsurge in awareness and satisfaction with life, after a crisis or illness confronts them with how short life can be. Harry feels this acutely at the end of *Hallows* when he thinks he's going to his death in the forest. "Every second he breathed, the smell of grass, the cool air on his face, was so precious: to think that people had years and years, time to waste, so much time it dragged, and he was clinging to each second."[22] Focussing in the moment, on what our senses bring us, on our breathing, can invoke awareness. In this state, we can later learn to focus beyond the physical senses to subtler kinds of perception.

Awareness brings freedom from negative mental states. The destructive power of thought pops up vividly in *Phoenix* when a magically disoriented Ron summons a brain trailing tendrils of thought from a tank at the Department of Mysteries. "Harry did not know what would happen if Ron touched the tentacles of thought now flying behind the brain, but he was sure it would not be anything good."[23] It wasn't. Ron was nearly strangled and smothered by thought. Many of us know the feeling. It's one reason that the wonderfully named pensieve is such an appealing implement.

Later, when Ron is recuperating, Madam Pomfrey notes that "thoughts could leave deeper scarring than anything else" though Dr Ubbly's Oblivious Unction brings some improvement.[24]

While many of us might like a gallon jug on hand, awareness can act in a similar way. As the therapist Rudolph Bauer says, "We can't intellectually resolve some problems, we have to energetically dissolve them."[25] Awareness does this in an alchemical sort of way.

One example is the level of understanding that comes to Harry after he sees Snape's memories in the pensieve in *Hallows*. The pensieve is another way that people enter alternate realities akin to the awareness state in the books. The bluish silvery substance that carries the memories is between a gas and a liquid. In magic, air tends to represent pure consciousness or mind, and water tends to represent emotions. Memory contains both. Here again, as with the cloak, a silvery liquid quality suggests alchemical mercury.

To experience the memories, you need to literally enter the alchemical vessel. The pensieve's name, from pensive or thoughtful, suggests it as the alchemical vessel of consciousness, sometimes even symbolized as a skull in old manuscripts. You fall into it, to sluice about in the memories. Harry experiences Snape's memories from the inside, from Snape's perspective. This invokes compassion but there's much more going on here. The process occurring in the pensieve also implies the alchemical *solutio*, an oceanic experience where the boundaries between self and other dissolve in awareness. Harry experiences Snape's absolute love for his mother, and his genuine despair at her death. He understands how Snape got where he was, and sees how, even as a

peculiarly dressed boy, Snape could strike "an oddly impressive figure."[26] Harry doesn't have time to fully process the experience in *Hallows*, but there are hints of compassion and even admiration.

Did this experience of Snape's memories, held in awareness, change the facts of the years of bullying and animosity between them? No. Harry would probably never have felt much better about that if he'd just thought about it. It's interesting to note the difference between the resolution of his feelings with the Dursleys and those with Snape.

Harry doesn't feel better about his abuse at the Dursleys' hands by thinking about it. Few who've experienced child abuse do. Being able to explain why Snape bullies him, or why Voldemort killed his parents, doesn't make Harry feel any happier about these situations. Even his first brief dip into Snape's memory in the pensieve doesn't make him feel much better about Snape, just temporarily worse about his father.

However, Harry's deeper understanding, borne of his lengthier sojourn in Snape's memories (and, of course, his greater maturity and other experiences) does change his feelings.

Awareness *dissolves* what we can't *resolve* by the intellect. It's the alchemical *solutio*, in which the elements we don't need wash away. Think of panning for gold. By this metaphor, the weightier elements of our being, our essential gold, stays in the pan while the lighter grit and dirt breaks into bits and gets sluiced away by the water.

One big difference between Harry's resolutions of his enmity with Snape and with the Dursleys is that he never had the chance to enter a pensieve of Vernon or Petunia's thoughts, to experience the *solutio* specifically in relation to them. He'd worked on himself, and entered awareness himself, which enabled him to rise above the "16 solid years of dislike" enough to encourage them to take magical protection from Voldemort.

He transcends his emotions about the abuse over time as he grows in power and knowledge through magical training and entering awareness. At times, his power gets a bit out of hand, like when he blows up his aunt in *Azkaban*. However, by the end, he's calmed enough that he even has a kind of reconciliation with his cousin Dudley, who'd made his early years hellish. There are many stories about how spiritual training and experience can transform personalities. However, Harry doesn't end up with children named Vernon or Petunia.

The Dursleys have less to recommend them than Snape on many levels, which is the other difference. Petunia, like her sister, adores her son enough to die for him, but her desperate love, untempered by discipline, damages the boy. Other than this rather warped redeeming feature, all the Dursleys do is consume. Snape gives his life for a higher good, yet Harry's hatred of Snape was much more venomous than his hatred of the Dursleys. Nonetheless, the resolution attained in awareness in the pensieve must have been profound, given the scene on Platform 9 ¾ that ends *Hallows*.

THE SPIRITUAL POWER TO TRANSFORM

There's a story about how a cruel Tibetan bandit went to a hermit's cave to rob him. When he found the old man meditating, radiating peace, love and compassion, his fierceness vanished and he stood in wonder. He asked the hermit for his blessing, and after that, whenever he thought of doing something horrid, the old man's serene face would appear before him and he'd abandon his plan. As Buddhist monk, Matthieu Ricard, notes, "Visualizing such scenes is not about having fun with autosuggestion, but about being in resonance with the basic goodness lying at our very core."[27]

A serious study of the long-term effects of meditation on the brain showed remarkable differences between twelve trained

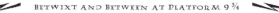

meditators of the Tibetan Buddhist tradition and the twelve control subjects studied. Where untrained subjects couldn't focus, trained meditators could actually pay attention to things, like wizards. For example, the meditators were able to read 'micro-expressions' of a thirtieth of a second more accurately than secret service agents, who'd previously done best at this task. This skill must be a facet of the legilimency that Dumbledore, Voldemort and Snape are so good at, which we're told usually requires eye contact.

Spiritual and mental training has other fringe benefits. As Ricard goes on to say, people who can recognize micro-expressions also tend to be "the most open to new experiences, the most curious about things in general, and the most reliable and efficient." They also tend to feel happier. Alternate states aren't just about entering other worlds; they're about helping us in this one. One study, reported in the *Proceedings of the National Academy of Sciences*, showed that novice meditators' levels of anxiety, depression, anger and fatigue went down, while their energy levels rose, after only five twenty-minute sessions of meditation training.[28]

Yet some people find something dangerous in entering alternate states. Despite the long tradition of meditation in Christianity, I remember hearing a priest vigorously argue against entering states where we weren't thinking rationally and intellectually. He said we shouldn't shut down the logical thought processes of the brain because God gave us our brains and meant us to use them. This is a rather silly argument. After all, God also gave us genitals, but no priest would argue that they're meant to be in constant use. Anyway, the brain is not *inactive* in meditation it's just doing something different from regular thinking. If some people find the idea of entering alternate realities through meditation dangerous, it shouldn't come as any surprise that they find the alternate reality presented

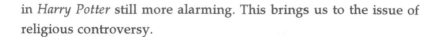

in *Harry Potter* still more alarming. This brings us to the issue of religious controversy.

HARRY AND ALTERNATE RELIGIOUS REALITIES

Harry has been a target of Evangelical dislike since the beginning, mostly in America. Church groups have burned and banned the books on the grounds that they 'recruit' for the devil. By the year 2000, the books had been challenged in 25 school districts in at least 17 states.[29] The revelation that Dumbledore was gay in 2007 only made matters worse.

The UK generally considers itself less parochial, but Carol Rookwood at St Mary's Island Church of England Primary School in Kent banned the books in 2000. She said that "Devils, demons and witches are real and pose the same threat as, say, a child molester."[30]

This must have been a deeply offensive comparison to a mother of young children, and indeed, a Rookwood later turns up as a Death Eater in one of the novels. As JK Rowling said, "You have to be careful if you get friendly with me because you tend to turn up in my books, and if you offend me, you often turn up as a nasty character."[31]

On a more serious note, Rowling has said that no one has ever told her that they have taken up witchcraft as a result of reading her books. The growth of Wicca and Neo-Paganism was underway long before *Harry Potter*. Both phenomena might be seen as responses to the same cultural void, the loss of meaning and magic. While some Pagans find a hero they can identify with in Harry, as do some Christians, other Pagan groups distance themselves and their ritual practice of magic from the books. They feel that the books trivialize ancient traditions.

One of the most important things to note up front is that, despite Rookwood's comments, the devil isn't in these books, any more than he's in Wiccan cosmology. Magic, in JK Rowling's universe, isn't based on conjuring spirits, good or bad, to do one's bidding. It's based on using a natural force that can be turned to positive or negative ends, much as Muggles use electricity.[32]

Of course, God isn't in the books either. The absence of a personified God is one of the main reasons that some Christians are so against the books. Yet, surely the story of a hero who holds to the good in a world where God's existence is unproved to many, *a world just like the real one,* is a more valuable lesson than telling the story of a hero who constantly uses an open line to the Almighty.

On some levels, it's surprising that there have been a greater number of Christian objections to Rowling's universe than to, say Philip Pullman's. Though he sets his story in a universe where there was no Creator, the figure of The Authority in the books, a feeble, ancient creature in a box, is God in many people's eyes. Much as I enjoyed the books, and think he raises important and intelligent questions, I could quite see why people might find the theology of *His Dark Materials* disturbing.

Even well-loved Christian authors like CS Lewis and JRR Tolkien have substantial Pagan elements in their work which haven't been scrutinized as thoroughly as similar elements in JK Rowling's work. Part of the reason may be that there's a Christian God figure 'in charge' in Narnia. The big lion, Aslan, stands in for Christ, though he didn't start out that way. Aslan came "bounding into" a previously directionless story, one that CS Lewis had been coming up with in disconnected images for a long time. He recalled having had some dreams of lions around that time, but "Apart from that, I don't know where the Lion came from or why He came." (Lewis' use of capitol letters.) He added that at first "there wasn't even anything Christian" about these images. In fact, CS Lewis uses many figures that were actually worshipped by the ancients, incorporating them into a Christian cosmology in a way that JK Rowling doesn't.[33]

Pro-Harry Potter Pagans get annoyed that some Christians claim Harry as a purely Christian culture hero. "Get your own Christian hero!" is the sentiment here, rather than Christianizing a wizard, a category of person that has been severely persecuted in the past by the Church. Witch burning was no joke, despite the way Harry's textbook in *Azkaban* says that it was harmless to real witches.

It's worth noting here that Ms. Rowling herself is Christian, and that Harry's Christening is an important plot point, in that it gives him his Godfather, Sirius. I was halfway expecting her to end the novels as an unambiguous Christian parable, but in fact, she stayed the course she has been on throughout, which is clearly spiritual, but not specifically religious. Although Harry does offer Voldemort quite a Christian exhortation to repentance in the last book, themes like repentance and sacrificial love appear in many other traditions as well.

She deliberately chose one Pagan and one Christian quote to begin her final book. One is from Aeschylus, and asks the "dark gods beneath the earth" to "bless the children" and give them triumph. The other is from William Penn, and speaks of death as a voyage, and of love and friendship as eternal. She said, "I really enjoyed choosing those two quotations because one is pagan, of course, and one is from a Christian tradition." She'd chosen the passages around the time of *Chamber*, and she knew that if they worked then she'd gotten the story to where it needed to be at that point.[34]

She's clearly an open-minded Christian, and has admitted to struggling with her faith yet her Christianity is far from incidental to the books. After *Hallows* she said she hadn't wanted to speak much about her religious beliefs earlier because it would have given away what was going to happen. Two Bible quotes also appear in *Hallows*. "The last enemy that shall be destroyed is death," 1 Corinthians 15:26, appears on James' and Lily's graves.

Dumbledore's mother and sister's graves are inscribed with Christ's words from Matthew 6:19, "Where your treasure is, there will your heart be also."[35]

Speaking about the quotes for the first time with journalist Shawn Adler, she said that Harry was going to find scripture on tombstones because the books were British. However, for her, the particular quotations he does find sum up the whole series. "They just say it all to me, they really do." she added. God doesn't speak from clouds but the idea of a 'Sacred' with a capitol 'S' is felt throughout the books. The fact that she doesn't get too specifically religious makes the books useful to seekers of all or no traditions.

JK Rowling created a fairly secular magical universe in *Harry Potter*, with levels or lacks of religious participation that mirror modern culture. Harry and his friends celebrate Christmas and Easter, as well as the Pagan festivals of Yule and Halloween. However, they celebrate these festivals in the secular way that many do in the modern West, with chocolate eggs at Easter, presents at Christmas, a party with bats and pumpkins at Halloween. (Some Scots feel she should really have featured the traditional turnip lanterns rather than the American imports. Hagrid could have engorged them just as easily, but never mind!)

You can imagine Hogwarts students coming from any religious background, or none. The Patils are Indian, so one might imagine that they're Hindu. Lee Jordan's dreadlocks may be a fashion statement or he may be Rastafarian. We see many nationalities at the Quidditch World Cup, and presumably, many religious backgrounds. There have been magical practitioners of every culture and just about every religion, including Christian.

Though a discussion of magic in Judeo-Christian tradition is *well* beyond the scope of this book, it's interesting to note that the verse of scripture that Christians most invoke to bash *Harry Potter* (and magic in general) is mistranslated. Exodus 22:18 was translated as "Thou shalt not suffer a witch to live." in the *King James Bible*, justifying centuries of persecution. However, it actually applies to a specific class of 'dark' magicians, not to all 'witches' or workers of magic.[36] Many European ritual magicians and alchemists were devout Christians who saw their magical work as part of fulfilling God's plan for creation.

Most cultures through most of human history have embraced a magical, holistic, world-view, just like most indigenous people today, and just like the wizards and witches in Harry's world. Our ancestors were just as smart as we are yet found a magical world-view intellectually and spiritually satisfying. They also didn't see any need to make progress for its own sake. There are periods of thousands of years where people simply stuck with the technology they had when it worked well enough to meet their needs.[37] It's similar to the way that wizards in the books are happy to use torches and candles instead of 'eckeltricity.' They cast a nicer light and they've probably been magically de-sooted as well![38]

Candles and torches are also renewable in a way that the fossil fuels we burn to generate 'eckeltricity' aren't. Cultures that practice magic today, like many indigenous cultures, reveal the ecological value of the magical world-view. Shamans and wizards see humans as one element in a greater whole. Magic wouldn't work if we weren't connected to the rest of the universe in denser and subtler ways. In the introduction to his seminal book, *The Reenchantment of the World*, Morris Berman spoke of the same need for 'reenchantment' that the *Harry Potter* phenomenon expresses.

Because disenchantment is intrinsic to the scientific worldview, the modern epoch contained, from its inception, an inherent instability that severely limited its ability to sustain itself for more than a few centuries. For more than 99% of human history, the world was enchanted and man saw himself as an integral part of it. The complete reversal of this perception in a mere four hundred years or so has destroyed the continuity of the human experience and the integrity of the human psyche. It has very nearly wrecked the planet as well. The only hope, or so it seems to me, lies in the reenchantment of the world.

The much-needed spiritual and ecological sense of participation in a greater whole is represented in part by the shaman or wizard's relationship with totemic animals. Harry has Hedwig, and is also represented by Gryffindor's totemic lion. The scheme of the four houses and their totems relates to questions of meaning, vital virtues, and to the wizard's role in the cosmos.

III

FOUR HOUSES, FOUR ELEMENTS

You know, the very first time I saw you, Harry, I recognized you immediately, not by your scar but by your eyes. They're your mother, Lily's...Your father James...had a certain, shall we say, talent for trouble, a talent that, rumor has it, he passed on to you. You're more like them than you know Harry. In time we'll come to see just how much.

Professor Lupin

Mortal man consists of water, earth, fire and air. Man is the child of two fathers — one father is the earth, the other is the heaven...From the earth he receives the material body, from heaven his character...Every man takes after his father; he is able to accomplish what is innate in him.

Paracelsus

ncestry plays a huge role in the *Harry Potter* novels, from Harry's family resemblance to issues of magical blood, or its lack. We see it raised by issues of wizards' treatment of other magical races and celebrated in the Weasleys family bonds. Students from the same families tend to end up in the same houses like the Weasleys, but the Black brothers are prominent exceptions. Although Slughorn, then head of Slytherin, would have 'liked the set,' Sirius was sorted into Gryffindor. Of course Sirius still turns out to have some Slytherin qualities. He's arrogant, a bit reckless and 'dark,' and has a definite sadistic streak. By contrast, Regulus demonstrates some 'Gryffindor' sacrificial bravery in his final act. Sirius and Regulus show that the lines aren't so easily drawn, we each have all the house qualities in different measure. They also show that we have families of blood and families of emotional or spiritual affinity.

The Hogwarts houses, as McGonagall tells Harry and the other first years in *Stone*, will become their families at the school, sharing their victories and suffering the dreaded point loss for their rule breaking. Our families of blood and affinity benefit or suffer from our actions, as we do from theirs, partly through traits we inherit. For example, Petunia and Lily are both devoted mothers, and it seems likely that their own mother was too. This quality saves Harry, but spoils Dudley, because of how Petunia expresses it. All elements of our character can be expressed in positive or negative ways.

The word 'element' can mean an essential component of something. The ancients believed that everything was made up of four elements: earth, air, fire and water. Paracelsus, the well known 16th century wizard and alchemist whose bust resides in a Hogwarts hallway, says, "Mortal man consists of the four elements not only — as some hold — because he has four tempers, but also because he partakes of the nature, essence and properties of these elements. In him there lies the 'young heaven'..."[1] However, each of us has a dominant element. Medieval wizards recognized four types of personality that they called "the four humours" or tempers as Paracelsus calls them above. Each one was associated with an element. There was the choleric or fiery and passionate temperament. There was the sanguine or airy and intellectual. There was the melancholic, associated both with the dark earth and dark moods. Finally there was the phlegmatic, or watery and emotional type. Think of Phlegm, er, Fleur, with her watery cascade of silvery hair and slavish devotion to Bill.

We can see that the humours and the elements relate to the Hogwarts houses. JK Rowling said, "It is the tradition to have four houses, but in this case, I wanted them to correspond roughly to the four elements. So Gryffindor is fire, Ravenclaw is air, Hufflepuff is earth, and Slytherin is water, hence the fact that their common room is under the lake. So again, it was this idea of harmony and balance, that you had four necessary components and by integrating them you would make a very strong place. But they remain fragmented, as we know."[2]

The Sorting Hat places students in the house that shares their essential dominant quality. By doing so, it connects them to their spiritual ancestors, the founders of that house, via a direct line of transmission, the very hat worn by Gryffindor and endowed with aspects of the minds of all the founders.

A totemic animal represents each house. In shamanic traditions, totems act as 'transformers' for spiritual power, allowing the shaman easier, safer access to the vast power of the universe. They also act as protectors, like the patronus does. Totems also act as animal alter egos for the shaman. Sometimes the shaman is an animagus who can transform into their totem animal, like James Potter. The animal you'd cast as a patronus seems to be the same one you'd become if you successfully trained to become an animagus. JK Rowling implied this in an interview and it was later confirmed just before the final battle in *Hallows* when Professor McGonagall produced three patronuses at once, all of which had the same distinctive markings that she has in her cat form as an animagus. The cat is, of course, a classic witch's familiar, one manifestation of the totem. Totems often run in families and tribes, just as James and Harry share the stag. These tribal totems ultimately gave us the animals that represent family lines on European heraldic crests.

Each lineage has something to offer, as does each house at Hogwarts. Much is made of Slytherin badness, but as McGonagall says in *Stone*, "Each house has its own noble history and each has produced outstanding witches and wizards."[3] Industrious students at each house seek to become an ideal manifestation of their house type. Harry and Neville both try, and succeed, in becoming 'true Gryffindors,' who can pull Godric's sword from the Sorting Hat.

The device of the four houses has several layers of meaning in the books. On a narrative level, house membership tells you something about the characters from the outset. As in the classic school stories, the houses also set up automatic narrative conflict between characters, in the enmity between Gryffindors and Slytherins, for example. The Hogwarts houses correspond to the elements, as we know, but they also have a variety of other correspondences that follow on from those as illustrated in the following table.

THE HOGWARTS HOUSES AND ELEMENTAL CORRESPONDENCES

	Ravenclaw	Gryffindor	Slytherin	Hufflepuff
Animals	Eagle	Lion	Snake	Badger
Elements	Air	Fire	Water	Earth
House colors	Blue, Bronze	Scarlet, Gold	Green, Silver	Yellow, Black
Ritual magic elemental colors	Blue or Gold	Red or Crimson	Sea Green or Deep Blue	Corn Yellow or Black
House qualities	Intelligent, Studious	Daring, Brave	Ambitious, Cunning	Loyal, Hard working
Magical Precepts	to know	to dare	to will	to keep silent
Ritual magic elemental directions	East	South	West	North
Elemental implements	Wand	Sword	Cauldron	Pentagram

There's a column for each house. First, I give the totemic animals of each house, then the elemental correspondences and house colors, as given by JK Rowling and found in the novels. We can see that they match the elemental colors used in ritual magic in the next row down. Of course, though there's some broad agreement, there are also differences between various schools of ritual magic. (For example, many assign the sword to air and wand to fire.) I've primarily chosen to use Dolores Ashcroft-Nowicki's attributions from *The Ritual Magic Workbook*, which bear the closest relationship to the symbolic associations in the novels.[4] Next, you'll see the Hogwarts house qualities, and below those, you'll see that they map well onto the four traditional precepts of ritual magic. This is particularly illuminating in Slytherin's case.

Next we have the directions corresponding to the elements in ritual magic. The Hogwarts crest as illustrated in the books isn't laid out quite as it would be for the directions to match. Gryffindor and Slytherin (South and West) would need to swap to match the directions. However, when Ms. Rowling first describes the crest in *Stone*, she puts them in a correct directional order if you were 'reading' them going around the design clockwise: "a lion, an eagle a badger and a snake, surrounding a large letter 'H.'"[5]

Finally we come to the magical implements traditionally associated with each element. Again, we'll look at their relationship to house characters and qualities and see that they work quite well. Without further ado, let's turn to Ravenclaw and the kind of 'wit' every wizard needs.

RAVENCLAW: KNOWLEDGE AND AIR

For Ravenclaw, the cleverest
Would always be the best...[6]

The 'airy' nature of Ravenclaw pops up a lot symbolically in the books. The eagle is their totemic symbol, and the raven is part of their name. Odin, the wizard deity of Old Norse tradition, has two ravens, *Hugin*, which means 'thought,' and *Munin*, which means 'memory.' The eagle has long been associated with heavenly and earthly royalty. Scottish chiefs wear eagle feathers, and the bird is associated with the Greek Zeus, king of the gods, whose lightning bolts the eagle carries. The eagle, like the lion, appears as one of the figures of the *Tetramorph*, the divine creature with the heads of an eagle, a lion, a bull and a man, seen in the visions of Ezekiel and St. John.[7]

In Celtic tradition, as in many others, the eagle is associated with the sun, but stories say that the bird also flies down to rejuvenate itself in a secret lake. Philip Carr-Gomm, Chief of the Order of Bards, Ovates and Druids, writing with his wife, Stephanie, says that the eagle represents "the intellect, the super-ego, the conscious self, the heights. The lake represents the emotions, the unconscious, the depths. To find renewal, spiritual and psychological refreshment and rejuvenation, we must periodically allow our intellects, our rational selves, the opportunity to plunge into the depths of feeling and the subconscious. In this way knowledge is transformed into wisdom."[8]

Adding to the airiness of their totemic animals, the first we really see of a Ravenclaw is Professor Flitwick teaching the first years to perform the levitation charm *wingardium leviosa* with feathers.[9] In *Hallows* he puts on a full show of air elemental power. When it's time to shore up Hogwarts' defenses against Voldemort, the Professor points his wand out of a smashed window, muttering complex incantations. "Harry heard a weird rushing noise, as though Flitwick had unleashed the power of the wind into the grounds." Likewise, McGonagall prominently uses fire in the battle and Professor Sprout uses plants, pelting the Death Eaters with mandrakes and other violent vegetables.[10]

We only learn that Professor Flitwick is the head of Ravenclaw late in the series. The Ravenclaws don't get that much of a look-in in the early books, but perhaps that's because the knowledge that they symbolize permeates the stories so thoroughly. Besides the fact that the whole series is framed by Harry's education, Harry, Ron and Hermione spend hours at the library, investigate mysteries, pass (or fail) exams, and read. (At least Hermione does, as she's always reminding her less studious friends!) Add to this all the information sought by and withheld from Harry and you end up with a story where knowledge is central.

The school song requests knowledge as well as comically referring to its airy quality. The students ask "Hoggy Warty Hogwarts" to "teach us something please." They go on to say, "Our heads could do with filling / with some interesting stuff / For now they're bare and full of air / Dead flies and bits of fluff."[11]

The four magical precepts, "to know, to will, to dare and to keep silent" have been used by everyone from the Masons to various magical orders. It's hard to say where they first came from. The order can vary, but in the version I was given, knowledge is the wizard's first quality.

The fake Mad Eye Moody's words are true: *"you've got to know."*[12] Wizards must know themselves, know magic and know the world. Their knowledge must encompass the unpleasant curses they may be hit with 'out there' and other unsavory information, like their own deepest fears, as revealed by the boggart in Professor Lupin's cabinet. What's more, the knowledge must be of a specific kind, personal and practical. Remember everyone's outrage at being taught 'theoretical' defense against the dark arts in *Phoenix*? Theory for theory's sake just isn't the wizarding way. The very name 'wizard' tells us why.

The term 'wizard' comes from the same root as 'wit,' 'witness' and 'wisdom.'[13] The motto engraved on Ravenclaw's diadem is "Wit beyond measure is man's greatest treasure." This isn't just being witty or intelligent. It means someone who has personal knowledge, often, knowledge of the sacred. A wizard is a person who can see spiritual reality personally and vividly and who is informed by this experience, so that he becomes wise. Witch may come from the same root. Wizardry is a form of magic based not just on reading books and relying on other people's experience of the sacred, but on our own. It's about shamanic knowledge of the sacred, or *Gnosis*, the kind of knowledge that the mystical Gnostic sect of Christianity were named for.

Let me return to Ravenclaw's totemic eagle for a moment. The great 7th century Irish theologian, John Scotus Eriugena, associates the 'voice of the Eagle' with the call "of that spiritual bird who, on swiftest wings of innermost theology and intuitions of most brilliant and high contemplation, transcends all vision and flies beyond all things that are and are not." He goes on to say that he, identified with this spiritual bird, "ascends beyond all visible and invisible creation, passes through all thought and intellect, and, deified, enters into God who deifies him."[14] It's all quite shamanic, and, unsurprisingly the eagle is also associated with shamans and their capacities for spiritual sight and flight. Bird imagery is one of the most common found in shamans' costumes.

This knowledge orients the wizard, literally. In rituals the wizard generally begins facing east towards the sunrise and, symbolically, the element of air, consciousness and knowledge. (To 'orient' just means to face east.) In ritual magic group workings, the wizard placed here consciously directs the power that has come into the temple. (The 'temple' may be an actual building or room, or simply a space consecrated for ritual use.)

The magical implement of air in some traditions is the wand, the one Harry most looks forward to receiving and the one that seems to exhibit the greatest degree of consciousness of all the magical 'inanimate' objects in the books. As Ollivander said, "The wand chooses the wizard." Wands with twin cores like Harry's and Voldemort's resist dueling each other.

In *Hallows*, Harry says that Ollivander speaks of wands as though they have feelings and can think for themselves. Ollivander responds that the connections between wizard and wand are complex, encompassing "an initial attraction, and then a mutual quest for experience, the wand learning from the wizard, the wizard from the wand."[15]

Cho and Luna are the two most prominent Ravenclaws in the books, and both reveal the positive and negative facets of this brainy bunch. Luna is an encyclopedic repository of information. The thing is, a lot of it is a bit 'airy fairy.' Ravenclaws can have trouble 'grounding' their knowledge. They can be the classical absent-minded Professors. Their minds are on loftier things than bills or burning porridge.

On the positive side, they're clever. Cho, the Seeker, thinks strategically and sharply. However, like all Ravenclaws, she can over think. We see it in her relationship with Harry. The poor girl has had an awful time, and Hermione has to explain to Ron and Harry why she'd be crying after Harry and she first kiss. She's confused because she liked Cedric and now likes Harry and guilty because kissing Harry may be disloyal. She's concerned with what everyone will say if she goes out with Harry, mixed up because Harry was with Cedric when he died and worried about getting kicked off her Quidditch team because she can't fly well with all this banging around in her head. After Hermione lays all this out for the lads, Ron responds, "One person can't feel all that at once, they'd explode."[16] However, Cho's problem actually has more to do with how many conflicting things a person can think.

Of course, Hermione's in a good position to know. She is the most intellectual of the Gryffindors, bringing a much-needed dose of "cool logic in the face of fire" as Dumbledore puts it at the end of *Stone*.[17]

GRYFFINDOR: DARING AND FIRE

By Gryffindor, the bravest were
Prized far above the rest...

Hermione isn't 'miscast' as a Gryffindor for narrative convenience, as some have said, but represents a clear elemental subcategory, well known in magic. Besides the four elements, medieval wizards recognized elements within elements. For example, the 'earth' of water might be the sand beneath the receding tide, and its symbolic qualities. You have fire, yes, but the holistic magical approach tells us that every piece of the universe is holographic, it contains a microcosm of the whole. So there's fire, but there's also a fire of fire, a water of fire, an air of fire and an earth of fire. Hermione is the air of fire. Her dominant quality is courage, as it is for all Gryffindors, but her secondary quality is airy intellect. Ambition is there too, and loyalty, but I think we're safe in assigning air dominance.

Ron is a straightforwardly fiery fire, with his red hair and his passionate moods. All Gryffindors seem to have tempers, unlike, for example, the airy Ravenclaw, Luna, who doesn't vex at all, even when people steal her things. As I'll discuss below, Harry is, for obvious reasons, the water of fire and Neville is, just as obviously, the earth of fire.

But what are fire's essential qualities? In ritual magic, the wizard placed in the south for group workings mediates the forces of love, honor and courage to those in the ritual. He also acts as the guardian of the group. Fire represents ardor, passion and vitality, our effective power. Passion and bravery were both highly valued by the ancient Celts and Northern Europeans, so it's not really surprising that many think of Gryffindor as the pre-eminent Hogwarts house. One of the oldest names for the Celts was the *Gál*, a word that the name of ancient Gaul, (now in France) and modern Gaelic derive from. It means to be hot, passionate, fiery and powerful in battle.

It's tempting to see this as a source of McGonagall's name. Her portrayal by Maggie Smith evokes a magical Miss Jean Brodie (a famous, earlier, Scottish schoolteacher role of hers). Brodie and McGonagall both evoke cool buttoned up proper Edinburgh on the outside but have fires within. McGonagall certainly isn't overtly romantically passionate like Brodie. (Though one does sense that it was different in her younger years. Under the influence of wine, she giggles and blushes at Christmas dinner in *Stone* when an equally tipsy Hagrid kisses her cheek, and in *Hallows* she notices that Harry was "gallant" to defend her when Avery spat on her.) In the final battle in *Hallows* she is absolutely willing to kill, even to kill students, who side with Voldemort. The volleys of knives and fire she pelts Snape with don't suggest a mild disposition, nor does her shrieking "Coward!" after him.

If we turn to the lion of Gryffindor, we see that it, too, is associated with warrior qualities. The ancient Egyptians saw it as a protective, solar animal. The god Horus took a leonine form as the god of the appearing sun. The goddess Sekhmet had the head of a lioness, and was sent down to act as the 'Eye of Ra,' and the 'enforcer' of this high deity. When humanity rebelled, and chaos reigned on earth, Ra sent down Sekhmet, and she laid waste to the world. Eventually priests desperate to stop her colored vast amounts of beer red, and, thinking it was blood, Sekhmet drank it and passed out. She was equally ferocious in destroying non-human agents of chaos, like disease, so she became associated with healing. The ancient Egyptians said, "What can kill, can heal." The lion was sacred to the sun deity, Mithras, and initiates into Mithraic mysteries were called lions and lionesses. The heraldic lion of Persia carries a sword and carries the sun on its back, combining some solar symbols we find in Gryffindor. It has the attributes of royalty, power, vigilance and of course, bravery.[18]

One web site that offers to sort students into houses uses bravery as its primary determiner by asking what you'd do if you encountered a troll. If you'd fight it, you automatically go into Gryffindor, if you'd go get help other questions follow to sift you into the three other houses.[19] This is a reasonable method. In some respects bravery is the first virtue. JK Rowling has said that it's the one she most admires.[20] As many have observed, bravery is the virtue that enables us to practice all the others. It's been advised that we should do something we're a little afraid of each day to practice bravery, so that when the hour of danger strikes, it will not find us unprepared.

The ritual implement of fire is the sword. (Think of the angel bearing the fiery sword outside the gate of the Garden of Eden, barring the way back.) The books give us Gryffindor's ruby hilted sword. In myth, the sword is always the weapon of choice for the brave young, dragon slaying, solar hero.

All martial arts cultivate bravery leading to qualities that the Samurai referred to as "immovable mind" and "rock body."[21] This is the ability to first, fix the mind on what is required, and second, make the body do what the mind has decided on. Harry has attained these two qualities by *Hallows*, or he wouldn't be able to make himself walk into the forest at the end. Harry was scared, but that doesn't matter. The brave man may be just as scared as the coward, no one can tell. And that's the point. The brave man (or woman) acts in spite of their fear. This is one of Gryffindor's great lessons. I imagine Neville, never portrayed as the epitome of natural heroism, was quite frightened in both *Phoenix* and *Hallows*, but it didn't change his actions. Neville's every-day heroism early on, as well as being willing to stand up to his friends, is of the order required by every bullied child just to exist at school, or wherever the bullying takes place.

Neville even found attending Professor Snape's classes scary, but he did it anyway.

Acting in spite of our feelings is one of the best things we can learn to do. Not in a self-repressive way (though even this has its place) but in a way that means we have power over feelings that don't serve us. Bravery and the warrior ethos isn't all about fighting. In the instructions the early Irish king Cormac gave to his son, he stresses flexible strength and appropriate actions. He says, "I was silent in the wilderness. I was talkative in a crowd. I was genial in Tara's banquet hall. I was violent in combat. I was gentle with the weak. I was forceful with the strong....I was not arrogant though I wounded. I did not speak of any in their absence. I did not blame. I praised. I did not ask. I gave. It is through these practices that young men become experienced warriors."[22]

Without flexible strength we tend to waver between being doormats and reactively deciding to be 'tough.' We then become brittle armored like a crab—an ineffective shield from a shattering blow, but an effective one from the pleasures of life and love. If we want to be strong *and* enjoy life, we must be open to feeling, but develop a core of steel within, unassailable in true combat. In Celtic tradition, the tree that carried the warrior quality of flexible strength was the holly, used to make bow shafts, the same wood Harry's wand is made from.

Harry's capacity for love, his vulnerability, does decisively help him in the battle, despite his doubts that it would. Not only does Voldemort's lack of understanding of love blind him to Snape's true loyalties, but it isolates him in a way that makes his immortal quest seem a bit pointless. But Voldemort does have one valuable quality, a quality shared by all Slytherins, and worthy of emulation.

SLYTHERIN: WILL AND WATER

And power-hungry Slytherin
Loved those of great ambition.

What is power? In the books, some prominent Slytherins see power purely in terms of power over others, what you can make others do, or what you can do to them. The young Tom Riddle embraced this idea of power as a boy, boasting to Dumbledore that he can hurt others if he wants to.

Power is always, ultimately, the ability to direct oneself. The wizard can actually do what he means to do, regardless of circumstance, no mean achievement. In the film of *The Fellowship of the Ring*, Frodo tells Gandalf he is late for Bilbo's birthday party and the wizard replies, "A wizard is never late, Frodo Baggins, nor is he early. He arrives precisely when he means to."[23]

In the books there's a lot about Slytherin wanting pureblooded students in his house. During the time of persecution in which Hogwarts was founded, this was framed (pretty reasonably, in my opinion) as a fear that children from Muggle households might be untrustworthy. However, the Sorting Hat (with some of Slytherin's consciousness in it, remember) chose half-blooded Tom Riddle, Severus Snape, and who knows how many others of mixed birth as Slytherins. Snape is even disappointed when Lily is sorted into Gryffindor. He seems well informed about Hogwarts and Slytherin, so can it be that even a Muggle-born could be selected? Clearly, whatever Voldemort chooses to think later, blood-status isn't essential. It's also not essential to be 'bad,' as Snape, Regulus and Slughorn show. Though Hagrid tells Harry that there isn't a wizard who went bad that wasn't in Slytherin, Peter Pettigrew proves that wrong.

It also doesn't make sense that the other founders would include someone in their quaternity who brought nothing positive to the table. Picture the four friends together, describing the students they each want in their houses. When it comes round to the "brooding, sometimes scary, but undeniably talented fellow with the dark, narrow eyes and well-groomed goatee" he responds, "Give me the evil ones from old families." As Steven Patterson points out, the three friends wouldn't be likely to say, "Oh good, let's get on with it then." Slytherin ambition is a necessary and important quality.[24] Harry isn't nearly sorted into Slytherin because he carries a bit of Voldemort. Harry has a thirst to prove himself, as the Sorting Hat points out, and Slytherin could help him to greatness.

Slytherins are described as cunning. In Scotland 'cunning folk' was a general term for practitioners of (usually) positive magic. Cunning is different from intelligence — it's street-smarts, Machiavellian savvy. Intellectuals may have no idea of the 'real world.' Slytherins are intellect 'on the ground,' like their totemic serpent. There's nothing wrong with cunning in and of itself. Even Jesus says "Be ye as wise as serpents and as harmless as doves."[25]

The serpent has been associated with cunning and immortality from at least the time of the Sumerian myth of Gilgamesh, written down around 2100 BC. *Harry Potter* shares many of this epic's perennial concerns, such as dealing with loss and the quest for immortality. Gilgamesh loses his friend Enkidu to death, and sets off to seek immortality. After the hero king finds a plant that will restore his youth, he goes for a swim and the wily serpent seizes its chance to take the herb, giving it the ability to shed its skin and apparently return to youth.[26]

From here on, the serpent was associated with cunning and immortality, but often in positive ways. For example, the ancient Egyptian uraeus, the rearing cobra, was associated with truth and light. It often appeared on either side of the winged sun disk.[27] Later, of course, it became associated with the serpent who tempted Eve to sin and resulted in the first couple's expulsion from paradise. But even after this, the serpent didn't shed all its positive associations. The caduceus, emblem of Mercury, features two serpents twining up a staff, and its healing associations remain in its use as a modern symbol for medicine.

Ambition is given as Slytherin's defining quality – but is it really? We might ask ourselves what lies beneath ambition. The will to succeed? Take away the qualifier. What lies beneath ambition is *will*. This can be the terrible will that enables Voldemort to make seven horcruxes, to kill any in his way (or any who simply happen to be passing) and to survive without a body, or it can be the will to love that inspires Snape. It can be a will to power that admits no bounds or a will to serve, to be ones' truest self. In other words it can be will or Will. It's experienced as an internal force, even if the person thinks of it as divine will.

Some traditions see true magical will or divine will as the highest quality with which a wizard can align.[28] Rabbi Aryeh Kaplan, writing about the Jewish magical tradition Kabbalah, describes divine will as even higher than wisdom, since it is the impulse that gives rise to all things, even thought.[29] Your own higher will is also divine will.

We see will at work in the 'oddly impressive' young Snape, in *Hallows*, confident in his future destiny at Slytherin.[30] We see it in spades in his school friend, Lucius. Jason Isaacs, who plays him in the films, says that Lucius is thoroughly unpleasant but is also "the most confident person I have ever stepped inside of, completely supreme in his arrogance and ruthlessness. There's nothing that he wouldn't do."[31]

Aligning with true will is a big part of the wizard's work. We do this by connecting with spirit in awareness in meditation, prayer and magical work. Growing up, my mother and grandmother always stressed the danger of working magic for narrow, selfish goals. Beyond how it may harm others, there's the fact that, as Dumbledore says, people have a knack of wanting precisely what's worst for them. By contrast, if we align our will with the sacred, we tend to experience synchronization with the world. Indian Tantric yogis sometimes develop this kind of synchronization, such that they find that each meal placed before them is exactly what they want to eat, and their other needs tend to be spontaneously met just as they'd like. The things they want from this 'higher will' tend to flow to them and they tend to flow effortlessly with life.

Slytherin is associated with the element of water. Psychologically it represents the watery regions of the subconscious mind and emotions. Like the Slytherin serpent, it can represent our deep, pre-conscious urges and desires.

In ritual magic, the temple officer who stands in the West, the place of water and the setting sun, mediates the powers of the Otherworld as they enter the temple. She or he acts as a contact point for these forces. This officer is usually a woman, so there's an interesting male / female switch, with McGonagall heading the 'fire' house and Snape heading the 'water' house. This may relate to the alchemical *rebis*, or hermaphrodite, which I'll discuss in chapter five. The officer of the West is the seer of the temple and must have particularly strong powers of will as well as psychic talent.

The magical implement associated with water is the chalice or cauldron. In magic, the cauldron can be seen as the principal of containment, with the potion being the power. You need both containment and power to create a predictable effect.

The more power, the more containment is needed. In *Stone* Neville manages to dissolve Seamus' cauldron by putting in porcupine quills at the wrong moment. Young wizards typically have more power than containment. It's one reason why Snape is always hammering Harry about his lack of mental control and discipline. As we see in the events at the end of *Phoenix*, Harry's fiery power to act and to draw followers and friends into acting with him, is a real danger to others and to himself when it's out of control.

Of course, Professor Snape is potions master for five of the seven books. He is a master of the cauldron and a master of containment. Dumbledore says that "To give Voldemort what appears to be valuable information while withholding the essentials is a job I would give to nobody but you."[32] He has a strong enough will that his occlumency can keep Voldemort out of his head.

By the end, despite the dismal failure of his lessons with Snape, Harry has cultivated his will. He has become the water of fire, and not just because he has a bit of Voldemort as an unwelcome lodger. He hasn't mastered will, few people of any age have, let alone a seventeen year old. But he has enough to make himself do what he has to, and the self-awareness to know the limits of his will. He doesn't seek out his friends to say good-bye before going into the forest, because he thinks he wouldn't still be able to go. He usually gets through by his other qualities, love, bravery and friends who make up for what he lacks, but that's okay.

No man's an island except Voldemort, and we see where that gets him. Voldemort, of course, insists on loyalty, and savagely punishes those who don't give it to him. Loyalty is a quality possessed by our final Hogwarts house, and Ms. Rowling emphasizes its importance throughout the books.

HUFFLEPUFF: SILENCE AND EARTH
For Hufflepuff, hard workers were
Most worthy of admission...

The Sorting Hat's Song in *Stone* says that Hufflepuffs aren't just hard working but are also just, loyal and patient.[33] Other than Professor Sprout and Cedric Diggory, there aren't many

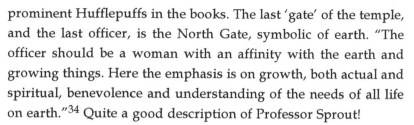
prominent Hufflepuffs in the books. The last 'gate' of the temple, and the last officer, is the North Gate, symbolic of earth. "The officer should be a woman with an affinity with the earth and growing things. Here the emphasis is on growth, both actual and spiritual, benevolence and understanding of the needs of all life on earth."[34] Quite a good description of Professor Sprout!

I've not found a huge amount of associated lore about the badger. It's actually a giant member of the weasel family, and not a tiny bear, as some people mistakenly say. However, it shares some obvious symbolism associated with bears in that it burrows, lives in holes in the earth and can be very fierce and determined. The bear is an important totem in many cultures. The term 'badgering' comes from the badger's savage and persistently determined quality.

The implement of earth in ritual magic is the pentagram. This can be the five-pointed star, usually made of clay or wood, with the three points upward symbolizing spirits' rule over the elements. The other way, with two points up, isn't necessarily diabolical but can have to do with manifesting desired results in the physical.

Ritual magician, Dolores Ashcroft-Nowicki suggests a more personal 'pantacle,' with one side painted with whatever the wizard's idea of God is, and the other painted with whatever they see as their relationship to that God. She advises changing pantacles as your idea of God changes.

In the books, we don't see any such symbol. Symbolic earth has been replaced by actual earth, with Professor Sprout teaching herbology in greenhouses filled with the stuff! The use of dragon dung as fertilizer relates nicely to alchemical symbolism. The dragon and dung can both symbolize the *prima materia*, the first material with which alchemists began their work.

The most prominent Hufflepuff student we know of is Cedric, a paragon of decency. He offered to give up Hufflepuff's

Quidditch win when he realized it came because the Dementors overwhelmed Harry in *Azkaban*. In the end, within reach of the Triwizard cup, he's willing to walk away from more glory than Hufflepuff has had in centuries in the spirit of fairness. He finally gives in to Harry's request to take the cup together, and as they say, the rest is history.

Neville has strong Hufflepuff tendencies. We can easily see Neville as the 'earth of fire,' with his gift for herbology and less than stellar early performance. His totemic toad is yet another symbol for the alchemical *prima materia*. Neville, too, is transformed by his diligent dedication to the alchemical process of transforming the self. Harry could certainly stand a bit more Hufflepuff stick-to-itiveness, of the kind Neville repeatedly demonstrates.

In *Phoenix* Neville works hard at his Dumbledore's Army lessons after learning that his parents' torturer, Bellatrix, has escaped from Azkaban. As Harry teaches him assorted methods of magical combat and self defense, he finds Neville's one pointed-focus alarming. "Neville barely spoke during DA meetings anymore, but worked relentlessly on every new jinx and counter-curse Harry taught them, his plump face screwed up in concentration, apparently indifferent to injuries and accidents and working harder than anyone else in the room." Only Hermione masters the shield charm faster than Neville.[35] In *Hallows*, when Harry returns to Hogwarts, Neville describes the tortures he and others have endured under the Carrows in such a matter-of-fact way that even Harry is unnerved.

Neville was such an intriguing figure, twinned with Harry by the prophecy, that many expected some sort of 'rug from under us' ending involving him. There was no huge shock, but Neville follows a clear heroic trajectory. He shows himself to be a true Gryffindor by pulling Gryffindor's sword from the Sorting Hat and slaying the final horcrux with it.

He also brings things down to earth. He's solid. In *Phoenix*, he insists on joining Harry on his mission to the Ministry. After all their training he doesn't take well to Harry asking him to stay behind. "We were all in the DA together," said Neville quietly. "It was all supposed to be about fighting You-Know-Who, wasn't it? And this is the first chance we've had to do something real—or was that all just a game or something?" He doesn't get angry or whine—just states the facts.

Neville doesn't waste words. The quality associated with earth in the magical precepts is silence, as in the old saying, 'silent as the grave.' At first I had a hard time thinking of what to say about this quality, and Hufflepuff in general. Like Hagrid says, I tended to think of Hufflepuffs as "a bunch o' duffers" and silence as the least interesting quality. I realized that I, like so many people, undervalue silence. I tend to meditate and take spirit journeys to music and play it in the background throughout the day, I have two voluble children and probably talk too much and too loudly myself. I think we all have to remind ourselves that conversation is not talking and waiting to talk, it's talking and *listening!*

Silence has a becoming humility about it. The wizard really doesn't want to boast. It's a bit like having the elder wand. It's tempting fate to run around saying "I have an unbeatable wand!" even if you do. Likewise, boasting about spiritual attainment pretty well means that you're not where you think you are. I once heard of a reporter asking a lama, "So, what's it like to be enlightened?" My informant (one of the lama's students) told me that if anyone was enlightened, this man was, but no enlightened person could respond to such a question. He said, "I don't know." My informant helped the reporter re-frame his question to ask, "What is the mind of enlightenment like?" That, he could answer. One facet of the answer is that the mind of enlightenment is a lot quieter than most people's minds. A well-trained lama or wizard

tends to find that when they aren't talking, or listening, it's actually quiet in their heads. Imagine that.

JK Rowling associates silence with both hard work and loyalty. Neville doesn't talk at DA meetings, he *works*. And of course, Peter Pettigrew betrays the Potters by speaking their secret when it was his job to keep it. When he says that Voldemort would have killed him, Sirius responds, "Then you should have died!" Peter's jabbered pleas and defenses to everyone are repulsive. Silence is dignified, where verbal diarrhea embarrasses those doing it and those listening.

Faithfulness unto death is an earthy quality. Will can be warped by ambition or fear or desire. Daring can see you pelting into rash acts, like Harry's 'rescue' of Sirius. Knowledge can be misused and information misinterpreted. Silence, by contrast, tends to obey Hippocrates dictum to doctors: "First, do no harm."

The head of Hufflepuff is a herbologist, growing plants for potions, the discipline that Professor Snape says you'd hardly think is magic. It's not flashy, but is a branch of 'magic' that remains in general practice. Each time we take an aspirin we benefit from some herbologist's discovery of the pain relieving properties of willow bark. The earthy element of magic endures.

Without the earthy qualities of silence, hard work and loyalty, the other elements are literally ungrounded. Fire spends itself in futile and changing passions, will becomes a guilty reproach and airy intellect builds castles in the sky. We need the ground beneath us, and Hogwarts needs Hufflepuff, and all the other houses.

All of us have thought about where we'd fit into the Hogwarts scheme. All houses have positives and negatives. In her article, *Ich bin ein Hufflepuff*, Susan Matthews said that although first drawn to Slytherin, she could finally happily admit to being the hard working loyal sort. Dark glamour just wasn't her style, nor, when she really looked at it, did she want it to be.

There's a real value in 'knowing your place' and an ultimate value in knowing yourself. Most traditional cultures 'sort' people in one way or another. Though rigid caste structures can be oppressive, a functional structure can actually be freeing, allowing each person to get on with doing what they do best, rather than being paralyzed by indecision.

Most people identify with a house from the start of reading the books. A little reflection on our own positives and negatives reveals both where we'd be most likely to end up and the dual side of our house attributes. You can also reflect on balancing your house type. Fiery Gryffindors benefit from an admixture of Slytherin will and cunning, Hufflepuff hard work and Ravenclaw awareness. All the houses benefit from mixing with the others

By using the house system as she does, JK Rowling acknowledges the positive qualities of many different types, the values of different groups to society and even the value of the less attractive people in those groups, like the geeks, underdogs and bullies. She acknowledges different kinds of heroism throughout the books as well. Quite a few people have noted her use of the heroic journey formula, popularized by Joseph Campbell. Tracing the heroic narratives of a few of the main characters can give us deeper insights into applying the positive qualities of the four houses in life.

IV

THROUGH THE MAZE: HEROIC JOURNEYS

It was, he thought, the difference between being dragged into the arena to face a battle to the death and walking into the arena with your head held high. Some people, perhaps, would say that there was little to choose between the two ways, but Dumbledore knew — and so do I, thought Harry, with a rush of fierce pride, and so did my parents — that there was all the difference in the world.
Harry Potter

The modern hero, the modern individual who dares heed the call and seek the mansion of that presence with whom it is our whole destiny to be atoned, cannot, indeed, must not, wait for his community to cast off its slough of pride, fear, rationalized avarice, and sanctified misunderstanding. "Live," Nietzsche says, "as though the day were here."
Joseph Campbell

he quotes above give us the two essential qualities of the hero. Joseph Campbell, that great scholar and *liver* of the heroic story, tells us that the hero works for others and doesn't wait around for his culture to approve of him (or her) saving it. The wizarding world doesn't always approve of Harry's efforts on its behalf, and often brands him a loony. This is typical. All you prospective and actual heroes out there (and that'd be all of you) had better accept this up front. As shaman, Simon Buxton's teacher told him, "A weak person always goes to where he is smiled at."[1]

The hero isn't weak, and also isn't focussed on his own personal survival. Like Harry, the hero may be keen to survive but, unlike Voldemort, he knows that there are more important things.

In a way, it's easier to define a hero by what he isn't. There are three 's' words. The hero isn't defined by narrow ideas of self, by surviving or by suffering. Modern people misuse the term. A hero isn't simply a victim who doesn't utterly collapse. A person doesn't become a hero by having a misfortune, say, by getting cancer. However, they may become heroic through their response to the disease if they behave in a way that gives hope and inspiration to others.

People aren't heroic for saving their own lives in a disaster. They're heroic if they save another. Harry is always saying that his scar and his survival don't make him special. He's right. Those things mean that his mother was special. However, his response to his circumstances does make him heroic. As Dumbledore points out during the discussion that gives rise to Harry's thoughts above, he could have responded differently. He could have turned to dark magic, or even to work with Voldemort, as the Dark Lord offered in *Stone*. He could have fled.

A big part of the reason he didn't was his concern for others. The hero acts for others. Whether or not the hero is a wizard or shaman, he acts out of a basic magical, mystical and ecological under-standing of reality: we're all connected. Of course, heroes like Harry don't reach this understanding, or gain the ability to act on it, instantly. They learn in stages, as we all do.

STAGES OF THE HEROIC JOURNEY

The hero's journey is a bit like the alchemical process of making the philosopher's stone. Different people describe different stages put them in different orders.[2] Stages can also be repeated, which can get confusing. For example, does Harry go through his 'winning the maiden' stage in *Chamber* when he rescues Ginny, in *Phoenix*, when he has his first romance with Cho, in *Prince*, where he gets involved with Ginny, or sometime after the series ends when he marries Ginny?

One way of looking at the heroic pattern, like the alchemical, is that we return to stages at different levels throughout our lives. Growth is more a spiral than a straight line. When he rescues Ginny from the dragon's den, he's not at the stage where he has romantic feelings. His flirtation with Cho is an immature attempt. His first real romantic engagement with Ginny is based in friendship, more mature, but he still can't give himself fully to it because of his circumstances. Obviously, sometime between Voldemort's death and the epilogue, their relationship moves to a deeper level.

The three 'basic' stages of the journey are separation, initiation and return. Harry, like all heroes, receives a call to adventure, goes to places where things happen to him, and returns changed, with gifts for his people.[3] These stages can correspond to the three aspects of joy, sorrow and higher awareness, discussed earlier. The hero experiences joy in departing for adventure. Harry re-invokes the euphorically happy memory of discovering he is a wizard and will be leaving the Dursleys to conjure a patronus. The hero experiences sorrow during his travails (no need to elaborate in Harry's case) and he then attains the higher awareness at the end to bring gifts to his people.

We can see the three stages of separation, initiation and return in the *Harry Potter* series as a whole and within each novel. In the series, Harry receives his call via the highly symbolic owls from Minerva bearing his letters and finally, in no uncertain terms, on his 11th birthday, from Hagrid.[4] He has all sorts of perilous and sometimes traumatic adventures, which include the heroic staple of dragon involvement. Finally, he returns spectacularly to his community delivering the biggest possible boon.

Each novel puts a slight twist in the theme. 'Home' is Hogwarts and his friends, rather than Number Four Privet Drive and the

Dursleys want nothing less than supernatural boons from Harry. Hence, the 'return' isn't tidily book ended in the stories. However, the 'call' is represented in each novel by his start-of-term letter with supply lists and OWL results. The call also takes the form of horrid newspaper articles that spur him to action in later books. He departs from the Dursleys and goes to Hogwarts in each novel. (Except in the last, where he goes on the camping holiday from hell before returning to Hogwarts.) The end of most of the novels features a summing up from Dumbledore, discussing the boons Harry's actions have given the wizarding community and other information. The wrap up in *Prince* comes earlier, when Harry reaches the conclusion above. Ms. Rowling herself said that we sort of skid out of *Prince* into *Hallows*. Reading one after another feels a bit more like reading one book, than say, reading *Azkaban* after *Chamber*.

If we go beyond these three stages we can look at an outline of other elements of the journey. Beginning at the very beginning, the hero is often conceived in an unusual way. The hero may be born out of wedlock or posthumously or supernaturally. Harry is a typical hero in that he has parents of unusual qualities and abilities from whom he is separated. One psychological way of reading the story is that of psychologist Sigmund Freud's 'family romance.' Freud realized that most, if not all, of us, fantasize that our parents are not our parents at some point during childhood. Like Harry, who keeps dreaming that some unknown relative will come to take him away, we may dream that we have perfect parents elsewhere who'll appreciate us much more than our current models.[5] In Harry's case, he knows he doesn't have parents, but he does find a family of affinity at Hogwarts who love and appreciate him much more than the Dursleys.

In the usual mythic way, there are tokens of his future greatness. First, there's the prophecy. This leads to Harry being imperiled as an infant, another heroic theme. Harry's scar symbolizes the lightning bolt power of truth and illumination. The books don't say precisely where it is, and the films place it off to one side, but illustrations seem to show it more in the middle. See, for example, the Mary Grandpré picture of Harry and his broken wand in Chapter 18 of the American edition of *Hallows*, which shows it central. (You'd certainly think that's where Voldemort would aim!) This gives it a relationship to the 'third eye,' the spiritual eye you see in the middle of the forehead of deities like Lord Shiva, of Hindu tradition. This eye has the power to see into the spiritual dimension, and also to transmit power. Some traditions even ritually 'open' this third eye by cutting the skin.

Harry's scar has initiatory, visionary and power giving functions. It 'initiates' him into Voldemort's very mind and soul, gives him the power of parseltongue and enhances some of his other talents. The price is, of course, an unwelcome 'lodger' and the loss of his parents. The way that Voldemort equips Harry to act by trying to murder him is a classical example of the 'reversals' we find in fairy tales and myths.

Tokens of Harry's future greatness continue throughout the books. Of course, Ollivander's comments, when the wand that chooses Harry turns out to be the 'twin' of Voldemort's, are a significant token. We must expect great things from Harry. Besides being a token, it also underscores Harry as Voldemort's light twin, just as Voldemort, on one level, is Harry's dark or shadow self.

The whole question of being chosen, being marked by prophecy, birth and life as special, raises an interesting issue. Magical children are born, not made, as Petunia Dursley discovers to her eternal resentment when she asks Dumbledore to be allowed to attend Hogwarts like her sister, Lily. Harry is even more special than this broader group of which he is a part. The anti-racist theme is a prominent 'text' of the books, but the wizard / Muggle divide, and Harry's 'Chosen One' status, are subtexts at odds with it.

After Harry answers the 'call,' delivered by owl post and by

Hagrid, he meets the snobbish, and racist, Draco Malfoy at Madam Malkin's robe-makers. Hagrid gets indignant over Draco's superior attitude. He says that Harry's not Muggle born, (though his mother was) and goes on to say "If he'd known who yeh were — " implying that Malfoy would have been impressed. Most wizards Harry meets are extremely impressed. Hagrid comments earlier that Harry will grow up to be "a thumpin' good" wizard, given who his parents were.[6]

The whole idea of better blood and birth either leads to racism or requires very careful thinking to avoid racism. Fairy tales have these kind of 'special' heroes yet always aim for a socially just reality. The hero can't be a swot. (This is the British term for a person as studious as Hermione.) Harry isn't universally good at everything, or universally good, as I'll discuss later. He's not that brainy, or hardworking. These lacks make Harry, and other heroes, 'every man' figures with whom the audience can identify. The conflict is that this makes the 'ordinary' hero's triumph more based on innate qualities like blood, birth and destiny. This, in turn, can reinforce racist assumptions. Elaine Ostry, a scholar of children's literature, says that Ms. Rowling has inherited an internal conflict in the fairy tale form itself.[7]

The hero often has a special upbringing. In another of JK Rowling's twists, the most special upbringing Dumbledore can give Harry is a resolutely ordinary one at the Dursleys that gives Harry humility and compassion. This miserable but useful beginning is followed by Hogwarts. Harry's adventures at Hogwarts follow the well-worn pattern of that favorite British hero-tale, the school story. Harry Potter compares with another school story, Rudyard Kipling's *Stalky and Co.*[8] Stalky and his friends, like Harry, Ron and Hermione, engage in 'house' rivalries, and forbidden activities. Harry and Stalky both become 'outcasts' at different points. However, their headmasters secretly expect great things from them.

The hero often acquires layers of magical protection and allies to help him. Harry certainly does, getting various objects, like his father's cloak, that magically help him. He also has friends who help him find the horcruxes and objects to destroy them with, like basilisk teeth. He and Ron get Gryffindor's sword from the frozen pool in a way that clearly alludes to Arthur receiving Excalibur from the Lady of the Lake. Arthur simply takes Excalibur, but Ron and Harry, like most modern heroes, need to dive beneath the waters of the subconscious to pull it forth.

Sometimes the hero acquires so much magical aid that he becomes invulnerable, at least for a time. Harry never acquires invulnerability but, as Dumbledore often tells him, paradoxically it's vulnerability, not invulnerability that Harry requires to triumph. Here we could more broadly say that the hero often gets what he needs to win at some stage of his journey.

The hero often fights a dragon or other monster. Of course, Voldemort is the primary serpentine monster, but there are others, notably the basilisk in *Chamber* and the dragon who he must defeat but not kill in *Goblet*. Dragons have a wealth of symbolism. The Asian ones, like the Chinese Fireball, can symbolize kingship and the vital powers of nature. However, European dragons, like the Hungarian Horntail, can sometimes symbolize evil, negative avarice. They hoard virgins and gold, neither of which they are capable of enjoying. Consequently, they can represent the most primitive and undesirable parts of us.

Harry goes through a revealing mythological shift in his dealings with dragons. His first encounter is with Norbert, who hatches out of a black dragon's egg before him. In alchemy, the dragon's egg can symbolize the black prima materia, the first substance, with which the alchemist began his transformative work.

This baby dragon proves unmanageable, even by Hagrid, who might be seen here as representing positive but unrefined aspects of the self. The primordial self, who's powerful but not always wise, and has poor impulse-control. In this case, Harry and his friends simply pass on the problem to someone older and better-equipped, Ron's dragon expert older brother. As children, we rely on older family members to control our dragons.

The next dragon is the classical one that needs slaying, and this is the next response we find within ourselves. At adolescence, the dragon can no longer be palmed off. As aggression and lust arise within us, our first impulse is to slay the monster, but it isn't all bad. Lust and aggression can be 'sublimated' into fuel for spiritual development, as in East Indian Tantra. This tradition sees the vital, but potentially destructive, spiritual power within us as a sleeping serpent called the *kundalini*. It can arise during adolescence and during spiritual 'growth spurts' as well. It has the power to help us grow and change or, if we don't control it, to drive us mad.[9] Twelve year old Harry takes no chances and, with the aid of Dumbledore's phoenix (symbol of the resurrected king, his aspirations to attaining the end of the alchemical process) and Gryffindor's sword, (elemental weapon of fire and the wizard's vital force) he kills it.

This is the response he's capable of at the time, and it's certainly better than letting it wreak havoc, but it's not the most constructive possible response. As Nietzsche says, "Be careful, lest, in casting out your demons, you cast out the best thing that is in you." It's often more useful to put them to work, or at least, to work your way around them. This is what Harry does in his next dragon encounter with the Hungarian Horntail in *Goblet*. She is a devouring mother archetype if ever there was one. She guards an egg that is no longer the black of Norbert's, but golden. This shows that Harry has gone some way towards transmuting his black *prima materia* into something more valuable.

Harry uses his broomstick and its power of flight to grasp this golden egg without hurting the dragon. We're told that Viktor Krum lost points because he harmed the dragon so that she trampled some of her own eggs. At this stage, we figure out how to get around the dragon, and take what is valuable from it to guide us, as the golden egg guides Harry on the next stage of his journey. As Harry goes to sleep after the contest, with his small, manageable model of the Horntail asleep on his night table, he reflects that dragons were really quite all right.

The final dragon is, of course, the one that he and his friends ride on their spectacular escape from Gringott's in *Hallows*. The dragon power is much more his own. In shamanic terms, any animal that allows you to ride it in a journey is likely to be your totem. The dragon is blind, which can represent the fact that Harry's knowledge is still incomplete. He also can't control it, and has to go where it takes him, so he still has a way to go. However, he's come a long way from shipping it off to Charlie to deal with!

Another of the hero's well-known adventures is a journey into the Underworld; a journey Harry makes many times, figuratively and actually, as in the Gringott's episode. The first is of course, his journey past Fluffy / Cerberus into the subterranean rooms that guard the philosopher's stone. The most vividly horrific is probably found in *Prince* with its corpse-filled lake and Harry having to obey Dumbledore's terrible orders. As the alchemist says, *Visita Interiora Terrae Rectificando Invenies Occultum Lapidem*, "Visit the interior of the earth, and by rectifying you will find the hidden stone which is the true medicine."[10]

The hero is often banished in youth to return later and triumph over his enemies. In some cases he must again leave the realm he won with difficulty. Harry's story gives many repetitions of this theme. Before the series concluded some fans had a theory that Harry was a horcrux (as he turned out to be) and would win the final battle with Voldemort only to discover that he'd lost his powers when the piece of Voldemort's soul left him. In this theory, Voldemort's transferred powers were what made Harry a powerful wizard. Stephen Fry put this theory to JK Rowling in a television interview and she pronounced, "Oh that's good!" It certainly would have been mythically sound.

The hero, as noted above, always returns with boons for his people. Dumbledore sets this up as a very basic premise from the start. In the first novel, he conceals the philosopher's stone within the Mirror of Erised in such a way that only a person who wanted to find the stone but not use it for himself could get hold of it. In other words, his root desire had to be for the good of others. He had to be a true hero.

Death is another component in the myth. The hero may die fighting for the good of others. He may attain 'immortal glory' and renown. He may even be resurrected and attain immortality and illumination. Having done so, he may transmit his powers to others.

It's worth noting that, where Campbell draws little distinction between fairy tale and myth, Bruno Bettelheim, a child psychologist and great authority on fairy tales, saw myths as generally pessimistic and fairy tales as optimistic. The hero at the end of the fairy tale reassures us by getting the girl (or boy) the castle and living happily ever after. The hero of myth faces insurmountable odds and dies heroically. The message of the fairy tale is "Do your best and good will be rewarded." The message of the myth is "Do your best even if you don't get rewarded. There are more important things." After all, we can only control our own actions, not guarantee outcome. We can, however, guarantee failure if we sit around waiting for a guaranteed success! Both of the messages above convey important truths and JK Rowling gives a nod to both in her ending. Harry's ending partakes of myth and fairy tale, myth in terms of his actions, fairy tale in terms of the outcome. Of course, many others in the series don't fare as well, and so, lean towards being mythological heroes. Let's have a look at the most prominent one.

PROFESSOR SEVERUS SNAPE

Professor Snape gets his own heading because, of all the characters, other than Harry, he's taken the greatest hold on the popular imagination. Other than Sirius, the *Prisoner of Azkaban*, he's the only other lone character to feature in a title. In America, when you ordered the final book at Borders bookshop, they gave you two stickers. One said, "Snape is loyal" and the other "Snape will betray." You could choose one to wear to declare your allegiance! This is a key to Snape's fascination. He's enigmatic. Everything he does always seems open to several interpretations.

That said, fan fiction picked up on many subtexts of his character, well before these became clear in the novels. Lily as the great love of his life, whose death catalyzed his turn to the good side, appeared in a number of places. JK Rowling also expressed shock when one caller to a phone in radio show asked her about Snape's "redemptive pattern" in 1999. She told them they'd understand her shock if they read book seven when it came out. Archetypes function in strange ways. When people latch on to them as adored personifications ('imaginary' figures that manifest a particular archetype or aspect of the psyche) they transmit more than their creators may have intended.

Joyce Millman wrote a brilliant examination of this character in the novels, films and fan fiction entitled *To Sir, With Love: How Fan Fiction Transformed Professor Snape from a Greasy Git to a Byronic Hero...Who's Really, Really Into S & M*. That rather says it all. Professor Snape is a great example of an archetype 'let loose' in the playground of popular imagination, and he hasn't always behaved himself. The Snape of fan fiction is the ultimate tall dark and tortured anti-hero. Ms. Rowling has not always appeared to be best pleased with fan responses to Snape.

In a 2004 talk at the Edinburgh Book Festival, she said, "You always see a lot of Snape, because he is a gift of a character. I hesitate to say that I love him."

An audience member responded, "I do!"

"You do?" Ms Rowling replied, and then continued:

> This is a very worrying thing. Are you thinking about Alan
> Rickman or about Snape? Isn't this life, though? I make this
> hero — Harry, obviously — and there he is on the screen, the
> perfect Harry, because Dan is very much as I imagine Harry, but
> who does every girl under the age of 15 fall in love with? Tom
> Felton as Draco Malfoy. Girls, stop going for the bad guy. Go for
> a nice man in the first place. It took me 35 years to learn that, but
> I am giving you that nugget free, right now, at the beginning of
> your love lives.

Personal advice aside, this seems a bit disingenuous now. After all
that, Severus did turn out to be a tortured romantic hero of the
precise sort she was warning young ladies away from.

It's worth noting that the fan fiction about Snape as a Byronic
hero began in earnest after Alan Rickman was cast in this role. He
has, of course, played wonderful romantic figures in films like
Truly, Madly, Deeply and *Sense and Sensibility* and evil yet enticing
villains in *Die Hard* and *Robin Hood, Prince of Thieves*. He has a Goth
look in the films, which make no effort to 'ugly him up.' His teeth
aren't horribly yellowed, his hair doesn't seem terribly greasy and
they've given him rather fetching robes.[11]

As Ms. Rowling notes in her comments above, it can be hard for
fans to separate the two now. I've wondered if it's even been hard
for her. A post-Rickman Snape gets a very 'charged' scene
comforting the distressed Narcissa in *Prince*. Ms. Rowling also titles
the chapter that reveals his deeper motivations of love for Lily *The
Prince's Tale*. Given her interest in numbers, I couldn't help but
notice that it's chapter 33, the age Christ was when he died. I also
found myself wondering if his self-chosen 'Prince' title was less
about a Voldemort type aspiration to nobility than a wish to be the

prince in a fairy tale involving Lily.

During a 'web chat' with fans on her British publisher, Bloomsbury's web site shortly after *Hallows* was released, one fan asked Ms. Rowling if she thought Snape was a hero. "Yes, I do; though a very flawed hero. An anti-hero, perhaps. He is not a particularly likeable man in many ways. He remains rather cruel...and yet he loved, and showed loyalty to that love, and, ultimately, laid down his life because of it. That's pretty heroic!" Later she goes on to say that Lily loved 'Sev,' and might even have returned his romantic feelings, "if he had not loved Dark Magic so much, and been drawn to such loathsome people and acts."

The narrative progression of Snape's character, his 'arc' in the stories, reminds me a bit of Darth Vader's in *Star Wars*. In the first three films he's a bad guy redeemed by saving Luke and destroying the emperor by dying a sacrificial death. Then, the prequel trilogy focussed on how he got there. The 'long story' in *Star Wars* turned out to be Vader's. In some respects, the 'long story' in *Harry Potter* feels a bit like Snape's, more even than Dumbledore's, though both names 'reincarnate' in Harry's son.

Harry eventually calls Snape the bravest man he ever knew. Harry has a hard time facing death at Voldemort's hands. He steels himself and confronts him a number of times, mostly unwillingly, but Snape walks into the old serpent's jaws repeatedly and picks his teeth for him. When we see the bloody death Voldemort gives Snape when he thinks Snape is loyal, we can only imagine what he'd have done if he'd found out about the betrayal. The quality that enabled his bravery was the central Slytherin quality of will. Slytherin Snape has will aplenty and Gryffindor Harry often lacks it until the later books.

One wonders if Snape's abuse of Harry was at least partly of the 'toughening up' variety. Re-read the occlumency lessons in *Phoenix* and they take on a different quality in retrospect. What seemed like bullying then, now strikes one more as a desperate attempt to shore up Harry's defenses. Snape is right in *Phoenix* when he says that people like Harry are easy prey for the Dark Lord. Harry proves to be so just a few chapters on. Even the final scene in *Prince*, where Harry pursues Snape, trying to curse him, reads more like a lesson in retrospect. He defends Harry against other Death Eaters and, while undoubtedly furious, seems to be making one last attempt to hammer some sense into Harry. Perhaps he's trying to use Harry's hatred of him to motivate him to control his mind and emotions at last.

Snape actually seems to have better mental control than Dumbledore, though he's a younger man. Is it that he has nothing left to lose? He's deeply emotional but his loved one is beyond help or harm. A hero with no personal stake has greater ease of action. Detachment can thus be an important heroic virtue.

Our model for the virtues of will and detachment for most of the *Harry Potter* series is Professor Snape, though we didn't know for sure until the end. Snape and Dumbledore are a bit like the yin and yang symbol. Snape is mainly dark with a little white dot of love for Lily, the best part of him, as Dumbledore says. Dumbledore, by contrast, is mainly light, as the name Albus indicates. It means whiteness or purity. However, he also has the black dot of his lust for power and dreadful culpability in his sister's death. We'll turn to his story next, followed by the arcs of some other prominent characters.

ARCHETYPAL CHARACTER ARCS

Albus' second name, Dumbledore, is an Old English word for 'bumblebee.' JK Rowling says that, given his love of music, she pictured him wandering around humming to himself. 'Honeybee' was also a title given to initiates who had attained an unquestioned degree of purity at Eleusis and Ephesus, centers of the ancient Greek mysteries.[12] The shamanic teacher, Simon Buxton, wrote of learning an indigenous European tradition of shamanism based around the bee as totem. His wise old teacher told him something that might have come out of Dumbledore's mouth. "As you continue to deepen into the Path of Pollen, your task is to become detached, but not indifferent — serene but not inactive."[13] This also describes Dumbledore himself.

Dumbledore's power is nicely understated in the first couple of books. Richard Harris conveys this well as Dumbledore in the film of *Chamber*, for example, in the scene where Snape tries to remind him of rules about under-age wizardry after Harry and Ron crash a flying car. "I am familiar with our bylaws, Severus, having written many of them myself." That look over the top of the glasses speaks volumes.

As the books progress, it's increasingly obvious that Dumbledore isn't just an eccentric old fellow. Like his namesake bee, he's tranquil unless roused by threat. Then, he is terrifying. JK Rowling hits you between the eyes with his power in *Goblet*, when he bursts in on Barty Crouch Jr. (disguised as Moody) and Harry.

At that moment, Harry fully understood for the first time why people said Dumbledore was the only wizard Voldemort had ever feared. The look upon Dumbledore's face as he stared down at the unconscious form of Mad-Eye-Moody was more terrible than Harry could have imagined. There was no benign smile upon Dumbledore's face, no twinkle in the eyes behind the spectacles. There was cold fury in every line of the ancient face; a sense of power radiated from Dumbledore as though he were giving off burning heat.[14]

Harry has Dumbledore like Frodo has Gandalf, Arthur has Merlin and Luke has Obi-Wan. As essential as these figures are, it's equally essential that the hero loses their support at some stage, for the journey to proceed. Originally, Obi Wan Kenobi made it all the way through the first *Star Wars* trilogy alive. Then, George Lucas, who modeled his saga on Campbell's model, realized he'd gotten it wrong. Alec Guinness, the eminent British actor who played Obi Wan, nearly quit when Lucas changed the script to better reflect the hero's journey, but decided to remain when Lucas assured him his absence would be as deeply felt and essential as his presence.

As science fiction writer Lawrence Watt-Evans noted in his article, *Why Dumbledore had to Die*, anyone who knew Campbell knew that Dumbledore was doomed well before *Prince*. JK Rowling follows the other features of the hero's journey too closely to alter this element. In fact, she disposes of mentors and potential mentors rather ruthlessly. As Harry realizes at the end of *Prince*, all the adults who stood between him and Voldemort have been taken from him one by one. In *Hallows* he even foregoes Lupin's help. The hero always faces the villain alone in the end, as Harry tells the crowd when he's about to duel Voldemort.

Neville also attains fully heroic stature in *Hallows*. Neville's life fits the heroic journey pattern just like Harry's, as Martha Wells discusses in her article, *Neville Longbottom: The Hero with 1000 Faces*. He's imperiled as an infant by the prophecy that could be about him. He's lost his parents to all intents and purposes. Certainly, he fulfilled his fans' hopes that he'd play a significant role in the books by the end. He also changed his grandmother's opinion of him. By the end, she expects him to be in the thick of the battle at Hogwarts. Neville is a good example of a person who wills himself to transcend negative family expectations.

His grandma would have been bereft after the loss of his parents, and would be seeking signs of their quality in him. Failing to find it, wondering, as we're told in *Stone*, if he was even magical enough to come to Hogwarts, would have been a huge disappointment. Parents trying to eradicate poor qualities often amplify the very qualities they dislike along with insecurity. The first few novels show the results in Neville's case, a pudgy, frightened and bullied lad. However, by *Phoenix* he has begun to change, and to her credit, so has his grandmother's opinion of him. Neville's initiatory process is nearly as brutal as Harry's is. In its own way it's worse. For one thing, Harry has times when he's admired, even revered, by others. Poor Neville remains the bullied chump for the first few novels — but not by the end.

One of the most heroic things Neville does in the books, in fact, one of the most heroic things any of us can do, is to transcend our self image, negative or even sometimes, positive. Neville forgets about the self-image of cowardly, bullied Neville, which he's carried from *Stone*. As he says, there's no need to tell him he's not brave enough for Gryffindor, Draco has done it already, and he does it to himself. He changes his self-image, not by trying to change it, but by focusing on the job at hand.

In *Phoenix*, he focuses on learning what he needs to and fighting when he has to. By *Hallows*, we discover the Neville has been standing up under torture to the repellent Carrows at Hogwarts. Later, when Harry tells him to kill Voldemort's snake if he gets a chance, he doesn't say, 'who, me?' he matter-of-factly agrees to do it. In the end, he even stands up to Voldemort, who recognizes his quality. Of course, Neville doesn't just decide to lose his self-image and become instantly brave. He goes through various initiatory processes, from his training to his traumatic experiences that temper and test his mettle. His heroic initiations combine the traditional horrors of young male initiations with the added intensity of the wizard's initiation.

Traditional cultures often subject boys to brutal initiations. There's a picture of an Aborigine initiation where the initiates are lying in a semi-circle on the ground. Some have white feathers at their heads. These ones have died. The methods used in boy's initiations include sleep deprivation, scarification, fasting, terrifying rituals, knocking out teeth and circumcision — and, as Campbell said, "there's no chance of relapsing back to boyhood after a show like that."[15] While all male initiations aren't that severe, there's a certain value to the male psyche in making a hard and fast line between boyhood and manhood. Harry and Neville's ordeals help make them into fine people. Some women in the books, like Hermione, go through similar initiatory heroic processes. However, for others, initiation, and the heroic journey, has a different quality.

WOMEN'S HEROIC JOURNEYS

Although painful rites of passage feature in women's initiations in some cultures, women have a quieter entry to womanhood in many others. Nature does it. This may be one reason why women tend to fare better without traditional rites of passage than men do. They still have some kind of initiation, though being handed a tampon by an embarrassed mother isn't as fulfilling as celebrating one's new womanhood more elaborately in a larger community of women.

So what is the heroic journey for women? One woman I knew said that the hero's journey wasn't her story, because the woman's story is more about relationship as opposed to boldly going. However, a woman's life, even one solely devoted to marriage and children includes heroic elements closer to home. Try giving birth, there's no question that it's an initiatory experience. The mother who gives her life over to others, in various ways, is the central heroic spine of the whole *Harry Potter* narrative. It's not surprising that JK Rowling focuses so much on maternal characters. Writing the books after losing her own mother and during the process of having her own family would tend to keep motherhood in the foreground.

The maternal focus is a big reason why some critics, like Christine Schoefer and others, have accused JK Rowling of depicting women in a sexist way. However, as Sarah Zettel writes in her essay on sexism (or its lack) in the series, it's unusual to find such a wide range of mothers in a fantasy novel. The women in the series aren't just generic mothers, defined by the fact of having children. They are fully fledged, multi-facetted characters.[16]

Lily becomes more defined as the series progresses. We hear about her from Slughorn, and get a more vivid sense of her through others' memories, especially Snape's. She also didn't go into hiding to save herself but for her son.

Even the more negative examples of motherhood are real, rounded people. Merope, Voldemort's mother, is a realistically portrayed victim of child abuse, who can only love a man who disdains her. Many recover from abuse, but poor Merope was one who didn't, and couldn't attach enough to her baby to raise her wand to save herself for him. Petunia, by contrast, is a bit too attached to Dudley. She is an over-adoring mother, who, like her sister, flings herself between her child and a wizard she thinks will harm her boy. This happens in the comical scene involving the 'ton-tongue-toffee' at the start of *Goblet*, but it's still a repeat of Lily's sacrificial gesture.

Narcissa is another devoted mother — one stuck in a very nasty situation. She's less sympathetic because her husband's actions have deprived who knows how many other mothers of children, but she's certainly devoted. The unbreakable vow she requests from Snape is an important plot point. Narcissa becomes more sympathetic through her love of Draco and this love helps save Harry and defeat Voldemort in the end. Her sister, Bellatrix, by contrast, is the 'anti-mother.' She relishes torturing Neville, the boy she effectively orphaned. She has no children, though she says she'd be happy to sacrifice them to Voldemort's cause if she did. It's probably no coincidence that this childless woman is apparently the only active female Death Eater.

Obviously 'childless' doesn't mean 'bad' in the books, however. McGonagall and Sprout don't appear to have families, though they act in a kind of maternal role as heads of house. McGonagall's cry when she thinks Harry is dead indicates a deeper maternal love for

Harry than she's let on. McGonagall and Sprout are also heroic. When Harry needs time to find the last horcrux, McGonagall and Sprout say that they'll help give him the time he needs. Flitwick says that they won't be able to stop Voldemort. "But we can hold him up." McGonagall replies, and she and Sprout exchange a "look of grim understanding."[17] They know that they're unlikely to survive.

The mother we see most of is, of course, Molly Weasley. Some critics read her as a bit of a caricature, or even a racist stereotype. A poor woman with an Irish first name and lots of children living in a house called the Burrow, as in a rabbit burrow, as in 'breeds like.' Her red-haired family root for Ireland at the Quidditch World Cup. Yes, we 'hear the pipes a callin'. Her temper and strictness complete the picture. However, as Zettel notes, she's a strict disciplinarian because she's raising seven prank-loving wizard children. We hear how teddies have been turned into tarantulas, tongues have been burned through with acid pops and how, once, Ron was nearly tricked into making an unbreakable vow that his dad only just prevented (with bad consequences to Fred's left buttock).

All those children also give her and Arthur more to lose than anyone else in the books. As Arthur says in *Goblet,* finding the dark mark over your home, and knowing that what remains of your family is inside, is the very worst thing a parent can imagine. Of course, a father can be as devastated as a mother can by the loss of a child. It's just that mothers have a particular, well-recognized, visceral bond with their children. In nature, a female defending her offspring is generally considered to be the most dangerous animal to encounter. Molly Weasley is never depicted as extraordinarily powerful, but she becomes so when defending her children.

Fear for children and other loved ones comes up again in *Phoenix* when the boggart appears to Molly as dead members of her family and a dead Harry. This is what JK Rowling says she'd see if a boggart appeared to her.[18] That's what it would be for most parents. The fact that Molly can continue to be the Order's 'house mother' in the face of this is extraordinary. In some ways if you're fighting, making battle plans or otherwise engaged directly with the grim reality of a situation, you can put on your armor and keep it on. Having to be a nurturing mother figure, to be 'soft,' while maintaining your own psychic defenses, is very hard. It must have been an enormous psychic relief to fight Bellatrix in *Hallows*. She had many years of seething fear and fury built up, a dead son and an imperiled daughter. Bellatrix had no chance.

Fleur is a younger example of the more relationally focussed woman. When Fenrir Greyback disfigures Bill, she's furious that Molly thinks she won't want to marry him. She says that the scars just show that he's brave and that she's good-looking enough for both of them. Finally, Molly, realizing (but not saying she realizes) that Fleur truly loves Bill, talks about loaning Fleur a family tiara for the wedding, leading to a teary embrace between them. Ms. Rowling manages to make Fleur heroic without altering her essential conceited character, and brings about a rapprochement between her and the usually hot-tempered Molly without compromising either character or resorting to overly sentimental language. It's very skilled writing.

Hermione isn't really at either of these stages of the woman's relational journey yet. She's still pretty well in the straight heroic journey mold, despite her obvious romantic attachment to Ron. Many women have little trouble approaching life from the hero's journey framework until they have children.

Though Ginny is classically heroic, dueling Bellatrix along with Hermione and Luna, her journey, like her mother's, is really all about relationship from the start. (Arthur and Molly got together at Hogwarts, though we're not told exactly what age they were.) Ginny loves Harry from the beginning. The lesson for young ladies here is to focus on being themselves, not on the boy. Cho is an interesting contrast. She's had a rough time, but also seems generally unwise in her choices. She brings Mariette into Dumbledore's Army when Mariette's attitude is suspect from the start. Mariette ends up giving them away to Umbridge. She's also depicted as a classically weepy and unreasonable teenage girl, though it has to be said that Harry acts like a classically callow and tactless youth at this point as well. Like so many teen relationships, theirs break up on the rocks of mutual mismanagement.

Cho and Ginny, like other prominent figures in the books, including Harry, are marked out with the obvious title of 'Seeker.' Quidditch Seekers don't invariably represent the classic heroic archetype in the books, but they are all, literally, seekers, people looking for something. The snitch is that something, and of course, its symbolism, and that of the Seeker, is bound up with the larger symbolism of the game.

SEEKING THE SNITCH IN A COSMIC CONTEST

The Quidditch Seeker is usually the best flier on the pitch but is also the player most likely to be fouled. He or she is idolized but remains a team player. As I've said above, the hero does what he does for others as part of a greater whole. The Seeker can win more points than anyone else, and often ends the game, by catching the tiny winged golden orb.

Let's begin with the symbolism of the snitch. In *Quidditch Through the Ages*, Kennilworthy Whisp tells us that the snitch was originally a tiny round bird called the golden snidget.[19] Hunting the snidget was a popular, though cruel, sport and on one occasion a snidget flew into the middle of a Quidditch game and ended up being included in play. The 'Seeker' was originally the 'Hunter' and the game ended with the death of the snidget.

A glance at the picture given in the above book along with this account makes it clear that hunting the snidget paralleled the British Muggle tradition of hunting the wren. There's a rich tradition of folklore around this tiny, rounded bird. It's called the

'King of birds,' and was protected most of the year. However, it was ritually hunted by boys on the day after Christmas and subsequently paraded with wreaths of holly around it. December 26th is the day of St. Stephen, the first Christian martyr. You'll have picked up on the link with Harry's holly wand.

The golden snidget became a regular feature of play, but was so depopulated by hunting and Quidditch that it was made a protected species. This led to the alternative, the golden snitch used in modern Quidditch. The first snitch was forged at Godric's Hollow, the home of both Harry's and Dumbledore's families.

The winged disk is found throughout the ancient Near East and in ancient Egypt. Masons, Ritual Magicians, Theosophists and others have used it in later times. On one level, it is simply the life-giving orb of the sun. Some have suggested that it symbolized the sun at eclipse, with wings of light appearing around it. This would represent the power of light even at the darkest hour. Sometimes it's seen as the symbol of a perfected soul flying back to its divine source.

In a legend cut into the walls of his temple of Edfu in Upper Egypt, Horus, young son of the mother goddess, Isis, takes the form of a winged disk to defeat evil doers, specifically Set, the "cunning and treacherous" being who murdered his father, Osiris. There are various endings to the story. In one, Set is killed but comes back to life as a serpent. In another Horus ultimately kills Set in the form of a child.[20]

Horus is sometimes shown as a child on Isis' lap, or with both Isis and Osiris, and sometimes as a young man. (The statue of the Potters at Godric's Hollow calls many iconic images of this Egyptian divine family to mind, as well as those of the Christian.) Harry is a hero out of the Horus mold. Horus later orders that the Winged-Disk, with Uraei, (the two serpent goddesses) should be brought into all his sanctuaries to drive away evil. The sun disk and the serpent combine into a potent image of highest united with lowest, the power of the union of opposites to drive away evil. (It appears on the epigram page at the front of this book.) This is a recurrent theme in *Harry Potter* that we'll return to.

The particular winged disk image I've placed at the head of this chapter is of the Assyrian deity Ashur. In his book, *The Aura of Kings*, Abolala Soudavar says that similar images may later represent the deity Ahura-Mazdâ and / or the *khvarnah* or *farr*, the divine glory, a quality attributed to the king.[21]

On one level the *farr* is simply the power of truth. Harry's truth is often pitted against others' falsehood. Rita Skeeter and the Ministry maligned him and Umbridge forced him to carve "I must not tell lies" into his hand, though he's the one telling the truth. Voldemort is, like Satan, 'father of lies.' For example, in *Hallows*, "there was relish in his voice for the lie," that Harry was "killed while trying to save himself."[22]

This symbol of the winged disk has come to be called the *faravahar* in modern Zoroastrian religion. *Faravahar* means 'to choose.' It represents the human soul. The three layers of feathers represent good words, good thoughts and good deeds. The two ribbon-like elements at the bottom represent duality, good and evil, left and right. In modern Zoroastrian tradition the man faces to his right, representing the prophet Zoroaster, and the choice to live a virtuous life. The themes of choice and sovereignty run all through the *Harry Potter* series, and we'll have reason to return to them in the following chapters.

Finally, the winged orb can symbolize both the beginning and end of the alchemical process. In the beginning, according to Jung, the winged orb can represent all the elements merged together in chaos. (See the illustration at the head of chapter six and the discussion of the *rebis*, the alchemical hermaphrodite, towards the end of chapter five.) At the end, it is yet another symbol of the philosopher's stone, the culmination of the alchemical process – the enlightened alchemist whose soul can soar beyond earth's confines.

(See the illustration at the head of chapter seven.) That's quite a lot of symbolism for a little winged marble!

In many seasonal games the ball represents the sun. Some games preserve more symbolic aspects than others do. The Kirkwall Ba' Game on the Hebridean Isle of Orkney pits the 'Uppies' against the 'Doonies.' Each team aims to get the handmade leather ball into the goal. The Uppies goal is the site of an old castle and the Doonies is the sea within the harbor basin. A similar ball game in Cornwall features a silver plated apple-wood ball.[23]

It's easy to see the cosmic symbolism. Uppies at hilltop and Doonies by the sea represent an obvious polarity, just as Gryffindor and Slytherin do, with one house in the tower and the other beneath the lake. The omens derived from an Uppie or Doonie win affirm their associations. A Doonies' win means good fishing in the coming year and an Uppies victory portends a successful potato and barley harvest. On this level, there are no real losers in the Orkney game.

The Mesoamerican ball game, by contrast, had losers. It was an important feature of Mayan and Aztec life, played from at least 250 AD. It re-enacted a tale of the gods of life defeating the gods of death. As Douglas Gillette tells us in *The Shaman's Secret*, the Mayans hoped to magically defeat death by rigging the game so that death always lost. The losing team representing the lords of death was probably sacrificed. All in all, not such a fun day out as Quidditch.

Of course, as I mentioned above, JK Rowling has put a parallel to the sacrifice of the 'king wren' in the earlier version of Quidditch. The Quidditch Seeker also seems to be a bit of a sacrificial figure in the books. The Seeker is the most frequently fouled player.

Significant matches often end with a heroically injured Seeker. In *Stone*, Harry misses the final match because he's unconscious after his fight with Voldemort. In *Chamber*, Harry catches a snitch after his arm is broken. In *Azkaban* his broom is destroyed and he nearly falls to his death. In *Goblet*, Viktor Krum catches the snitch but loses the match in the Quidditch World Cup. Badly injured, he'd realized Bulgaria couldn't win, but wanted to "end it on his terms" as Harry observed. Viktor has the same heroic, kingly character that seems to be shared by most Seekers. He's able to make the best possible choice even when the one he wants, winning, isn't available to him. He can follow through on that choice even when it costs him something to do it.

Two Seekers in the novels make bigger sacrifices. Regulus Black, Sirius' brother, dies to thwart Voldemort. Regulus, like the rest of his family, is named for a star. The name itself can mean king or prince.[24] He demonstrates the quality of sovereignty to the greatest degree. He's totally uncompelled by fear and desire.

The other sacrificed Seeker is Cedric, who comes through all the Triwizard tasks only to be killed so quickly that he doesn't even get the chance to raise his wand. He seems to exist to give a first taster of just how casual killing is for Voldemort, and also reminds us that however heroic someone is they can encounter a force more powerful, or quicker, than they are.

As Harry becomes the captain of his team in *Prince*, the hero becomes 'captain of his soul.' The symbolic snitch and the 'Seeker' term come up repeatedly in the books. When he's coming to, after his ordeal with Quirrell and Voldemort in *Stone*, he thinks he's sees the snitch but it's the golden glint off Dumbledore's glasses. It calls to mind the kingly and perfected soul that the winged disk can symbolize. The snitch returns even without Quidditch in the final book. Of course, in the last battle, Harry is also described as catching his opponent's wand "with the unerring skill of the Seeker." The game ending catch.[25]

Other Seekers in the books give us different perspectives on the quest. Other than Harry, Draco is the one we know best. He fits the school bully archetype to a T, and as such, is a staple in all British school stories. He's the Seeker drawn to the false glamour of the dark arts. Draco desperately wants to be cool and powerful, and would, as the Slytherin description goes, use any means to attain his ends. Then he sees what evil really looks like. Like his parents, he learns that he liked the idea of Voldemort a lot better than the real thing.

Cho, as discussed above, is a much more minor figure. Her story reiterates the theme of trusting the wrong person, and of the Seeker's need to develop emotional control. The fact that she can't fly well because she's such a wreck is significant. Flight is to the Quidditch Seeker what higher spiritual awareness is to the spiritual seeker — the basic skill that enables attainment of the goal.

Ginny by contrast, always flies well. She realizes over time that the kind of person she wanted to be with was also the kind of person she wanted to *be*. This is one of the most important lessons we can learn. Ginny doesn't just make cow eyes at Harry as he zooms around the Quidditch pitch. She gets some zooming in herself. Ultimately, a Quidditch win, with her as Seeker, precipitates her first kiss with Harry.

Ginny also doesn't just admire Harry's magical prowess. She develops impressive abilities of her own. Ginny, Harry, Ron and Hermione aren't just heroes; they're witches and wizards.

Some people have argued that the use of magic is incidental and purely mechanical in the stories. The earlier books especially tend to ignore some of the implications of the magic, and treat it as a simple tool, rather than a way of being. Later, the magic becomes a bit more like magic as traditional cultures experience it. Let's see what Harry and the sources his story draws from reveal about the use and nature of magic.

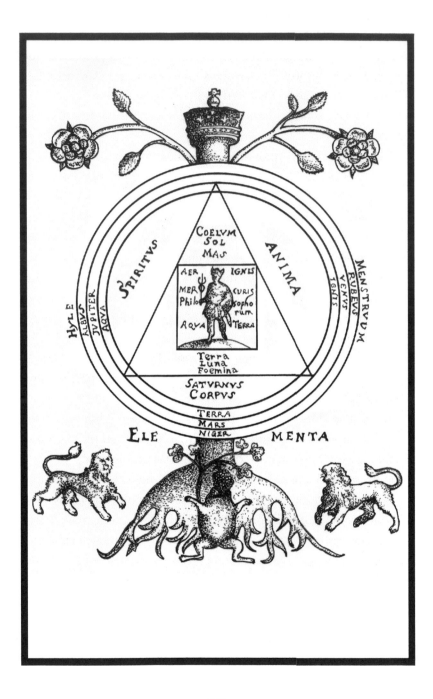

V

THE ART

A philosopher acts not what nature does; for nature where she rules, forms all vegetables, animals, and minerals, in their own degrees. Men, do not after the same sort, by their arts make natural things. When nature has finished her work about them; then by our art they are made more perfect.
Nicholas Flamel

Memory, prophesy and fantasy
The past, the future and the dreaming moment between
Are all one country, living one immortal day.
To know that is wisdom.
To use it is the Art.
Clive Barker

K Rowling spoke in 2003 at the Royal Albert Hall with Stephen Fry (the insightful actor who reads the novels on the British audio books) and questioners from around the world. A child in Hong Kong asked if she believed in magic. She replied, "I'm sorry to say, because often when I answer this question I get a groan, that I don't believe in magic." The audience did, indeed, groan. She continued, "I really don't in magic the way that it appears in the book. I could be slightly corny and say I do believe in other kinds of magic; the magic of the imagination for example, and love, but magic as in waving a wand — no. I'd love to believe in it but I'm afraid I can't."

Stephen Fry responded, "But it doesn't matter that it sounds corny ... it's desperately important that the way Harry solves all his problems is really through his courage, his friendship, and his loyalty and stoutness of heart." Rowling agreed. "Harry is not a good enough wizard yet to even attempt to take on Voldemort as wizard to wizard. He's escaped him three, four times if you count the encounter with Tom Riddle. He keeps doing it because there is one thing that Voldemort doesn't understand and that's the power that keeps Harry going. And we all know what that power is."[1] The power of love, particularly maternal love, and the power of magic are related.

The womb 'magically' responds to our needs and when we emerge, we continue to learn magic, or fail to learn it, at our mother's breast. It's deeply bound up with the magic of love. The child psychologist, DW Winnicott, described how the baby and mother enter 'transitional space,' a special kind of awareness, together and experience a sense of unity that we can call magical.[2] In a good mother and baby relationship, like Harry had with his mother, Lily would have experienced Harry in some ways, as part of herself, as she loved him and met his needs. Harry would also have experienced Lily in some ways as part of himself. As Professor Colwyn Trevarthen, a child development specialist, notes, mothers and infants can naturally develop a wonderful synchronization in their interactions. They are "as tightly organized as well matched...musicians in a duet."[3]

Musical babbling, play, conversation and improvisation build enjoyment, trust, and companionship. Mother and baby fall in sync emotionally and physically. The breast fills just before the baby cries with hunger and Mum knows it's time for a feed. The baby receives it happily. To a well cared for baby, as Harry was, the world began as a place where his needs weren't just met, but were 'magically' anticipated in a synchronized flow between himself, those he loved and his world. The film of *Azkaban*, probably the most psychologically resonant of the first five films, had Harry use the memory of a loving exchange with his parents as the happy memory that empowers him to cast a patronus. He's not even sure if it's a 'real' memory, but it enables him to perform the most advanced magic he's done to that point.

There's great truth here. First, in magic, objectively real is far less important than useful. If a thought is positively empowering, then it's as real as it needs to be. Next, we can see that Harry learnt magic, love, trust and playfulness, all together – everything a great wizard (or a great person) needs. He gained the confidence to play with reality in a world responsive to his actions.

This is one reason why Harry always had a better shot at being a truly great wizard than Voldemort. Harry's first year was full of love's magic and the experience of a magically wish-fulfilling universe that parental love and awareness create for the baby. His family was in hiding, so he had two full time parents at home and plenty of love and attention before he was orphaned. Of course, he then went to a hostile and loveless home, but that first year stayed with him. As Dumbledore tells him, "To have been loved so deeply, even though the person who loved us is gone, will give us some protection forever."[4]

Voldemort, by contrast, had no experience of being deeply loved in his first year or at any other time. The orphanage might well have been a better environment than the Dursleys, but his mother chose to die (presumably from her misery at being dumped) rather than save herself for her son. Somewhere deep down Voldemort must have been horribly jealous of Harry, whose mother had died for Harry when his own mother wouldn't live for him. He never learned trust, so his magic was all force against force. He never trusted the world to respond to him, so his life became an act of forcing what he wanted from it, against nature, against the greater whole.

Dumbledore, of course, was always concerned with the greater whole, the 'greater good' as he put it in his youth. I'll discuss the ambivalent aspects of this in the next chapter. Here I'll

SEEKER'S GUIDE TO HARRY POTTER

just say that Dumbledore keeps testing Harry's trust, and keeps emphasizing how important it is. He wants Harry to trust him, in part, to strengthen the trust that Harry needs to work magic. Harry must trust that the world can, and will, respond to him, trust that magic will answer when he calls.

It's well known that trust and belief help magic work. When Harry is desperately trying to master a summoning charm in *Goblet*, so he can get his broom and evade the dragon in the first task of the Triwizard Tournament, Hermione stays up most of the night helping him learn it. At the end, Harry is still not sure he's got it, but Hermione tells him, "Just as long as you're concentrating really, really, hard on it, it'll come." Ron plays Quidditch better when he *thinks* he's drunk the lucky potion felix felices in *Prince* and later comments that it's really just the same as having actually taken it. One of *The Tales of Beedle the Bard*, *The Fountain of Fair Fortune*, features an ending that underscores the point even more than Ron's comments. [5]

The 'natural magic' of *Harry Potter* is based first upon an idea of the underlying unity of all things throughout nature, expressed in the quotes above. The first is from Nicholas Flamel, who you'll remember was Dumbledore's alchemical partner in *Stone*. (As I've noted, he was also a real person.) Flamel saw the alchemist as perfecting nature, working with nature, respectfully, reverently, to bring forth its best potential, much as parents work to bring forth the best in their child. This is a very different process from imposing an outside idea of 'best.' In fact, on a very obvious level, alchemical symbolism is simply about the natural process of producing a child. A 'philosophical orphan,' like Harry, arises from the union of the king and queen in the womb-like alchemical vessel.

The second quote, from Clive Barker, a fantasy and horror writer, has always been a favorite of mine. To know the underlying unity of creation is wisdom, the personally and profoundly experienced wisdom of the wizard. Using this knowledge is the Art: magic.

I've been speaking of magic in one way or another throughout this book. For example, in chapter two, I discussed 'awareness,' the magical state of consciousness we enter to do spiritual work. I've spoken of magical perception as a useful parallel mode of perception to scientific approaches. As Paracelsus said, "Magic has power to experience and fathom things which are inaccessible to human reason. For magic is a great secret wisdom, just as reason is a great public folly. Therefore it would be desirable and good for the doctors of theology to know something about it and to understand what it actually is, and cease unjustly and unfoundedly to call it witchcraft."[6] No wonder he made it onto a chocolate frog card!

Here we'll look at both magic and alchemy, as both arts fell under the patronage of Mercury or Hermes, the central figure in the mandala at the start of this chapter. Hence, they're often called the Hermetic arts. Wizards and alchemists apply spiritual principals to bring about magical changes in the world and their experience of it. The difference between these two and the mystic is one of approach. The mystic may stop at knowledge or *gnosis*. The wizard and alchemist apply that knowledge in some way. They are more active; the mystic is more passive. Both approaches have value and exist on a continuum.

To make the distinction clear, we'll use Trelawney as a mystical example and Dumbledore as a magical one. Trelawney, upon seeing a snail, might say something like "Why has the Universe sent me a snail, can I read some meaning in its silvery trail? Must I move slower in life, avoid the sun, or apply more unguents?" Dumbledore, on seeing a snail, would simply think, "How may I use this snail?"[7] He might have escargot, but at least he'd take it off the roses. The wizard is pro-active and practical. He's often closer kin to the scientist than to the mystic.

One approach also often leads to the other. The magician's experience reveals the wonders of the universe and he may come to feel less of a need to act on it all the time. The mystic's experience of an all-pervasive Divine often leads him or her to want to take compassionate action for others in one way or another, like doing charitable work or healing. Despite being a pre-eminent wizard Dumbledore has mystic qualities, when he touches on ideas of 'magic at its most mysterious.' The mystic knows that he can't know nor do it all. The mystic is also prepared to let the reins slip a little, or a lot, in life. Sometimes, when we stop striving, it allows for something better than we could have consciously planned. The down side of the mystic approach is that the mystic can become passive or even paralyzed.

Because the mystical approach tends not to focus on applying techniques to produce results, they can also end up being credulous, believing anything. Yes, Mr. Lovegood, it really is an erumpent horn! Occam's razor applies; the simplest solution is likely to be correct. The mystic has fewer checks and balances. They can easily deny what's before them. It's like the scene where Trelawney is wandering down the hall and Harry hears her reading cards. She reads the knave of spades as a dark young man, possibly troubled, who dislikes the questioner. "Well, that can't be right." she says, with the very young man she's divined hiding behind a statue near by.[8]

Ms. Rowling doesn't really give us a positive 'pure' mystic figure, just as she gives us no positive clergy, which may give us a sense of her own approach. The centaur, Firenze probably comes closest. He echoes a wounded healer and teacher figure of Greek myth, the centaur Chiron. (Firenze is also wounded in the last battle.) However, he was also a more pro-active member of his species. When he carries Harry out of the forest in *Stone*, Bane, another centaur, criticizes him for intervening, saying, "Remember, Firenze, we have sworn not to set ourselves against the heavens. Have we not read what is to come in the movement of the planets?" Firenze responds, "I set myself against what is lurking in this forest, Bane, yes, with humans alongside me if I must."[9]

Yet, the practical and active wizard's approach also has a down side: just because we can do something doesn't mean we should. Voldemort is nothing if not active, his activities extend beyond the grave, but they are far from wholesome. (In the deepest sense, relating to wholeness and health.) As McGonagall says, there are some kinds of action that Dumbledore, for one, is too 'noble' to take. But it goes beyond good and evil. Just as Sirius tells Harry that there are more than two kinds of people in the world, good people and Death Eaters, there are more than two kinds of magic, and it isn't just the blatantly 'evil' kind that can get us into a mess.

JK Rowling is right to depict magic as potentially dangerous in the books. Magic can make a mess of life through simple bad management and poor choices. We may be trying to force things to happen that won't make us happy or confusing means with ends. The magic she depicts positively in the books is aligned with some kind of morality or true will.

Ritual magicians have many different perspectives on this. Some believe that it's okay to do as you please. As Quirrell says in *Stone*, some go to the extreme of only seeing power and weakness, not good or evil. Scottish magical tradition, by contrast, even felt that it was important for a person not to "indulge in strong wishes, lest he overstep proper bounds and wish what providence has not designed to be." This was especially true of people with 'the sight' or other spiritually powerful people. It was felt that we should work to align our will with the sacred rather than use sacred power to manifest our unaligned will. Hogwarts is a Scottish school, and takes the stand that magic should be aligned with morality.[10] The wizard's character is thus highly important.

MAGIC FLOWS FROM THE MAN

In a Stephen Fry talk with JK Rowling on the Bloomsbury web site he said, "In many ways the stories would hold together even if there were no magic in them, because what people really come away with seems to be the relationships — particularly, obviously, Hermione, Harry and Ron." She agreed, and commented that readers seem to enjoy it most when the magic went wrong.[11] In *Charmed Life: the Spirituality of Potterworld*, Christian theologian, Francis Bridger argues that the magic is more broadly symbolic of power in general in JK Rowling's work, as in JRR Tolkien's *Lord of the Rings* and CS Lewis's *Narnia* series. When power is used badly a few benefit and most suffer. When it is used well most benefit and a few suffer.[12]

Certainly, the human qualities of the magicians are depicted as more important than the magic itself. For example, while Harry, Hermione and Ron try to get to the philosopher's stone, they use some magic, but that's not the main thing that gets them through. It's not what Dumbledore awards the points for at the end, either. Ron plays a great game of chess (at personal sacrifice), Hermione applies logic to a problem, Harry flies well enough to catch a key, and Neville stands up to his friends when he thinks they're wrong.

Before Harry goes off alone in the final stage, Hermione tells this eleven-year-old boy he's a great wizard and hugs him. Embarrassed, he says that he's not as good as her. She responds, "Books! And cleverness! There are more important things — friendship and bravery and — oh Harry, be careful!"[13]

At the end, there's no special trick or even skill to Harry getting the stone. He doesn't know the right spell. It's his internal state, that he wants the stone but not for himself, that gets it. In principal, throughout the books, as here, the truly significant magic flows from the man, rather than the magic being a pure technique. The same sort of thing happens at the end of *Goblet*. It's his gut feeling that tells him to force the current of light back into Voldemort's wand and it's his dual Slytherin / Gryffindor qualities of will and courage that enable him to do so.

Magic becomes more essential to the story as the series progresses. It also becomes less mechanical. When we begin, the magic seems to involve simply repeating words (with the correct pronunciation and emphasis, of course) and waving a wand or assembling ingredients in a cauldron in the right order. There's a lack of any kind of internal focus or process for most spells, though, like anything, practice makes perfect. There's certain shallowness to most of the magic in the first few novels. The Booker prize-winning novelist, AS Byatt, a particularly harsh critic of the books, went so far as to call it 'ersatz.'[14]

For example, we're introduced to Transfiguration, 'turning something into something else,' in *Stone*. It begins gamely enough, turning matchsticks into needles. Then we go on to animate to inanimate transformations that, quite frankly, give me the creeps. If I was in McGonagall's class, I'd find the beetles into coat buttons bad enough, but by the time we got to hedgehogs into pincushions I'd be calling the MSPCA. (Magical Society for the Prevention of Cruelty to Animals – if there is one!) Especially when the imperfectly transfigured hedgehogs curled up when approached with pins. It's obviously all played for laughs, but it just never sat comfortably with me. What would the consciousness of a formerly sentient being become if its body was made into a coat button or pincushion? Would it cease? Would it still be 'in there' horribly immobile? The students, and teachers, don't seem bothered.

By contrast, Ursula K. LeGuin's *Earthsea* quartet never dodges the implications of the Art. In the first novel, *The Wizard of Earthsea*, Ged, the young wizard, goes to study on the Isle of

Roke. He learns the arts of Change (what would be called Transfiguration at Hogwarts) from Master Hand. However, the things changed don't remain changed. One day, while holding a particularly nice jewel he's made from a rock, he asks if he can make the change permanent.

Master Hand responds, in part:

> To change this rock into a jewel, you must change its true name. And to do that, my son, even to so small a scrap of the world, is to change the world. It can be done...It is the art of the Master Changer, and you will learn it, when you are ready to learn it. But you must not change one thing, one pebble, one grain of sand, until you know what good and evil will follow on the act. The world is in balance, in Equilibrium. A wizard's power of Changing and of Summoning can shake the balance of the world. It is dangerous, that power...It must follow knowledge and serve need. To light a candle is to cast a shadow.

To Ged's annoyance, he also notes that "A rock is a good thing, too." If all the islands of Earthsea were made of diamond, life would be impossible. You can't grow crops or graze livestock on solid diamond.[15]

Transfiguration scenes in the *Harry Potter* books are amusing, but offer little that you could use in life. The Changing lessons in the *Earthsea* books, by contrast, come with a message that works in life as in Art: don't change things unless you've deeply considered the consequences. Change "must follow knowledge and serve need." That's a real mantra for life and Art.

Part of the issue in *Harry Potter* may simply be that these are young wizards and they start with the basics. The Department of Mysteries at the ministry of Magic has a tank full of brains, a gateway to death, a room of love and time in a big glass globe for research purposes. From early on we get a sense that there are much deeper magical levels, but obviously, these aren't necessarily accessible to a 13-year-old, just as the restricted section at library isn't.

When we get into 'advanced' magic, like occlumency, the patronus charm and the killing curse, internal states become much more important. As the fake Mad-Eye Moody says in *Goblet*, the killing curse needs "a powerful bit of magic behind it." All the students could point a wand at Moody and shout *avada kedavra* at him without giving him "so much as a nosebleed."[16] So what is magic, and how does one acquire a powerful bit?

POWERS YOU DIDN'T KNOW YOU HAD

You can answer the above question in dozens of ways. You might end up settling on writer and ritual magician Alan Moore's definition of magic as a "personal ecology of energy." You might end up with something more prosaic, like "Magic is the power of positive thinking." The controversial occultist Aleister Crowley said that "Magick is the Science and Art of causing Change to occur in conformity with Will."[17]

This brings up two important points. First, all attempts to create change in conformity with true will, that important Slytherin quality, can be seen as magical acts, whether they're ritual, psychological or physical. By Crowley's definition, turning on a light switch can be seen as a magical act. The second point is that we don't need to perfectly understand the process to make it work. How many of us can honestly say we understand how turning on a light happens from the power station through to the switch? That doesn't stop us doing it. People who believe 'it's all in their heads' can effectively use magic as a tool for personal growth. People who believe in a spiritual reality can use it. The beauty of magic is that it doesn't demand that you have any *particular* belief system for it to be effective.

Magic changes the world *or our experience of it.* The ritual magician and teacher, Lon Milo Duquette stresses the capacity of magic to change the self.[18] Magical techniques have been drawn into psychology and 'self-help.' Just like science, psychology hasn't so much displaced magic as absorbed much of it into itself. For example, cognitive behavioral therapy tells us to change how we think about events and emotions as a first step to changing our lives. Why is there 'power' in positive thinking? There's no completely rational reason that thought should change our circumstances, yet it's generally accepted that it does.

Gestalt therapy can 're-invoke' the 'demons' of the past; traumatic events and the 'ghosts' of people who hurt us. In one famous technique, the patient might picture their mother or father sitting in an empty chair and confront them with the support of a therapist and sometimes a group. Ultimately, they 'banish' the bad influence, just as Harry and his classmates learn to banish boggarts in Professor Lupin's class.

There are few other episodes in the books that involve anything like conjuring spirits, which means that Harry and his friends primarily practice what's called 'natural magic.' This is working with magic as a natural force rather than interacting with spirits on different levels of being, which is sometimes called 'high magic.' Harry and his friends don't align with a 'higher power' of any kind, as in many devotional mystical and magical traditions, but they still try to adhere to higher values of love, loyalty and right action in their magical practice.

Magic begins with thought. As mentioned above, if we think positively, things tend to go better. 'Creating our own reality' is a popular phrase. However, bear in mind the fact that we're not alone. There's a nice exchange in the discussion between the outgoing Minister of Magic and the Muggle Prime Minister at the start of *Prince.* As the Minister is leaving, the Prime Minister desperately asks why they can't sort Voldemort out — after all, they can do magic. The Minister responds, "The trouble is, the other side can do magic too, Prime Minister."[19] The same could be said to all the positive thinking gurus who claim to have the secret of omnipotence. We can indeed, go a long way to creating a better reality by thinking positively. However, *other people are thinking too.*

Magic can manifest through the power of the word. As the inspirational writer, Florence Scovel Shinn said, "Your word is your wand."[20] In some ways all language is magical. As Alan Moore says, "The very language of magic seems to be talking as much about writing or art as it is about supernatural events. A *grimoire*, for example, the book of spells, is simply a fancy way of saying grammar, to cast a spell is simply to spell, to manipulate words to change people's consciousness."[21]

The way that the spells only work if properly pronounced emphasizes the importance of language in *Harry Potter*. Flitwick tells them to "never forget Wizard Baruffio who said 's' instead of 'f' and found himself on the floor with a buffalo on his chest." When learning *wingardium leviosa* in *Stone*, Hermione counsels Ron to make the 'gar' nice and long, and she's the first to succeed.[22]

We come to an interesting point if we compare the magical use of words in the *Earthsea* novels with their use in *Harry Potter*. Both use sacred language. Many traditions hold the idea that some languages, whether Tibetan, Latin or Hebrew, have particular power. Partly it's simply because any language that isn't our day to day language can help take us out of our usual frame of mind. Latin has always been a popular magical language, at Hogwarts and elsewhere.

In *Earthsea*, wizards learn an ancient and primordial 'true' language. Wizards create magical effects mainly by learning a thing's true name in this language. While they're walking, Ogion, the young wizard Ged's first teacher, asks his apprentice what certain plants are. Ged doesn't know one and Ogion tells him it is fourfoil. Ged asks what use it has. Ogion replies, "None that I know of." After they walk a bit further, Ogion says. "'When you know the fourfoil in all its seasons by root and leaf and flower, by sight and scent and seed, then you may learn its true name, know its being: which is more than its use. What, after all, is the use of you? Or of myself?"[23]

In *Earthsea* the use of magical names affirms the value of each being in itself, not in its actions. It's a bit of a paradox. The wizard's way is a path of action that values being above action, at least as it's conveyed in *Earthsea*.

Have you spotted the difference with Hogwarts yet? Where *Earthsea* uses nouns of power, *Harry Potter* uses verbs. The Latin phrases are almost entirely words of command. *Accio*, the summoning charm, means 'I summon' and can be used to summon everything from brooms to prophecies to ton tongue toffees. The magic is about creating an outer effect, not knowing an inner essence.

The most prominent 'noun of power' in the books is Voldemort's name. The use of "You-Know-Who" and other epithets reflects Scottish and other traditions, which hold that to name is to invoke. Hence, you'd never say, 'the devil,' but rather, 'the wee man,' a term that has the advantage of making his power seem smaller as well as not invoking it. Voldemort's name is made into a 'taboo' in the final book, meaning that those who use it do in fact summon his minions, if not the man himself. Yet nouns of power don't only invoke Voldemort. They also invoke the positive power of the patronus. We invoke positive or negative forces with words all the time.

One of the most magical activities Harry practices in the books is positive self-talk. He often encourages himself and reminds himself that he's triumphed against overwhelming odds before, in fact, from his babyhood. For example, in *Azkaban* he thinks to himself, "Did they think he couldn't look after himself? He'd escaped Lord Voldemort three times, he wasn't totally useless..." Looking in the mirror in his room at the Leaky Cauldron, he even says, "I'm not going to be murdered." to which it replies, "That's the spirit, dear."[24] When he mounts his broom and soars aloft to get the golden egg from the dragon in *Goblet*, he reflects that the dragon isn't so different from an opposing team in Quidditch. He can get the egg easily.

Harry gives us extraordinary and ordinary examples of a power we all possess. Whether he's trying to prepare himself for a Quidditch match or a duel to the death, he most often focuses on the positive and he triumphs. Thoughts and words shape our reality too. The magic of mental attitude, of love and imagination are all pervasive. They are true magic, because they change things, internally and externally. As the eminent anthropologist Bronislaw Malinowski said, "The function of magic is to ritualize man's optimism."[25]

JK Rowling certainly created positive change for herself and others through her use of language, from giving enjoyment to transforming lives through her charitable works. It's good to be aware of how others use the word's magical power to influence us in less positive ways.

Alan Moore has a lot to say about this. In one interview he contrasted some ancient and modern applications of magic, saying that, "Art, like magic, is the science of manipulating symbols, words or images, to achieve changes in consciousness... The fact that in present times this magical power has degenerated to the level of cheap entertainment and manipulation is, I think, a tragedy." Advertisers, through the 'magic box' of television, use magic to tranquilize people, "and their magic words, their jingles, can cause everybody in the country to be thinking the same words and have the same banal thoughts all at exactly the same moment."[26]

Maybe that's why wizarding houses don't have televisions! Wizards are clever enough not to subject themselves to that particular form of unconscious enchantment. All seekers need to become aware of how others are using their magical abilities to influence us so that we can tell our own true will from theirs, and find our proper place in the universe. Aleister Crowley said that "The order of nature provides an orbit for each star" and "A clash proves that one or the other has strayed from its true course." However, it's not always easy to tell which one.[27]

That's why most magical systems impose some kind of 'magical law enforcement,' like the department of that name at the Ministry of Magic. To paraphrase a dictum of Muggle law, (my right to extend my fist ends where your nose begins) my right to extend my magical will ends where your will begins.

THE UNFORGIVABLE CURSES, MAGIC AND MORALITY

The importance of each individual's self-determination is under-scored by the curses the Ministry deems unforgivable. The unforgivable curses all infringe upon a person's free will and interfere with them at a level of essence. The imperius curse is quite obvious, the curse of command, to make a person do whatever you want. The cruciatus curse tortures, which is something that few would wish to experience. The killing curse is definitely against most people's will.

It should be noted that the books don't say that these are the only curses or deeds that would get you a life term in Azkaban, just that they're the ones that would automatically result in such a sentence. This obviously doesn't always follow either, because Harry, Hermione, Molly Weasley and *numerous* others perform these curses in the final battle of Hogwarts and none of them are jailed for life. Susan Hall gives a legal perspective on the wizarding world in her article *Harry Potter and the Rule of Law: The Central Weakness of Legal Concepts in the Wizard World.* Muggle law distinguishes between *actus reus*, acts which may be criminal, and *mens rea*, the mental attitude that determines whether or not a crime has been committed. For example, stabbing a person may be a criminal act, but not if the person doing the stabbing slipped and fell, stabbing the victim by accident.[28]

It's the sort of difficulty that would have been involved if the magical brawl between Grindelwald and the Dumbledore brothers, leading to Ariana's death, had gone to trial. (It seemingly wasn't even investigated. This is one of many dubious law enforcement situations that arise in the books, from the elf-smashed pudding incident to various kinds of summary justice being meted out at a whim. JK Rowling has said that Hermione beefs up the Department of Magical Law Enforcement in later years. We can only hope so!)

Obviously, the link between thought and deed in spell casting complicates matters. The imperius curse complicates them still further, as the fake Moody noted in *Goblet*. Here we're less concerned with particular points of law than with their underlying principals.

Ms. Rowling draws upon both Christian and magical tradition in placing interference with free will as the central kind of wrong-doing that lands you in Azkaban for the rest of your life. The unforgivable curses can be subtly distinguished from others that might seem to be similar by their relationship to will. Let's look at each curse in turn.

The one that most obviously interferes with free will is the imperius curse. Andrew Sims writing on Emerson Spartz's *Mugglenet* web site, says it comes from the Latin *impero*, meaning 'to give orders, rule, hold sway,' or *imperium*, meaning 'power to command, rule, control.'[29] It's described as feeling wonderfully peaceful and pleasant as long as you don't fight back. Harry successfully fights the curse, but many can't, or don't choose to try. One message here is that it's seductively pleasant to let others control you. It's a great relief to be free from choice and responsibility, but 'just following orders' is a bad idea.

The *avada kedavra* is obviously a variant of *abracadabra*. As Sims notes, "Its likely source is either the Arabic *abra kadabra*, 'may the things be destroyed,' or the Aramaic *abhadda kedhabhra*, 'disappear with these words.' I'd vote for the second, given that the word was used in talismans to treat disease, written in a diminishing triangle to reduce diseases to nothing.

This curse and *crucio* are less obvious violations of free will. However, as the fake Moody and Bellatrix note at various points in the books, you really have to get behind them to work them. Your whole magical will and desire must be focussed on torturing or killing. This indicates quite clear *mens rea*, or criminal intent.

Crucio simply means 'to torture' in Latin. This curse is far from the only one to cause pain. *Sectum sempra* (meaning something to the effect of 'always cuts') both hurts and injures. We could assume that the 'bat bogey' hex doesn't feel particularly pleasant. Of course, as Hermione points out, *sectum sempra* has not been Ministry approved, it's a 'home-made' curse. However, Hermione isn't averse to using painful curses when provoked. She uses *oppugno* (Latin, meaning, 'to attack,' the same root as 'pugnacious') to set her flock of little yellow birds on Ron after he's kissed Lavender Brown.

How do these differ from *crucio*? There's a question of degree. The cruciatus curse is depicted as the most agonizing pain possible, but I don't think this is a key distinction. *Sectum sempra* must be very painful; *oppugno* could be depending on what you 'set' on your object, a flock of eagles rather than a few canaries, for example.

Curses of combat seem to be dealt with case by case depending on circumstance, or not even dealt with at all. Harry and his friends curse with some impunity, even when Malfoy, Crabbe and Goyle are left unconscious, Crabbe with tentacles growing from his face at the end of *Goblet*.[30] Adult wizards seem to expect and allow for a bit of mayhem amongst the youth. Malfoy even gets away with petrifying Harry and kicking his nose in on the train at the start of *Prince* without any consequences.

As I've mentioned above, to effectively cast the cruciatus curse you must really want to cause pain. By contrast, Harry can cast *sectum sempra* with no clue as to what it will do, other than that it's 'for enemies,' when Draco is about to hit him with the cruciatus curse. *Crucio* also indicates clear and fixed malefic intent in another way. To torture is different from cutting or defending. Where other curses may be applied in differing combat situations, the name here says it all, this one is to torture for a potentially limitless period, as it causes no physical damage.

Only Snape's speedy spell work saves Draco's life after Harry uses *sectum sempra*. As with any curse that produces physical damage, you couldn't use it for ages. Because *crucio* is limitless, it allows a level of deliberate cruelty other curses don't. Harry uses it briefly against a Death Eater in the final book, but, as Neville's parents' condition shows, when used for a longer period it can torture a person into insanity. And this is the key; like the other unforgivable curses, it has the power to separate someone from their own essential self and so their true will.

It's interesting that *obliviate*, the curse to remove a person's memory, doesn't carry the same penalty. It goes along with what many magical and contemplative traditions say, that thought and memory aren't who we are at a level of essence. Meditation can begin with a process of withdrawing attention from inessentials, like thought, memory and physical sensation to enable us to focus on that spark within us, the magic, the divine essence of our being.

The bad effects of crimes against free will can damage us at an essential level. Voldemort's conception is a foundational example. Merope enchants Tom Riddle Senior with a love potion or spell. Voldemort results from a union against a person's free will. If Merope had been a Muggle, and the sexes of Merope and Tom were swapped, it would look more like what it was, drug-assisted rape. Romilda Vane's attempt to drug Harry in *Prince* is played for laughs at first but nearly has deadly consequences. Professor Slughorn correctly emphasized the terrible dangers of obsessive love in *Prince*. As he says, amortentia is indeed the most dangerous potion in that room. Harry, by contrast, is conceived from a love match. He's depicted as being different in his very essence, from the start.

Of course, JK Rowling has said that she thinks "we all have a little magic in us." The alchemists agreed, and sought to transform our magical essence into its highest possible form, the alchemical gold or the philosopher's stone. The processes Harry goes through owe much to alchemy and alchemical symbolism brings additional richness to our reading of the tales.

ALCHEMICAL SYMBOLS AND TRANSFORMATIONS

Alchemy is an art of transformation with physical, psychological and spiritual aspects. In an article on alchemical bird symbolism, the Glasgow based scholar, artist and practicing alchemist, Adam McLean, discusses how the physical aspects of alchemy relate to the psychological.

In the early alchemical texts...this picture of soul alchemy is developed in parallel with descriptions of what was a sore physical process. Thus it was that the soul development of the alchemist went hand in hand with an actual physical operation, and this operation, the details of which have not been wholly lost, involved color and form changes within a sealed flask, isomorphic to the inner changes of soul alchemy, described by these bird symbols. Thus we had a physical process which involved a blackening, a whitening, a rapid iridescence of colors, a circular distillation stage, and a final sublimation.[31]

The physical parts of the process evolved into modern chemistry, but as John Granger points out in *Unlocking Harry Potter*, it's much more than a kind of 'stupid chemistry' that gave rise to today's chemistry. Jung used it as an important basis for interpreting symbols in his school of psychology and many others have 'mined' alchemical symbols to express their own philosophies. As McLean points out, most interpreters have such personal axes to grind that they don't let the symbols speak for themselves. The seeker's best approach to alchemical symbols is to simply meditate on them and let them speak personally. (McLean gives helpful guidance and background on his web site and in his other works.)

Granger gives one of the fullest discussions of alchemical themes and characters in the *Harry Potter* books. Another author who treats these themes in great detail is Hans Andréa on his fascinating web site *Harry Potter for Seekers*. Both of these authors note that alchemical symbols stand out a mile in the *Harry Potter* books

While some of JK Rowling's use of alchemical symbols fits patterns and sequences, she also drops in alchemical symbols from time to time like street signs saying 'this is where we are,' just like she drops in tarot symbols, like the lightning struck tower or hanged man. At the start of *Hallows* she 'flags' the alchemical stage we're at with a white peacock. It's significant enough that the color frontispiece of the deluxe American edition features it. The *cauda pavonis* or peacock's tail is a very significant stage in the alchemical process, like the *albus*, the whitening.

In Adam McLean's article on bird symbolism in alchemy, he says that five birds, crow, swan, peacock, pelican and phoenix, symbolize five stages of soul development. Birds, like the winged golden snitch, represent the soul's power to ascend heavenwards. The crow represents death and the *nigredo*, the initial darkness of turning within. In Harry's case, this could be seen as his parents' death and his years of exile, as well as, of course, his returns to the *nigredo* at other points in his story.

A white swan, representing the alchemist's experience of a light filled inner-world, "the initial inner brightness which is often erroneously mistaken for true illumination," often represents the next stage.[32] When Harry receives his white owl and leaves the Dursleys for Hogwarts, he thinks his troubles are over. He thinks the first illuminating glimpse of the wizarding world is illumination itself. Then he discovers that there are many more stages and processes to go through. An actual white swan appears briefly in the form of Cho's patronus in *Phoenix*. This 'swan maiden' is Harry's first glimpse of romantic love and the spiritual union it tantalizingly offers, but this glimpse of light also proves imperfect.

As part of the same 'white swan' complex, Harry's confidence in his spiritual powers increases in *Phoenix*. Alchemy associates the phoenix with the king who appears at the end of the process, of which more, later. He really is grasping at the phoenix in this book, trying to jump forward to the final stage. Many teens, like many spiritual seekers, reach a stage where they falsely think they know ever so much more than their teachers. Harry certainly thinks he knows more than Dumbledore at certain points, never mind Snape. The end of the novel offers a fiery comeuppance to heroic presumption.

Many seekers get a first bright 'hit' of a tradition or practice and think they're there. Then, this hit fades. They think they've picked the wrong path, and go on to the next one, the next hit, and so on. They never get beyond this very surface level of illumination, so they think that's all any tradition has to offer.

If a seeker follows through on the alchemical path, however, they reach the next stage, represented by the peacock, a real turning point. Here, the alchemist becomes more conscious of previously unconscious spiritual and psychological realms and forces. McLean says that it represents the "the conscious experience of the astral body," the aspect of the spirit body that can travel in spiritual realms. It means that here we become more fully conscious of this level of the subtle body, aware of ourselves as more than physical.

He says this stage was sometimes split into two aspects, "an initial winged dragon phase which resolved into the Peacock's Tail." We have, of course, seen dragons aplenty in *Harry Potter* as I discussed in the last chapter. Here's another layer of their meaning. "In the initial encounter with the astral body, the negative distorted aspects of one's being can dominate, and these can be pictured as the winged dragon, but through soul purification, ultimately the full beauty and splendor of the astral body are revealed in the Peacock's Tail." Draco is named for the dragon, of course, and he typifies some of the most negative aspects of ego-based consciousness.

To progress, the alchemical seeker must engage in the difficult and sacrificial work of the white pelican, depicted as tearing its own breast to feed its young. This image was used as a Christ symbol in medieval times. "One's image of one's self must be changed, transformed, sacrificed to the developing spiritual self. This is almost invariably a deeply painful experience, which tests one's inner resources." There are no pelicans in *Harry Potter* but Hedwig (a white female bird named for a saint) dies shortly after we see the white peacock. The books are also *loaded* with other sacrificial symbolism.

Finally, the phoenix stage shows that the alchemist "has integrated his being so much, that he is no longer dependent upon his physical body as a foundation for his being. He now stands upon the sureness of the spiritual—he has in this sense attained the Philosopher's Stone, the Spiritual core of his being." As Dumbledore says, "To the well-organized mind, death is but the next great adventure."[33]

The white peacock in *Hallows* indicates that Harry is at an intermediate stage between peacock and pelican. He's on his way towards becoming the self-sacrificing pelican, capable of using all the powers he's aware of.

Another metaphor alchemists used for this stage was 'the white stone.' As you might surmise, this may be the stage Dumbledore paused at. Though he made the philosopher's stone with Nicholas Flamel, he doesn't seem to have used it, at least not to the same extent. This is perhaps for the same reason that he shied away from opportunities at the Ministry. He felt himself unworthy to hold a lot of power, like uniting the Deathly Hallows, and so, during life, 'stalled' at the white stone that crystallized in the form of his tomb at the end of *Prince*. However, of course, the phoenix, the red representative of the *rubeus* or final stage of the work, is seen flying from it at the end and a phoenix acted as both a totem and patronus for him in life.

Ms. Rowling is also not a slave to alchemy. There were a few online debates after *Hallows* between readers who were surprised she killed one character, or left another standing, because of what they felt those characters symbolized. By contrast, I think that, despite the vast amount of underlying symbolism, her characters have always been characters first, and her story has always been her first priority, not metaphysics. However, Hermetic symbolism and stages served her narrative needs very well.

ALCHEMICAL CHARACTERS, ELEMENTS AND STAGES

Harry is the salt of the earth. The alchemical salt was said to originate in the *prima materia* as a 'blood-red' substance, which then became a bright white substance called "the salt of wisdom" by the sages.[34] Here we can see that the alchemical salt, mercury and sulfur aren't necessarily the same substances that go by these names in ordinary chemistry, but the natural properties of these elements can still tell us something about their symbolism. In a sense, then, this 'salt' is already the philosopher's stone, it just doesn't know it yet, but the knowing makes all the difference. Salt is like spirit, the stone is like soul. As my first alchemical teacher, psychologist Rudolph Bauer, says, "Spirit is given, soul we create."

Affirming Harry as the hidden stone, end product of the work, his wand core is made of phoenix feather — the phoenix being another symbol for the end of the process. His wand being broken, exposing the feather, is a 'darkest before the dawn' moment, showing us that the stone will soon be revealed within Harry. The red of the phoenix feather (phoenix may come from the Greek *foinix* meaning crimson) also echoes the red of sacrificial blood, essential to the alchemical process in many accounts.[35] For many seekers, the absolute worst comes before the greatest leap forwards towards the goal.

Salt is revealed as the stone by the transmuting actions of two other substances, sulfur and mercury. The easiest of these elements to see in Harry and his two best friends is, as John Granger points out, Mercury. Another name for Mercury is Hermes, Hermione's namesake. Mercury's designation on the periodic table is Hg, Hermione's initials. Her parents are both dentists. (Think Mercury fillings.) Mercury is often pictured as androgynous or feminine.[36] Mercury is most often associated with the alchemical serpent or dragon that twines up the caduceus of the deity Mercury, and sure enough, Hermione's wand core is dragon heartstring.

JK Rowling says on her web site that she wanted the three friends' wands to unite the three wand cores Ollivander used: phoenix feather, dragon heart string and unicorn hair. Interestingly, some alchemists discerned three forms of

Mercurius, the dragon represented the lowest, the unicorn the middle and the phoenix the highest.[37]

Mercury is more than a substance, in a sense it stands for the entire art of alchemy itself. In one alchemical text, the *Aurelia Occulta*, Mercury speaks, saying "I bestow on you the powers of the male and female, and also those of heaven and earth. The mysteries of my art must be handled with courage and greatness of mind if you would conquer me by the power of fire...by virtue of the sun's rays all colors shine in me and all metals." No wonder Ms. Rowling said "They couldn't do it without Hermione."[38]

As Mercury is associated with water, sulfur is associated with fire, which brings us to Ron, our red-haired, emotional sulfur, the *prima materia* of the sun. As Jung notes, on one level, sulfur is burning and corrosive to the matter of the stone. This quality is typified in Harry and Ron's conflicts, particularly in *Goblet* and *Hallows*. For example, in *Hallows*, Harry feels a "corrosive hatred" towards Ron, right before Ron leaves Hermione and him.[39] On another level, when sulfur is purified, as Ron is by his *separatio*, or separation stage, in *Hallows*, it is the very same matter as the stone itself.[40] Ron comes to understand this in an all-important exchange. Ron returns at a dramatic moment to save Harry. Then, after the dust has settled a bit, he apologizes for his bad behavior.

"You've sort of made up for it tonight," said Harry, "Getting the sword. Finishing off the horcrux. Saving my life."
"That makes me sound a lot cooler than I was," Ron mumbled.
"Stuff like that always sounds cooler than it really was," said Harry, "I've been trying to tell you that for years."
Simultaneously they walked forward and hugged...[41]

Ron, like Harry, can wield Gryffindor's sword and finally transcends jealousy to understand his heroism and Harry's by the same terms. The sulfur and the stone are one. Jung thought of sulfur as "the motive factor in consciousness" which can, on the one hand, be the consciously directed will that aids us, or, on the other, unconscious compulsion which hinders us. By the end of *Hallows*, Ron has shown both sides to his character.[42]

By turns, as one would expect, sulfur and mercury do battle and unite as well, as Ron and Hermione do throughout the series. Their definitive embrace of union during the final battle typifies how union is often depicted in alchemy as the passionate melding of opposing elements in combat situations.

In the novels, Ron acts on Harry to burn away impurity in sulphurous, fiery solar exchange. Hermione dissolves impurities more gently in her cool, lunar, Mercurial waters. Harry is the stone. But there's also one missing implied element – that of the *prima materia*, the 'first matter' with which alchemists began their work.

I'll give you a hint who represents that. It's often symbolized, as it is in the drawing that heads this chapter, as a toad, Neville's pet.[43] Like the lowly toad, and Neville at the start of the series, the *prima materia* is often said to be beneath most people's notice. (The toad is related to Harry as well in *Chamber*. One of Lockhart's dwarf cupids recites Ginny's poem to him, which begins, "His eyes are as green as a fresh pickled toad.") Harry most prominently, but Ron, Hermione and Neville as well, all go through their own transmutations throughout the series. Each, in his, or her, own way, evolves towards being the stone, though Harry is obviously the main protagonist who fully attains the transformation.

As these four represent alchemical elements, other characters represent alchemical stages. You'll have probably also noticed that the alchemical image at the head of this chapter includes the names 'Albus' and 'Rubeus.' The fact that the books feel so fresh and yet resonate so powerfully owes something to the fact that while most people know nothing of alchemy, its symbols still strike a powerful chord. Ms. Rowling has put old potion in fresh flasks and added some peppermint.

Let's start with the aforementioned alchemical mandala. It's drawn after one found in Samuel Norton's *Mercurius Redivivus*, written in 1630.[44] The first thing you'll notice is its similarity to the symbol of the Deathly Hallows. The triangle in the circle is there. The lettering, figure of Mercury and the tree trunk give us a strong vertical like the line.

Adam McLean gives an interesting interpretation of this symbol in his book *The Alchemical Mandala*. As we'll see, it all relates very well to our hero and his three primary mentors, Dumbledore, Hagrid and Sirius.

The mandala integrates the three, four and two. The two is duality, high and low, light and dark, male and female, and so on. Uniting polarities is probably the biggest theme in alchemy, and we see it repeatedly in the *Harry Potter* novels. Think about the connections and re-connections between Harry and Voldemort, or the relationships of various battling and uniting pairs like Ron and Hermione. Hogwarts unites Slytherin under the lake and Hufflepuff by the kitchens with the 'towers' of Ravenclaw and Gryffindor. In the mandala above Mercury we see *Coelum, Sol, Mas*, Heaven, Sun, Masculine, written, below, *Terra, Luna, Foemina*, Earth, Moon, Feminine.

UNION OF OPPOSITES

Harry's parents represent just such a solar and lunar union. James and Lily as a stag and doe bring in a wealth of mystical and alchemical symbolism. Not only was the stag frequently depicted as the enemy of the serpent, but also various components of the deer were said to provide cures for many ailments and injuries, particularly snakebite. Like Lily's protective charm, the deer's 'virtue' or power continues to be effective after its death.

The lily is a symbol for the Blessed Mother, Mary. Before

her, the lily was the symbol of Juno. According to the Romans, the first lily sprang from the goddess' breast milk, so it's deeply symbolic of nurturing maternal love. The alchemists believed the lily to have an incorruptible nature, and its juice to be incombustible. In alchemy, the male and female who become 'conjunct' and create the *hieros gamos* or 'sacred marriage' in the vessel, are often represented as a solar king and lunar queen who unite and then die to create the stone, or one of its earlier stages. Hermes Trismegistus, the early mythological alchemist, called the stone the philosophical orphan.[45] No prizes for guessing who *he* is.

The esoteric and alchemical theme of the 'chemical wedding' is repeated a few times in different ways in the books. For example, *Harry Potter* has many interesting correspondences with the 1459 initiatory tale *The Chemical Wedding of Christian Rosenkreutz*, as Hans Andréa discusses on his web site.[46] The last words in *Prince* are Harry's thoughts of looking forward to Bill and Fleur's wedding. He "felt his heart lift at the thought that there was still one last golden day of peace to enjoy with Ron and Hermione." And a golden day it turns out to be, from the white and gold roses to the liquid gold dance floor. Fleur and Bill's wedding is also full of opposites uniting, especially solar and lunar ones. The red haired groom wears a white rose, representing the white, lunar stage of the work, and his bride, with her hair that's always compared to cascading water, emits 'a strong silvery glow.'

The moon even symbolically 'becomes' the sun. Harry's friend, Luna, tells Harry that her father believes in dressing in 'sun colors' for weddings for luck![47] Not only is she named for the moon, but her patronus is a hare, associated with the moon in folk tradition. An alchemist wrote that Luna is the 'mother in this art' and 'Sol is hidden like a fire" in her.[48] Luna's yellow clad father also gives Harry his first sight of the symbol of the Deathly

Hallows at the wedding.

Luna's solar fire emerging shows that we're nearing the resolution of opposites that concludes 'the great work.' Imprisoning her in a dungeon is a natural course for the forces of darkness to take to thwart the process. Her symbolism is why Harry really did have to go on at least one alchemical date with her, even if only 'as a friend.' Their mutual knowledge of death and suffering and Luna's consequently compassionate nature makes them a real alchemical pair. You'll remember that it's only her actions in *Hallows* that allow him to escape for some well earned rest after the final showdown.

Three Circles and Three Stages: Albus, Rubeus and Niger

If we return to our alchemical drawing, we arrive at the circles. Here we see three phases, described as *albus*, *rubeus* and *niger*. *Albus* is obviously Albus Dumbledore and the white, lunar stage of the alchemical work. *Rubeus* is Hagrid, the red solar stage, and *Niger* means 'black,' Sirius and the 'black' stage of the work, sometimes called the *nigredo*. You may remember that his ancestor, the Hogwarts headmaster's name is Nigellus.

At the start of *Azkaban*, Sirius is almost always referred to as Black or less often, 'Sirius Black.' then, after Harry realizes that his godfather is innocent, he becomes Sirius — the light that comes out of the darkness. Sirius becomes a 'guiding star' to Harry just as the *nigredo* that initially seems to want to destroy us becomes a kind of godfather, protecting, strengthening and guiding when its true purpose is revealed.

When we move on to the next alchemical stage and character, we see that Albus is associated with spirit, *hyle*, the primal energy of creation, the element water and the expansive energy of the 'father of the gods,' Jupiter, wielder of the celestial lightning bolt with which Harry is marked. The *albus* or *albedo* is a stage of 'whitening,' a purification we come to out of the oscillations of union and loss we experience in life. Water is associated with washing and the *baptismo* or *solutio*, where all impurities are dissolved and washed away.

Harry goes through a lot of purification and watery elemental lessons in *Prince*. A newfound success in potions features prominently in the book. Of course, he doesn't know he owes this success to the head of the 'water' house, Severus Snape. Felix felicis, the golden essence of liquid luck, guides his steps, and saves the lives of his friends in the last conflict.

He also finally sheds the last of his child-like qualities. Having put off getting the memory Albus needs from Slughorn, he is overwhelmed by guilt. He realizes that he's been irresponsible. Despite everything, he hasn't taken Dumbledore's request seriously enough. After Dumbledore's death he comes to a realization most of us, thankfully, come to more gently and older. He realizes it's up to him, there's no one 'above him' anymore. His mentors and protectors are gone.

Of course, he still has Hagrid, but he can't really go around with him and Hagrid also isn't much good for sage advice. Rubeus is a wild man, unrefined, but he also prefigures the psychic 'giant' among men, the king, and the red of the stone, the returning of spiritual power to earth. JK Rowling gave Hagrid an oak wand though by the Celtic system she followed for Harry, Ron and Hermione, he should have had an elder wand. She said, "In Britain, the oak is 'King of the Forest' and symbolizes strength, protection and fecundity; what other wood could 'choose' Hagrid?"[49]

Rubeus, unlike the representatives of the *albus* and *niger* stages, doesn't have to die because the process ends with him, as much as it can be said ever to end.[50] He represents the earthly manifestation of all the good the alchemist has gained in his transformations. Of course, the 'Fallen Warrior' chapter gave people a turn and Ms. Rowling's sister told her she'd never forgive her if Hagrid died. That said, one 'red' figure does die in *Hallows*, Rufus Scrimgeour. (Rufus means 'the red one.')

The alchemical Rubeus is associated with solar fire, Venus, the goddess, and with the *menstruum*, the "womb of form" that contained the *hyle* or primal energy. In this womb, the elements combine from the union of force and source, masculine and feminine. Albus directs, Rubeus delivers, protects and nurtures.

Now, something may strike you as odd here. Hagrid associated with Venus? Come on! Well, it is odd, but in Albus, Snape and yes, even Hagrid, we can clearly see a frequent symbol of the alchemical union of polarities, the hermaphrodite, often depicted as a two headed masculine and feminine crowned being standing on a winged sphere.

The alchemical hermaphrodite, the *rebis*, often represented the end of the alchemical process, the philosopher's stone. It represented the union of all opposites. The process begins in unity with the 'confused mass' of the *prima materia* and ends in unity with the *rebis*. (The winged sphere can represent both kinds of unity. See the pictures at the heads of the next two chapters.) What's the difference then? The difference is between unconscious and conscious union. The material, the soul, having gone through the process of individuation, initiation and return, experiences a quality of union unimaginable at the start.

John Granger devotes a lot of attention to this alchemical theme in *Unlocking Harry Potter*. Hagrid proves to be a surprisingly androgynous figure. He nurtures horrible beasties like acromantulas and acts as the alchemical womb for the blast-ended screwts, experimentally crossbred from manticores and fire crabs. He's a mix of giant and human. When he hatches the horrible Norbert the dragon, his first response to its snapping at him is, "Bless him, look, he knows his mummy!" He demonstrates extreme sacrificial love in relation to his brother, Grawp. He knits, he cooks (badly) in a flowery apron — and don't forget the fact that his oak 'king of the forest' wand is concealed in a small pink umbrella.

Ms. Rowling plays with androgyny and united polarities throughout the books. The story structure resembles *Cinderella*, making Harry 'Cinderfella,' a character that girls and boys alike have been able to identify with.[51] Harry is also a Gryffindor / Slytherin *rebis* and Voldemort unwittingly becomes a Slytherin / Gryffindor one by using Harry's blood for his rebirth.

Like Hagrid, Snape appears with feminine accoutrements for laughs. The Snape boggart in *Azkaban* wears a woman's dress with a vulture hat. As I mentioned in chapter three Snape is also the head of Slytherin, the 'water' house. Water is an element usually associated with the feminine. Snape is another Slytherin / Gryffindor *rebis*. Albus, as mentioned in the last chapter, is a 'white hat' with a black band as Snape is a 'black hat' with a white band. Granger correctly predicted that Snape wasn't a 'fence straddler,' but was "living as a conscious conduit between the electrical poles that define the wizarding world." He went on to say that "Severus Snape is the alchemist's apprentice and great-souled man...He isn't an artificial or accidental hermaphrodite like Voldemort and Harry but a man who has deliberately and sacrificially bridged the Gryffindor / Slytherin divide."[52]

Albus is also a hermaphroditic figure devoted to love. Shortly after *Hallows*, JK Rowling revealed that she'd always seen him as gay and that the great love of his life had been the dark wizard Grindelwald.[53] This certainly made sense of Skeeter's glee at uncovering their relationship and her nasty comment about Dumbledore taking an 'unnatural' interest in Harry.

It also, however, makes perfect sense alchemically and even magically. From the most ancient times, some magical traditions have included elements of androgyny, bisexuality, cross-dressing or homosexuality to symbolize that practitioners were 'between the worlds.' Being between the worlds sexually symbolized that they were also between the physical and spiritual worlds, and could therefore act as intermediaries. This sort of thing is far from universal, but it's not an anomaly either, it's a significant strand of symbolism. It's not, however, necessary to cross dress or be gay to embody the union of opposites that Dumbledore does!

If we go beyond the surface level of the *rebis* symbolism, we see that Dumbledore has united polarities within himself to so great an extent that he can see beyond the surface polarities in everyone around him. The good, the bad and the ugly are all treated with courtesy and respect, even the repulsive people who come to kill him in *Hallows*. As the embodiment of the *albus* or *albedo*, he represents clear sight and purified motives. He sees people as what they are at heart, the stone itself, the divine essence. The stone may be covered in mud, blood, tar or anything else, but that doesn't change it one bit. It is still the stone.

Dumbledore is a force of love, but not love specifically and soppily directed at evildoers. He doesn't want to cuddle Fenrir Greyback and isn't afraid to admit his disgust towards him. The quality of love attained in the *albus* is love as a purified and radiant state of being, a sun that shines on just and unjust and isn't dimmed on anyone's account. This is one point of forgiveness; it's remaining aligned with the sacred, with love and harmony, regardless of what other people choose to do.

As Dumbledore says, the pure power of love, as held in that sealed room at the Department of Mysteries, is "more wonderful and more terrible than death, than human intelligence, than human nature."[54]

Albus is ruthless as an angel, and not the benignities of new age greeting cards. At heart, he's more like the Old Testament angels or the fierce Sumerian kerubs with lion's bodies and wings behind their dignified bearded faces. The *albus* is a point of frightening purity. It sees through the dearest illusions, destroys sentiment, dissolves everything that is not the stone. Like so many of the themes that run through the books, it is both terrible and great.

VI

THE TERRIBLE AND THE GREAT

I think we must expect great things from you, Mister Potter…After all, He Who Must Not Be Named did great things — terrible, yes, but great.
Ollivander

Everything is Poison. Nothing is Poison.
Paracelsus

Iphias Doge's obituary for Dumbledore said, "No wizarding duel ever matched that between Dumbledore and Grindelwald in 1945. Those who witnessed it have written of the terror and the awe they felt as they watched those two extraordinary wizards do battle."[1] Dumbledore and Grindelwald are like the warring and uniting elements in the alchemical vessel. Each wanted to become a *rebis*, to unite the polarities of life and death through the Hallows. JK Rowling has said that Dumbledore loved Grindelwald and was then horribly disappointed in him — not to mention in himself. Grindelwald was like Dumbledore's shadow; the boundless will to power that led to his sister's death.

He put the fight off because he feared learning that he'd actually cast the killing curse that felled his sister. Many seekers are afraid of what horrible truths about themselves will appear through the walls of the vessel as the elements do battle. The spectacle of transformation is not always peaceful, or beautiful.

Placing this battle in 1945 obviously refers to the end of WWII, which yields more interesting parallels than the obvious. Some of those who fought and who were bombed in European cities described similar mixed feelings of fear and horror and awe. The journalist Bill Moyers asked a veteran who'd fought in the Battle of the Bulge, where a German surprise assault nearly succeeded, what the experience was like. He responded, "It was sublime."[2]

That's not to say it was good, or pleasant, yet the awful may be awe-full. Awe-some is another word for the same thing. An experience of prodigious power and energy and scale can be sublime, regardless of its moral content. It's an experience of expansiveness and scale.

The alchemical *sublimatio* was the process of heating a liquid so that it turned into a vapor, expanded in the vessel and coagulated into a solid again, its impurities reduced. To sublimate came to mean to raise a quality within the self to a higher, subtler level, to expand the self, since a vapor takes up more space than the same substance as a liquid or solid. (The molecules are farther apart.)

This is not described as a painless process, as I noted in the last chapter. Seeing things on a bigger scale is awe-full. There's a classical example in the *Bhagavad Gita*, the 14th book of the *Mahabharata*, a vast Indian epic describing the war of the Pandavas and the Kauravas, who represent the forces of order and chaos, respectively. However, the epic poem's 90 thousand verses are packed with ambiguity. (Just for comparison, that's about 1.8 million words to the *Harry Potter* series' substantial 1.1 million.) Most of the 'white hats' in the *Mahabharata*, like Dumbledore, have black bands, and vice versa. Every person fighting on the Kaurava side isn't 'bad.' Some of them are only there because of circumstances, duty and loyalty. They're doing a bad thing for morally impeccable reasons.

In the *Bhagavad Gita*, the Pandava, Arjuna was about to fight relatives, friends and teachers on the Kaurava side. Overwhelmed, he refused and sat down on the battlefield. His friend, the deity Krishna, appealed to him in various ways to do his duty, and finally revealed himself in all his vastness. Krishna is Lord of Yoga, which means to 'yoke,' to harness polarities together to pull you towards illumination, as oxen yoked to a cart pull it. Arjuna sees Krishna as a huge being with myriad eyes and arms and faces and divine weapons.

He sees all things, all forces, foes and friends, flowing like endless rivers into his vast jaws to be destroyed. Krishna is Vishnu, the Creator and Destroyer of All. He is Time. Arjuna says, "Gazing upon thy mighty form…the worlds all shudder—how much more I!" He continues, "I see Thee and my inmost self is shaken, I cannot bear it, I find no peace, Oh Vishnu." Yet still, he is devoted to this being who has also been his benevolent friend. "Fain would I know Thee as Thou art in the beginning, for what Thou workest, I do not understand."[3]

If seeing on a bigger scale is this uncomfortable, *being* on a bigger scale can also be painful. When the seeker begins to expand himself so that he feels for others and truly experiences the scale of the terror and joy of the world, it sometimes seems unbearable. Greater awareness brings the seeker into uncomfortable intimacy with black, white and all shades of gray, the polarities and every point between.

JK Rowling doesn't sidestep this dynamic, but repeatedly returns to it. Ollivander, named for the olive tree of peace, is quite an ambivalent character. His words above resonate throughout the books. Even though Voldemort tortures and imprisons him, he still seems awed by the 'formidable' image of the power Voldemort would wield with the elder wand. Ollivander is never a Death Eater, far from it, but he obviously feels some attraction to Voldemort's qualities.

In one of the conversations between Dumbledore and Voldemort that Harry views in the pensieve in *Prince*, Voldemort says that his greatness has inspired jealousy and bad rumors. Dumbledore asks, "You call it 'greatness,' what you have been doing, do you?" Ms. Rowling often asks us to question what we call greatness. As Sirius tells Harry, there are more kinds of people in the world than good people and Death Eaters. Even good people have to break the rules in her novels, just like the heroes in the *Mahabharata*.[4]

Krishna has Arjuna and the other Pandavas break just about every rule of fair combat to win against the Kauravas. Where they don't break the rules, they turn the Kauravas adherence to the rules against them. For example, Arjuna's brother, Bhima, kills one Kaurava by striking him illegally below the belt during a duel with clubs. In the battle, the Pandavas often become what they despise, the Kauravas often hold to the code. When confronted by Arjuna and the others, Krishna simply says that he did what had to be done to win.

Similarly, Harry finds that he must perform unforgivable curses in *Hallows* to win. He has to perform the imperius curse at Gringott's to get into the vaults. He also performs the cruciatus curse when he doesn't absolutely have to. By that point, of course, he'd been through a lot. This raises another point; the warrior's actions for society can't help but place him on its fringes.

We've already discussed the ambivalent qualities of Dumbledore, Snape and Sirius. Harry's Dad was a bully as a lad, and even Hagrid, who's quite cuddly in many ways, loves monstrous, destructive creatures, an affection that nearly gets Ron and Harry killed when they go into the forest to speak with Aragog, the acromantula.

Barty Crouch Jr., when posing as Mad-Eye Moody, is another fantastic example. Who didn't cheer when he turned Malfoy into a ferret? He seemed truly angry at the lack of fair play in attacking an opponent from behind. Most of us would see his adherence to fair play as positive. He also actually teaches them quite well (even to throw off the imperius curse) and is genuinely kind to Neville. There are subtexts to his actions, to be sure, but that doesn't entirely undo their positive aspects. He's also unquestionably loyal and true, positive qualities, although he's fixed his devotion on an evil object.

There are many more examples of the 'terrible and the great,' like when Dumbledore speaks of love as a force more wonder-full and more terrible than death, and of course, the power of sacrifice itself.

Sacrifice is bound up with our whole conception of God and the universe. Ms. Rowling knowingly invokes all these levels of meaning, though she never speaks specifically of God. She doesn't really need to. Like all great authors, her deep concerns come through without her hitting us on the head with them. In her case, she's interested in themes of love, sacrifice, death and Deity. She could probably write a recipe book and we'd find them there.

Dumbledore spends the last book 'crucified' between the polarities of love and death. His love and guilt over Ariana puts him there when he tries to use Voldemort's cursed ring. As Snape promised in the first book, he could 'stopper,' though not stop death. Dumbledore is between the worlds, between life and death, a liminal or 'boundary' person, neither one thing nor the other. His 'dead' hand is a constant reminder. Many wizards and shamans, though not in Dumbledore's exact position, have been thought of as being between life and death in their role as intermediaries between this world and the Otherworld.

Dumbledore, in his state of 'stoppered' death, is an extreme example of a 'liminal' or boundary occupying figure in the books. The other two who represent alchemical stages also deserve a mention. Rubeus Hagrid is a half-giant living protectively between the castle and the Forbidden Forest. Many shamans live in such places, and as David Abram notes, they see their primary role as maintaining the boundary between polarities of wild and tame, this world and the Other.[5]

Communication between realms is important, but so is containment. Only a person between polarities can act as both intermediary and enforcer. Think of policemen. They're also liminal figures, with the evil doer's capacity for violence and the citizen's will to good. Without both polarities, they couldn't protect the latter from the former. They must literally and symbolically stand between the two.

Both Hagrid and Dumbledore do this. Hagrid is sent to mediate between the giants and humans, and is the only one who can control his giant brother, though that control is tenuous at first and results in numerous injuries. He can go everywhere in the forest and interact with all the creatures there — until his 'pet' acromantula dies and its descendants won't allow it. Similarly, Dumbledore can go in and rescue Umbridge from the centaur herd when no one else would dare.

Sirius Black is another figure with mixed qualities. He's another Gryffindor / Slytherin *rebis*, with qualities of both houses. He's also between human and animal worlds as an animagus. This liminal quality enables him to escape from Azkaban, to do what was thought to be impossible. He even returns as more than a ghost, but less than a physical person in the final book, to help Harry over the final boundary between worlds. Harry, of course, is another liminal character — the most liminal of the liminal.

THE PHILOSOPHICAL ORPHAN: HARRY BETWEEN POLARITIES

Harry's ambivalent qualities are part of what enables him to triumph. For example, his inner Voldemort's ability to speak parseltongue gets him into the Chamber of Secrets to rescue Ginny and defeat Voldemort's younger self. This is a layer of Paracelsus' meaning in the quote above, when he said, "Everything is Poison. Nothing is Poison." Cobra venom is used to make anti-venom, to cure the bitten.

Conversely, eat enough of anything and it can kill you. The most positive motives become poisonous if, like Barty Crouch

Senior's desire to fight the Dark Arts, or Dolores Umbridge's desire for order, they're taken to extreme.

It's similar to the way that the qualities of the Hogwarts houses can manifest positively or negatively. Even Gryffindor bravery can become rashness, just as Slytherin cunning can help manifest true will. This tells us that even our worst qualities, what we may think of as our personal 'demons' may be used for good. If we think of them as untapped potentials in the psyche, we'll see that they can wreck our lives if left unmastered, or be of use if mastered.[6]

A 'demon' of ambition can serve us if its power is channeled into the desire to do good for others. A 'demon' of rage can be sublimated through vigorous exercise that gets us in great shape or channeled via righteous anger to challenge injustice. Of course, the idea can be taken too far, as Quirrell does in *Stone*, when he tells Harry that there's no good and evil, only power and those too weak to use it. Certain uses of power are evil. Harry is constantly being challenged to define what those are, and his story challenges us to reflect on them.

Harry is marked with a symbol of creative and destructive power and polarities, his lightning bolt scar. It appears in the mystical 'third eye' position in many illustrations and serves as a spiritual 'third eye' through which he sees Voldemort. Lightning destroys things and makes the soil more fertile, as well as heralding the life-giving rain.

Paracelsus says that a flash of lightning appears towards the end of the alchemical process — the lightning that changes the dark 'contraction' of Saturn into the bright expansion of Jupiter. It brings a degree of calm to the turbulence in the vessel, though Harry doesn't really experience this much till the very end.[7]

After he gets to Bill and Fleur's house, after Dobby's death, he feels his scar burning, "but he was master of the pain; he felt it, yet he was apart from it. He had learned control at last, learned to shut his mind to Voldemort, the very thing Dumbledore had wanted him to learn from Snape." His grief for Dobby, like his grief for Sirius in *Phoenix*, seemed to drive Voldemort out, "...though Dumbledore, of course, would have said it was love..."[8]

He no longer feels the obsessive desire for the Deathly Hallows, like someone had slapped him and snapped him out of it. He's free of desperate fear and desire. After digging Dobby's grave, he washes his hands, watching the sunrise through the window and listening to the murmuring of his friends' conversation. "He looked out over the ocean and felt closer, this dawn, than ever before, closer to the heart of it all." The pile of red earth on Dobby's grave and the "bright-gold rim" of the sun tells us he's near to the *rubedo* and attaining the stone, or has actually done so. When Fleur tells him he can't talk to Griphook and Ollivander, he responds that he simply needs to, *without heat*. Emotions aren't dictating his course and he has no need to bully or get angry to attain his true will.[9]

Revealingly, before Harry learns how he got his lightning scar, it's the one physical feature he likes about himself. The seeker is often attracted to the idea of uniting the polarities, as Dumbledore and Grindelwald are. They like the sense that they have the power to do so *in potentia* — before they realize what the process will demand from them.

When Harry begins to learn what his scar means, he no longer likes it. It symbolizes both the 'terrible' fact of Voldemort's murder of his parents, his attempt on Harry's life and the 'taint' (and more) of Voldemort's touch, as well as the 'great' love his mother bore him. Harry's role as philosophical orphan, survivor and *product* of the king and queen's death, confronts him each time he looks in the mirror and each time someone's eyes do the familiar flicker up to his scar.

Beyond all these facts, Harry doesn't really want to have within him the capacity to be terrible, great and everything in between that the scar symbolizes. Most seekers would prefer narrower parameters of experience and emotion, say, benevolent to peeved, and leave off qualities like perversity, venomous hatred and wrath—but that's not entirely possible. We may sublimate them, but they're present in all of us.

Some of Harry's fury and the negative qualities he displays in the books come from Voldemort. Various people have theorized that Harry's bad behavior in *Phoenix* and elsewhere is just the Voldemort inside him, but I think that's an easy answer. Adolescents don't need to be possessed to be moody. Harry knows he's not inevitably good. He recognizes his own bad qualities and distinguishes them from Voldemort's, experienced through his scar. He slowly discovers that the scar is a painful power source that brings new meaning to the phrase 'double edged sword.' When yet another layer of its meaning is revealed in *Hallows*, he realizes that he, like Dumbledore, has been in a state of 'stoppered' death.

Adolescence is a well-recognized liminal phase of life when we (at least some of us) try to sublimate our rage and lust and destructive impulses. In the process we become very trying indeed. Rule breaking is a big feature of adolescence, and a big feature of Harry's life. Even conscientious Hermione is willing to "break at least a dozen school rules" to make the polyjuice potion in *Chamber*.

However, Harry and his friends seldom break rules for trivial reasons. One of the few occasions I can think of is when he uses his father's invisibility cloak and the Marauder's Map to sneak into Hogsmeade in *Azkaban*. When he's caught, and Lupin confronts him with the fact that he'd gambled his parents' sacrifices "for a bag of tricks," he's properly ashamed. He also feels badly after the flying car crash in *Chamber*. Interestingly, the later American edition of *Chamber* also features a longer discussion

between Ron and Harry before the 'theft,' where Harry doesn't agree so readily to it.[10]

The books have come under fire from conservative critics for encouraging children to break rules. Some Christian and even secular commentators have latched on to Harry's disregard for rules as the most 'subversive' message in *Harry Potter*.[11] But as the example above shows, the books don't tell children to break rules for any old reason. They allow that breaking a rule is a possible choice in serious situations. It's not just permissible but essential (for their safety and other reasons) to teach children that they *can* say no to adults if it's necessary. Harry is just confronted with these choices far more than the average child is. Even so, Harry doesn't throw the rules, or his own morals, out the window, even when it might be justifiable to do so. For example, when he tries to disarm rather than kill or stun an opponent during the ambush scene at the start of *Hallows*. Again, he's scolded by Lupin, this time, for his scruples.

Harry generally adheres quite rigidly to the spirit of the rules even when he's a bit cavalier with their letter. The spirit is about working for the triumph of a positive world order. He may question particular means, but *he never questions the good of the order itself.* He's not truly tempted by evil, although he does find the raw power of the elder wand attractive, as most would. He remains "Dumbledore's man, through and through," regardless of circumstances. He holds to the good that Dumbledore represents despite his mentor's imperfections, his death, or even, as Harry discovers towards the end of *Hallows*, his willingness to lead Harry to a possible sacrificial death via a tissue of lies. He follows Dumbledore even unto his own death. His trust and loyalty were ultimately justified, but they were tested to the extreme.

Harry's story encourages the seeker not to do what everyone says, but to also hold to the perennial values of love and self-sacrifice. Now, of course, I'm making a big value judgement by placing these highest, but I think it's a safe bet! Common sense tells us that our existence owes much less to 'selfish genes' than to altruistic ancestors. There's also the basic fact of the earth's vast generosity and each generation giving way to the next. The magic of love and sacrifice is the way of the world, not some theological symbol we have to squint at to see in it.

Holding to these perennial truths while not blindly following rules gives seekers like Harry the best of both worlds. A vine that is pruned, fertilized and trained up a trellis will bear more fruit than one growing wild, because it doesn't spend a lot of energy finding its way. Conversely, an unlimited search for self can be destructive. The ivy, Hermione's wand wood, is a symbol of the spiraling search for self. It can force the roof off a house and splinter the foundation if it grows wild against it.

The books underscore the idea that seekers shouldn't reinvent morality to suit themselves. They need to follow some higher ideal and limit personal power. Dumbledore tried to reinvent morals in his youth, to leave his sister and brother, to follow a 'greater,' ego-based, good. This shows the flaw in ever putting what we might deem greater good above the goods that the perennial wisdom describes as greatest: love, harmony and sacrifice in their service.

People who claim to stand for a greater good can deceive us all — and they tend to stand on social authority. As the fantasy author Mercedes Lackey rightly says in her introduction to *Mapping the World of Harry Potter*, "The narrow-minded, and those who would like to 'educate' children into submission, have a lot to fear from Harry Potter...I hope they are shaking in their shoes. With luck, the kids who grow up reading these books will not settle for 'Because I am the boss, 'because this book says so,' 'because that's the way it is. With luck, they will march out there determined to figure out what is wrong or right, and to right the wrongs."[12] Causes espoused by the Dursleys and Umbridges of the world have some reasons to worry about Harry's effect on *their* social order, but the rest of us don't.

Righting wrongs can be a morally difficult process. Harry keenly feels the ambivalence of his role as a liminal enforcer and breaker of boundaries like many policemen and soldiers do. As the saying goes, the idea of fighting for peace is akin to the idea of having sex for chastity. And yet the world confronts us with such situations, like WWII. Knowing this doesn't solve the problem internally, however.

Many of Harry's combative encounters seem to be battles within himself as much as with someone else. In the scene where Lupin chides him for his refusal to kill or even stun in certain circumstances, fourteen friends have just risked their lives to save him, one has died and Lupin has a point. An added irony is that the person he wouldn't stun, Stan Shunpike, was one of the major sticking points between him and any possible alliance with the Ministry. Although Stan was seemingly under the imperius curse when he was imprisoned, he was still actually working for Voldemort. *Hallows* even sees Harry try and save Malfoy, Crabbe and Goyle from an inferno of their own making. Here, Ron understandably says, "If we die for them, I'll kill you, Harry!"

There's a narrative tradition of victory via the liminal that Ms. Rowling also plugs into here. For example, liminal figures defeat the Witch King, leader of the Nazgul in *Lord of the Rings*. He can't be killed by a man and thinks he's safe. In the end, however, a hobbit wounds him and a woman, Eowyn, delivers the killing blow.[13] Harry, as an under age wizard, like Kreacher as a house elf, can breach the defenses Voldemort has set up around his horcrux in the cave because they're beneath Voldemort's notice and so, outside the parameters of his enchantment.

Voldemort's inter-species liminal 'gift' of parseltongue enables Harry to enter the Chamber of Secrets and defeat Voldemort there, and his 'inner Voldemort,' his 'scar-o-scope,' as John Granger puts it, gives him insights that help him win.[14] The 'head splitting' pain that accompanies these visions can symbolize the internal 'splitting' that people may experience in schizophrenia or during and after trauma. It also refers to the fact that Harry has a 'lodger,' a chunk of Voldemort wedged in that lightning bolt scar. Harry's relationship to Voldemort is, of course, his most unpleasantly liminal quality.

Voldemort isn't Harry's father in a Darth Vader biological way, but he is in a psychological way. Harry's psyche has been formed as much by Voldemort's negatives as by his parents' positives. This entwined relationship points to Voldemort as the symbolic shadow figure we all carry around within us. Everything repressed, everything hated and unacknowledged in the self. This internal foe is more to be feared than the external ones. But, like the external ones, our best course is to embrace and transform it.

Sometimes this means erring on the side of mercy. Some may find Harry's doing so irritating or foolish at points, like when he spares Pettigrew in *Azkaban*. Even Harry felt he'd made a mistake there, despite Dumbledore's reassurance. However, the sort of Harry who would have killed Pettigrew would have been the sort that would have killed Sirius a few moments before. That would have lost him one of his most important relationships.

By exhorting Voldemort to repentance Harry may be intuitively seeking a deeper victory. Morihei Ueshiba, the founder of Aikido, said "True victory is not defeating an enemy. True victory gives love and changes the enemy's heart."[15] Doing so, he echoes an earlier sentiment of Dumbledore's. In one of the memories that Harry experiences through the pensieve in *Prince*, we see Tom Riddle return to Hogwarts, apparently to ask for a job. Dumbledore refuses to give him one and he's furious. Before he storms out, Dumbledore says, with great sadness, "The time is long gone when I could frighten you with a burning wardrobe and force you to make repayment for your crimes. But I wish I could, Tom...I wish I could..."[16] Dumbledore sees past the maimed, evil

thing Voldemort has become to that unpleasant but not yet doomed boy and beyond him to the abandoned, unloved baby.

FALLING APART: HORCRUXES AND SOUL LOSS

It's significant that Ms. Rowling uses the deeply unpleasant image of a flayed child abandoned under a bench to depict the piece of Voldemort's soul that was lodged in Harry when *he* was a screaming baby who'd lost his parents. She used a similar image to convey Voldemort's appearance before his rebirth in *Goblet*. There, she softened it by saying that while he's like a crouched human child in some respects, "Harry had never seen anything less like a child."[17] No such softening occurs in *Hallows*. As a mother and children's charity founder, she must have found the image at least as horrible as the rest of us.

She uses it deliberately to convey a few things. First: what goes around comes around. He who flees death and deals it to others gets multiple doses via the rebounding curses that 'book end' the story and the destruction of his soul parts via horcruxes. Voldemort created a helpless, parentless orphan in Harry (and who knows how many others) and that is what his severed soul part becomes. We get Voldemort's point of view in *Hallows*, when he is in pain and terror, fleeing the rubble where the screaming Harry is trapped, "He had killed the boy, and yet he *was* the boy..."[18]

Dumbledore still pities him because he knows that within most evil doers is an 'evil done to.' The vast majority of those who end up harming others were unloved or abused. There are psychological reasons for this, but there are also spiritual ones.

From a shamanic perspective, trauma can create something called 'soul loss.' Soul loss can occur when trauma 'splinters off' part of a person's soul.[19] Shamanic cultures think of it as a kind of spiritual defense mechanism that prevents the full person from experiencing the trauma. Say someone's driving a car when a big truck comes at them head on — at that moment, part of them says, "I'm *out* of here." They wake up later in hospital remembering nothing, a sign of soul loss. For their healing to be complete, a traditional shamanic culture would treat the broken soul along with the broken bones.

Soul loss doesn't always occur through violent trauma. If a person 'dies a little' each day at work, they may be having soul loss. There are many other ways to lose or damage our souls. Alan Moore addresses the issue in modern Western culture. He speaks of how the search for our true self, our soul, our 'inner diamond,' is the 'the great work,' the gold the alchemists sought. It's the most important thing that we can attain, yet there are many "who seem to have the urge not just to ignore the self but actually…obliterate themselves."

> This is horrific but you can almost understand it. The desire to simply wipe out that awareness because it's too much of a responsibility to actually possess such a thing as a soul, such a precious thing. What if you break it, what if you lose it? Mightn't it be best to anaesthetize it, to deaden it, to destroy it — to not have to live with the pain of struggling towards it and trying to keep it pure? I think that the way that people immerse themselves in alcohol, in drugs, in television, in any of the addictions that our culture throws up, can be seen as a deliberate attempt to destroy any connection between themselves and the responsibility of accepting and owning a higher self and then having to maintain it.[20]

This may be part of what's behind Voldemort's hurry to mutilate his own soul. Lost soul parts typically take the form of the person as they were at the time of the trauma that caused the soul loss. The fact that two of the 'bits' of Voldemort take an infant form may have something to do with the fact that his defining trauma was the loss of his mother. The only other two pieces we actually see are the teen Voldemort at the age he was when he killed his father and grandparents, when that part splintered off, and eyes of an indeterminate age — the windows of the soul. The horrible 'infants' are also reminiscent of a botched alchemical process, a badly made philosophical orphan. Of course, the first time we see this image is before Voldemort's alchemical rebirth from the vast stone cauldron by his father's grave.

As Slughorn says, the soul is meant to remain intact. Splitting it is "an act of violation, it's against nature." The wizard "intent upon making a horcrux would use the damage to his advantage" by encasing the torn portion in an object.[21]

In *Harry Potter*, murdering another person under specific circumstances splinters off a piece of Voldemort's soul to safeguard within a horcrux. *Crux* is, obviously 'cross,' and my best guess is that *hor* relates to the Latin word that gives us 'horrible.' Like *crucio*, the horcruxes are full of Christian symbolism. It is the 'horrible cross,' the horrible sacrifice, that kills a victim and breaks the perpetrators soul, to acquire eternal life in a body for the murderer. It's easy to see the process as the antithesis of Christ's sacrifice to give others life at the cost of his own, to heal souls broken by sin and grant eternal life to everyone who chooses it. The making of a horcrux entails a horrible sacrifice. Of course, sacrifices of different kinds are central to Harry's story.

THE MAGIC OF LOVE, WILL AND SACRIFICE

Sacrifice is a huge theme in *Harry Potter* — and of course, in many spiritual traditions. The most obvious one is Christianity, but many indigenous and magical traditions also see sacrifice as a central element in creation. Modern Western culture is rather uncomfortable with the concept, however.

Many of us mistakenly feel like we're protecting ourselves somehow when we resist sacrifice and fearfully cling to all we have. We may resist a sense of inner prompting to make a sacrifice that we may think of as God's will or our own true will. I'll simply refer to it here as will, which you can read as you please. Will always calls us to do the highest good for others and ultimately, for ourselves. It calls us to be our biggest, best selves. Yet we often resist our true, higher will, for some perceived short term, smaller good. Peter Pettigrew thought he was taking care of himself by betraying Lily and James, but the life he gained wasn't worth living. He also gained no real power but diminished himself into a pet rat, the Weasley's and Voldemort's. By betraying true will, he identified with, and became, his smallest ego-based self.

That's because there's no way we can resist true will in one area of life without resisting it in all areas. It's like the way electrical current moves through a wire. Electrical wires have an impedance, that is, a degree of resistance offered by the material itself to the current passing through it. We can look at our own resistance to will in the same way. We can't resist the power as it might manifest in a specific way, any more than a wire can resist the current if it powers a blender but not a toaster. Energy is energy and resistance is resistance. Resisting *any* facet of will is to resist *all*, which limits our power to create the life we want.

Time for the big let go. We might call it the sacrificial posture, an internal posture of total love and non-resistance. The sacrificial posture that Lily and Harry adopted works through the magic of love and the magic of unhindered will. To open fully to true will, like Harry's to defeat Voldemort and save those he loves, or Lily's will to save Harry, opens us fully to spiritual power making us phenomenally effective. This is the specific mechanism through which Lily and Harry's sacrifices worked.

Interestingly, Snape's request of Voldemort is why Lily was able to save Harry. His love for her and his will for her survival worked together with hers for Harry to save him. Other people must have thrown themselves between Voldemort and their loved ones to no effect. It happens again in *Hallows* when he's looking for Gregorovitch at his old home. Harry is the only one to survive the killing curse because Lily is the only one Voldemort offers the choice to stand aside and live. She won't, and her willing sacrifice brings through vast power. This is why Voldemort says he should have known what would happen in *Goblet*. It wasn't a freak occurrence, but the simple operation of an ancient spiritual principal.

Later, Harry also adopts the sacrificial posture. In the forest at the end of *Hallows* Harry opens the snitch, symbolizing right choice and the perfected soul, with his sacrificial words, "I am about to die." Through sacrifice he opens to his true, divine, eternal self, with all its power. His sacrifice is even broader and more powerful than Lily's, because he has some time to reflect on and accept it, and he doesn't just do it for a specific loved one, but for everyone who Voldemort could potentially harm—in short, ultimately, *everyone*.

More specifically, as Harry tells Voldemort, he was prepared to die to stop Voldemort hurting those who'd arrived at Hogwarts to fight him. Voldemort responds that Harry did not die. Harry responds, "I meant to, and that's what did it. I've done what my mother did." None of the spells that Voldemort tries on the Hogwarts defenders bind them. He can no longer torture or touch them, because Harry offered himself completely.[22]

But wait a minute, you may say, Harry certainly lets go, but he also keeps fighting, he's not a gelatinous blob of non-resistance. This is a key point. Entering the sacrificial posture is a means to an end, not an end in and of itself. If we release the small, ego-based will, we can see what we should work for, even fight for, with clarity and simultaneously gain the power to do so. It's an exquisite spiritual mechanism, like Dumbledore's that only allows an altruist to get the stone from the Mirror of Erised.

Paradoxically, sacrifice is less of a sacrifice when it's embraced; though it may be a choice of lesser evil. Lily would have preferred to live, but failing that, dying was better than surviving Harry by standing aside. Harry could have fled Hogwarts on that fateful night, but the consequent fear and self-loathing would have been more unpleasant than the sacrifice, than flowing with the true will that directed his course.

Of course, Harry's sacrifice relates to the symbolism of Christ's blood sacrifice. In a 2007 interview JK Rowling said that because of the magic in the books' world, Voldemort "did have a chance for redemption because he had taken into his body this — this drop of hope or love…"

"Harry's blood." The interviewer, Meredith Vieira, prompted.

"Right," Ms. Rowling responded, "So that meant that if he could have mustered the courage to repent, he would have been okay. But, of course, he wouldn't. And that's his choice."[23] It's not too far a leap to the magic of Christ's blood sacrifice. We can, however, also see other traditions reflected, consciously or unconsciously.

Many magical traditions like the Celtic, Indian or Kabbalistic see creation as emanation. That is, if there was only Deity in the beginning, then it had to create everything out of itself, because there was nothing else to use. In this world-view, everything is part of God and God is therefore 'sacrificed' in all that is. This is part of the underlying unity that makes magic work.

JK Rowling places all of the Potters' sacrifices at times of the old Celtic year that were associated with Deity's primordial sacrifice in creation. Celtic literature and folk traditions also say that other sacrifices may have occurred during these festivals in ancient times. James and Lily die at Halloween or Samhain, the Old Celtic New Year. It began the 'dark half' of the year. The 'light half' began at Beltane, observed on the first of May. JK Rowling said that Voldemort died on the second of May, which places Harry's sacrifice on Beltane. This time of the year is also associated with the Death Eaters.

DEFENDING AGAINST THE DARK ARTS

In an early interview, JK Rowling said that the Death Eaters existed before Voldemort came along, and that they were known as the Knights of Walpurgis.[24] This is a reference to Walpurgis Night, an ancient German fertility festival when all the witches were supposed to gather together and have orgies. It occurred on the 30th of April, the day before Beltane.

Calling the Death Eaters the Knights of Walpurgis identifies them with the forces of chaos that can manifest as fertilizing or as destructive. The dark womb of the earth is a nurturing place. Remember her quote at the start of *Hallows* from Aeschylus that asks the 'dark gods' beneath the earth to bless the children? She clearly doesn't simplistically identify dark with 'bad.'

Many traditions make the deities of death the deities of sexuality and generation. In Celtic tradition, the Fomoire can be evil deities but are also in charge of the land's fertility, so they can't be gotten rid of altogether.[25] One of them, Bres the Beautiful, was very attractive, and they've certainly cast some 'lookers' as Death Eaters in the films. The chaotic twinning of sex and death in the psyche may be part of the attraction women feel for 'bad boys' that JK Rowling lamented in one talk.

Why should this be so? I can't go into great detail here, but on one level it's a no-brainer. With sex comes death. Amoebas don't really die they divide. With sexual reproduction part of our genetic material is discarded with each throw of the reproductive dice. Additionally, the destruction of chaos, the breaking up and rotting down of materials to make soil, for example, is a necessary destruction that comes before fresh generation. By contrast, the destruction of evil is unnecessary and gangrenous, generating nothing but rot. Most people wouldn't consider it evil to pull up a carrot. Many wouldn't consider it evil to kill an animal to eat, but it would be evil to pull up plants for no reason, or take pot shots at animals or humans for fun.

It can be easier to deal with evil if we 'personify' it. For example, personifying a depression as a demon or Dementor can help by placing it at a remove. You can then interpose your patronus or another positive force between you and it.

We find the utility of personifying the negative in the way Lupin teaches Harry to deal with a Boggart. The Boggart is just a Northern English variant of the Bogeyman of childhood.[26] This character (like most 'demons') likes to take the form we are most frightened of. It first appears in a wardrobe, the dark place where childhood fears often place such things. As Lupin says, the way to get rid of it is to *interact* with it, not ignore it or tell yourself it's not real.

In the Boggart's case, you have to "make it assume a form you find amusing" with the charm *riddikulus*. An age-old technique for banishing any fear is to have a bit of a chuckle about it. One method of 'banishing,' of clearing the space of any residual energy after a ritual in modern Chaos magic is to have a good laugh.

Personifying the bad, whether on the way to making it funny, or dealing with it in some other way, gives us a handle on it and often makes it less frightening. As any film director will tell you, the thing you can't quite see, the implied thing, is always more frightening than the thing in your face, however horrible.

JK Rowling has said that the Dementors 'personify' her own battle with depression. As such they're a pretty good example of putting personification to work for us. Unmastered and nebulous they made her miserable. Personified and used as characters in a book, they've help earn her lots of money, banishing some of her reasons for depression. Nicely done!

In what follows, I'm not saying that evil forces are all psychological projections. Nor am I saying that they're all ravening minions of Lucifer out to get us. I am saying that what we experience as 'evil' in our lives can be seen and dealt with in a variety of ways, and that such flexibility is highly useful.

A detailed analysis of evil's nasty little tricks is beyond our scope here, but most of us don't need that much detail. The forces of evil are often pretty blunt instruments, and we don't need to be that clever (or that holy) to avoid or combat them. For the most part, all that's necessary is staying close to the sacred through spiritual practice and to act on the awareness it generates and the perennial guidelines for right action.

When Harry is trying to learn occlumency to shield himself from Voldemort's influence, Professor Snape tells him to spend time each night before sleep ridding his mind of all emotion, emptying it and making it blank and calm.[27] Calming and strengthening ourselves is our first and best defense against evil.

Evil often enters our lives through plain old selfishness – the idea that my desires override other beings' desires. It begins innocuously enough. I want to see *Harry Potter* at the cinema, while a friend wants to see something else. *Of course* I think we should see *Harry Potter* because that's what *I* want to see, just like I might want fish, not chicken, for dinner or a child might want to play with a toy another child has. When we want things, we may negotiate, compromise, manipulate, bribe, bully or cajole. One child might snatch the toy from another, I might make a deal to see one film and then my friend picks next time.

I'd do well throughout to bear the Buddhist 'noble truth' in mind that desire causes suffering. The more violently I desire, the more self-absorbed I become as a consequence, the less happy I'm likely to be. If I haven't learned enough or if I go too far down the road of desire, it may not bother me much if my fulfilled desire is hurtful to another. A child snatching a toy may not care if the other child cries. A grown-up may not care if they seduce someone who has a family. If I continue along that road, my pleasure or even my convenience is worth more than another's life. "Kill the spare" as Voldemort tells Wormtail – but of course there are no spares, we're all one of a kind. To kill off a species, which we do around fifty times a day, is to *devolve* God's creation—which puts a whole different slant on the bio-diversity argument.[28]

For those of us who at least see the folly of living for personal desire, evil's first favorite thing to invoke in us is inertia. Voldemort infinitely prefers to take over quietly behind the scenes while most people sit on their hands. Sins of omission are the most common ones. Those of us who'd like to see the world become better are a host of billions—almost all of us, in fact. Yet a statistically teeny number of evil-inspired people are wrecking our planet. Why? Because, as the saying often attributed to the British statesman Edmund Burke goes, "All that is necessary for evil to triumph is for good men to do nothing."

Dementors paralyze prisoners at Azkaban by instilling feelings of hopelessness, the sense that one person can do nothing, or that, as Ron says after his first encounter, the sense that he'd never feel happy again. If we're reliving the worst things that ever happened to us, as Hagrid describes doing at Azkaban, we're not likely to do anything else. But summon your inner Ravenclaw, use logic, whatever's happened to us has nothing to do with our actions right now. Combat inertia through action, as Harry does, and as I'll discuss further in the next chapter.

Evil also likes to make you think it's you. We all have negative qualities, but evil forces can amplify them. Remember how Ron acted when he was wearing the horcrux in *Hallows*? It was Hermione who picked up on the fact that it was making him behave horribly. However, it didn't make him want to do something utterly alien, but played on the jealousies and insecurities that he was used to feeling. The same is true for us. If you've suffered from depression in the past, feeling your mood start to sink again after a period of feeling happy wouldn't make you think that there must be Dementors about. You'd be more likely to think, "Oh no, here this is again, guess I'll never get over it." Cue the hopelessness.

Obviously, evil also seeks our assent. Why would anyone say 'yes' to evil? For a short sighted good. JK Rowling speaks of people being drawn to Voldemort "for protection, for power, sadism." People like the Malfoys make a clear choice, and she thinks it's "always worth examining why people choose to make those decisions."[29] The Malfoys are going for a warped idea of 'purity' amongst other things. Bullies like Draco feel frightened at heart, or they wouldn't be so desperate for power. Pettigrew wants to live, reasonable in itself, but the life he gains isn't worth having. By contrast, Tonks and Lupin die to create a better world for their son to live in.

Evil seeks to 'make the worst of it,' to take what's loftiest and bring it low. In *Hallows*, with the aid of the horcrux, Ron's love for Hermione becomes fear, anger and jealousy that drives a wedge between the three friends. This is one of evil's favorite tricks. Combat making the worst of it by making the best of it. Just as the greatest evil is to take something good and twist it to bad, the highest good is to take something evil and turn it to good. The greatest evils that have befallen us are our own greatest opportunities for triumph. They're chances to make those experiences useful. Harry is never happy that he's lost his parents, but he does everything possible to make their sacrifice useful and meaningful, by defeating Voldemort and going on to lead the happy, productive life they would have wished for him.

DEMENTORS AND DARK NIGHT

JK Rowling is obviously not alone in wrestling with Dementors. Many people have experienced depression and an unusually high percentage of artists, writers, wizards and spiritual seekers do. In a way, it's part of their illuminating function — as the psychologist and concentration camp survivor, Viktor Frankl said, "That which would give light must endure burning."

Above, I spoke of resistance to the sacred as being like electrical impedance. We remove our resistance as we'd purify a material to carry an electrical current. A physicist in one of my workshops said that if you try and put a lot of power through material with impurities in it, the material would heat up and melt down. But, if you heat the material and cool it gradually, over and over, it will burn out the impurities so that more current can come through. The alchemical process is described just this way. The dark night of the soul, as St. John of the Cross called it, can be thought of as similar to the alchemical *nigredo* we discussed in the last chapter, or the *calcinatio*, a phase that burns away all impurities.

The Dementors are just one symbol of this experience in the books. In *Hallows*, Harry is forced to use a blackthorn wand after his holly is broken. In Celtic lore, blackthorn symbolizes the cleansing and traumatic change of the *nigredo*, the harshest 'blackthorn winter.' No wonder he dislikes the wand! (It so happens that he's wandering in the wilderness in the dead of winter at this point.) Yet folk tradition says that a man with a blackthorn stick is never lost, all he has to do is throw it in the air and it points the way. The energy of *straif*, blackthorn, and strife, a word derived from the plant's name, point the way, making our priorities crystal clear.

Traditional Western psychiatry has tended to see spiritual crisis as a manifestation of mental illnesses like schizophrenia or psychosis.[30] Harry's sensitivity to the Dementors, his scar-related experiences and his unusual abilities often make others think he's mad or untrustworthy. It's another of his liminal features.

Much of artists', teens' and seekers' vulnerability to Dementor attack has to do with sensitivity. The Francis Ford Coppola film, *Rumblefish*, is about a kind of messiah without a cause, the Motorcycle Boy. This character's brother asks their dad if the Motorcycle Boy is crazy. "No," his Dad responds, "The Motorcycle Boy's got a keen sensitivity. A keen sensitivity don't make you crazy — but it can *drive* you crazy, it can drive you crazy."

Of course, part of Harry's sensitivity comes from past trauma. As Lupin says, what he's been through is enough to make anyone fall off their broom — or act like a loon. Reliving his parents' murder each time Dementors are near is horrific, but so is the ambivalence of wanting to hear his parents' voices, as he can't remember doing in life. Harry isn't just sensitive because he's experienced trauma, but because he's a wizard, a practitioner of the Art. All forms of art require sensitivity to environment, to patterns and to emotions. During adolescence we all get more sensitive as nature propels us to breed. For some, it's the last hurrah of sensitivity before a big shut down. For others it lingers as emotional fragility.

No one stands a chance against Dementors or other dark forces, internal or external, without a modicum of mental control. If a wizard summons a 'demon' or other spirit in some schools of magic, they summon it into a triangle while they stand in a protective circle. This is all about control and containment. You'll remember that Hermione or Harry casts a circle of protective enchantments around each of their campsites when they're on the run in *Hallows*. Circle casting is one of the oldest magical rituals we know of. Ronald Hutton says that a striking feature of late medieval ritual magic is the use of a quartered circle, a circle marked with the directions, as the vital unit of sacred space.[31]

The circle represents the divine whole, the horizon, the sun, the moon and the cosmos. Magicians from Sumer to Assyria to Israel have used it from very ancient times. In the late 14th century, Antonious de Monte Ulmi called the circle the most perfect figure for magical operations and the symbol of the Prime Mover of the universe.[32] By surrounding themselves with a circle, Harry, Ron and Hermione encompassed themselves symbolically with the power of entire cosmos, the underlying wholeness of all being.

Both Snape and Lupin try to teach Harry ways to combat the dark arts. Snape's attempt to teach Harry occlumency, however much of a fiasco it turned out to be, was on a par with Lupin's patronus instruction in terms of its potential utility. Snape effectively encourages Harry to enter awareness, where we let go of everything inessential about ourselves, especially our emotions.

After witnessing a vision of Harry's involving Lily, Snape looks paler than usual, no doubt due to his own feelings, but he continues nonetheless. He tells Harry he's to empty himself of emotion, which Harry says he's finding hard at that point. "Then you will find yourself easy prey for the Dark Lord!" said Snape savagely. "Fools who wear their hearts proudly on their sleeves, who cannot control their emotions, who wallow in sad memories and allow themselves to be provoked so easily — weak people, in other words — they stand no chance against his powers!"[33]

Essential qualities of all the Hogwarts houses can defend us from Dementors and other dark creatures. We can apply Ravenclaw knowledge in a few ways. We can read about spiritual crisis and the kind of depression or anxiety it creates in us. Magical knowledge is also important. There are many ways, like Hermione's circle casting in Hallows or the techniques of mental control taught by Professor Snape, to protect ourselves from bad influences.

Gryffindor daring has obvious uses here. You can encourage yourself or act as if you were brave or cheerful, even when you don't feel so good. This isn't suppression, it's allowing the denser level to contain and direct the subtler, the body to educate the mind. Applying Slytherin will is essential. When Harry is trying to escape from a Gringott's vault with a horcrux in Hallows he paraphrases a Samurai saying, "The only way out is through."[34] If it's your true magical will to get through, you can and you will.

To do so you also need your inner Hufflepuff to keep going. It's often the case that a Dementor attack makes you fall back in your spiritual practice, or exercise or whatever else supports your positive state of mind but that's exactly what you need to stick with to get through those marshes. Neville must have felt frightened when he learnt that his parents' torturer, Bellatrix, had escaped from Azkaban. However, his Hufflepuff-like determination got him through any temptation to get paralyzed, along with his bravery and will. On the positive side, if we can approach the dark night or the Dementor attack as initiatory, it becomes so. As I said above, evil likes to work by turning the best things to the worst. When we turn the worst to the best, it's a double victory. It's the alchemical process of making gold of dung.

In alchemy, the gold of the self is revealed when all that isn't gold is burned away. In *The Way of Transformation*, the psychotherapist and diplomat, Karlfried Graf Von Dürckheim said something that makes me think of Harry and his relationship with Dumbledore.

> The man, who, being really on the Way, falls upon hard times in the world will not, as a consequence, turn to that friend who offers him refuge and comfort and encourages his old self to survive. Rather, he will seek out someone who will faithfully and inexorably help him to risk himself, so that he may endure the suffering and pass courageously through it. Only to the extent that man exposes himself over and over again to annihilation, can that which is indestructible arise within him. In this lies the dignity of daring.

Life gives us no complete way of avoiding initiatory processes, though some of us experience more dramatic ones than others. However, we needn't go alone.

The Patronus: Personifying the Positive

JK Rowling focused on the protective aspect of the patronus when the journalist Emma Coad asked her what spell she'd like to bring to life and why. She responded that "the outstanding spell is

Expecto Patronum...It creates the patronus...a kind of spirit guardian...and you could protect yourself and other people that you cared about with a patronus, but it's also because it's such a beautiful spell. You know, the image of the silver patronus emerging from a wand. I really like that."[35]

It's certainly a spell that's caught the popular imagination. Kris Chadderton, a music student at Swarthmore College in America says she uses it "any time I'm under pressure," pacing the halls before piano recitals chanting *expecto patronum*.[36] On Andrew Sims' useful spell list on *Mugglenet's Harry Potter Encyclopedia*, we see that *patronus* is Latin for protector and the phrase *expecto patronum* means, "I expect a guardian."[37]

Lupin describes the patronus as a "kind of positive force, a projection of the very things a Dementor feeds upon — hope, happiness, the desire to survive — but it cannot feel despair, as real humans can, so the Dementors can't hurt it."[38] The patronus is one of the clearest and most traditional manifestations of sacred power we find in the books. It's the only thing we might call a spirit that's regularly summoned in the books. On one level it seems to come from within the wizard, but on another it relates to things outside the wizard, particularly to people they love. It is the divine with and within the wizard. Let's unravel these elements a bit.

An underlying animistic idea behind working with a totem, patronus or guardian angel is that if God is manifest in everything then God is accessible through everything. (You can use the word 'Spirit' 'Being' or 'Goddess' if you prefer.) The ultimate 'great' alchemical antidote to the 'terrible' *nigredo* of the dark night or Dementor attack is the *coniunctio*, sacred union.

Alchemical texts often symbolize the *coniunctio* sexually, for example, by a naked king and queen embracing. In fact, it's a bit difficult not to read the patronus in a slightly Freudian light. It is, after all, a positive force relating to survival manifest as an enormous silvery white thing bursting out of a wand.

It also seems joined to love in some way. This may be romantic love. Snape's patronus always takes the form of Lily's, a beautiful doe. In some ways it even seems to *be* Lily's patronus, taken over by Snape in some mysterious way. After all, Harry senses nothing but benevolence from it. He's so keenly sensitized to Snape that you'd imagine he'd pick up on Snape behind the patronus but he doesn't. What he seems to feel is his mother's love. In Harry's case, of course, his patronus is very bound up with his love for, and identification with, his father, 'Prongs.'

Tonks patronus changes to reflect Lupin's werewolf form and Snape belittles it, saying it looks weak, simultaneously insulting her power and her love. We don't know what association each character's patronus has for them, but it's significant that the only ones we know about relate to love. This isn't just Freudian. A very important part of deepening magical and mystical practice has to do with cultivating some sort of personal devotion to the sacred.

I wouldn't be surprised if the happy memories many people use to invoke their patronuses are memories of romantic love. The emotions that many people feel only in the first throes of romantic love arise from moments of what the Hindu tradition calls *darshan*, the revelation of Deity through a statue or another form in a moment of pure perception. We're never mistaken in seeing the divine in someone; it's always there. Of course, we may be wrong in our subsequent actions, but never in our perception.

The memory Harry uses in the film of *Azkaban* is that of his parents talking to him. He's not even sure if it's real or not, but it works. In the books, he uses the joy he felt when he learned that he was a wizard in the first instance. In *Phoenix*, when Dementors attack him and Dudley, it's his love for Ron and Hermione that does the trick.[39]

The patronus' role as a protector and its relationship to love conjures up yet another magical association: that of the Holy Guardian Angel. In fact, the patronus seems very like a cross between the shamanic totem animal and the Holy Guardian Angel of ritual magic. Union with the Holy Guardian Angel places the wizard's heart firmly and passionately with the sacred. It also shows them clearly what else they might safely and soundly aspire to.

A ritual to unite with the Holy Guardian Angel is found in *The Book of Abramelin*. Abraham of Worms (sometimes called Abraham the Jew) wrote it in Germany between 1387 and 1427 based on teachings from Abramelin, an "old wise father" he met in Egypt. Ritual magician Lon Milo Duquette says that until a wizard is wedded to their Holy Guardian Angel, it is useless for them "to even attempt to manipulate the circumstances of life." A wizard who hasn't wedded their lowest to their highest natures is spiritually unprepared to know their true will, let alone exercise that will on the cosmos.[40]

The wizard who has attained "knowledge and conversation" of the Holy Guardian Angel has a spiritual magnetic north that points them towards their true will and an advisor with the "view from above" who can counsel them on how best to attain it in harmony with the cosmos. Dumbledore wasn't just too 'noble' to use dark, unaligned magic. As Harry says to Voldemort at the end, Dumbledore was too clever. He was a "better wizard, a better man."[41] Why try to force something from the universe when you don't even know if you truly want that thing? Passionate love for the Holy Guardian Angel can be the only force strong enough to control the wizard's other passions and desires.

For the knowledge of the wizard to be intimately useful to us, it must be bound up with love, engagement and personification. This means that Harry's trinity of pursuits, for love, knowledge and survival, are all bound up together. It's also why his lessons are best learned in a magical environment. This environment isn't just magical by virtue of all those unicorns and centaurs, but by virtue of his engagement with those he learns with and from, people like Lupin, Ron, Hermione and Dumbledore.

Harry's experience says something about the magic inherent in all good education. It relies on shared meaning and companionship, something Umbridge would never understand in her quest for authority, and something that JK Rowling, as a teacher, parent and activist obviously feels strongly about. Harry's experience also says something about the way we all embody facets of the Divine to each other.

Harry experiences Deity through Dumbledore. He also experiences 'divine' qualities of love and companionship through Ron, Hermione, Ginny, Luna, Molly and others. He experiences it through his parents' love. The image of comfort and union that Harry 'invokes', before his 'death' in the forest, is kissing Ginny. I have no idea if the idea of God in everything is a subtext of God's overt 'absence' in the books, or if it's conscious or unconscious on JK Rowling's part. We've seen that she uses characters as symbols of spiritual processes and plugs into all kinds of archetypes. It's only a step further to trace these figures back to their divine source.

In some ways the patronus seems to relate to our highest selves, just as the Holy Guardian Angel does. The Holy Guardian Angel can be seen as the wizard's higher self, their inner diamond, their Buddha or Christ consciousness. The idea that the patronus relates to this aspect of the self is implied in a few ways in the books.

We know that Snape's patronus was chosen out of love. Interestingly, a few pages before we learn this, Dumbledore implies that Snape's love for Lily is his highest quality. When Snape begs Dumbledore for his word that he'll keep the truth of the situation from "Potter's son," Dumbledore says, "My word, Severus, that I shall never reveal the best of you?"[42] So Snape's patronus can be seen to relate to both the higher self and to identity with the beloved, just like the Holy Guardian Angel.

One person attaining the knowledge and conversation of the Holy Guardian Angel, or illumination by any other name, creates such momentum that others get drawn along in their wake. Harry can transmit what he's been given, indeed, he feels compelled to. Attaining knowledge and conversation of the Holy Guardian Angel is supposed to inspire and enable the wizard to transmit the sacred powers he has received. I hadn't realized quite how explicit the books make this until I saw an interview with Steve Vander Ark.[43]

He noted that Harry teaches a large number of other students how to perform the patronus charm. This is after Lupin has told him that it's ridiculously advanced and that even many fully trained wizards have difficulty producing a patronus. In his hearing in *Phoenix*, one of the judges, Madam Amelia Bones, expresses surprise that Harry can produce a fully corporeal patronus.[44] Manifesting our spiritual power in a concrete and positive form in the world is, of course, the most important and sometimes the most difficult thing we can do.

We don't ultimately go through great and terrible magical transformations just for ourselves. We go through them in the service of others. Mahatma Gandhi said, "God demands nothing less than complete self-surrender as the price for the only freedom that is worth having. When a person loses himself/herself, they immediately find themselves in the service of all that lives. It becomes their delight and recreation. They are a new people never weary of spending themselves in the service of God's creation."[45] These 'new people' have attained the stone.

VII

USING THE PHILOSOPHER'S STONE

Remember, if the time should come when you have to make a choice between what is right, and what is easy, remember what happened to a boy who was good, and kind, and brave, because he strayed across the path of Lord Voldemort. Remember Cedric Diggory.
Albus Dumbledore

The difference between what we do and what we are capable of doing would suffice to change the world.
Mahatma Gandhi

here are a lot of Cedric Diggorys out there; young people who, through no fault of their own, stray across evil's path, or otherwise meet a sad fate. The wizard or alchemist who truly attains the power of the stone dedicates that power to saving the Cedrics of the world. On one level, the philosopher's stone is simply the enlightened wizard or alchemist—the person who, like Harry, at the end of *Hallows*, has transformed himself and so, can transform others in real ways. He or she becomes a catalyst for change.

We get much more than a hint of Harry as the stone at the beginning of *Hallows*, when the polyjuice potion that transforms Harry's six friends into him turns a beautiful gold. (Tastier than Crabbe and Goyle!) When his friends drink 'him,' they become him. The stone isn't just something special in and of itself, it's special by virtue of its effects on other things. It calls a quote from

The Gospel of Thomas to mind. Christ says, "He who drinks from my mouth shall become like me; and I myself will become him, and the hidden things shall manifest to him."[1] We'll find ourselves returning to Christian symbolism a few times in this chapter. JK Rowling was able to discuss her Christianity freely after *Hallows*. Before then, she felt it would give too much of the plot away. However, it's also obvious that she's a very open minded Christian.

Many European alchemists were also Christian and, unsurprisingly after all the dying and resurrecting that took place in the alchemical vessel, they sometimes pictured the philosopher's stone as Christ. Yet, attaining the stone is more a movement towards earth than towards heaven. It's called a philosopher's stone, not a philosopher's vapor, which tells us that attaining the stone is about grounding the seeker's spiritual attainment.

It's about putting all that spiritual awareness to the practical goal of recreating the world. The stone is the revealed diamond of the self that becomes the foundation stone of the 'New Jerusalem,' to give it a Christian name, though the idea of a sacred city bringing heaven to earth is found in numerous pre-Christian traditions as well.

JK Rowling's interviews after *Hallows* made clear what's implied by the *Hallows* epilogue. Harry, Ron, Hermione and their friends recreate the wizarding world. When their tale began, it didn't seem likely that a few children would triumph over Voldemort or that they'd transform the Ministry of Magic. When Harry began his journey to becoming the stone, he was only a baby, not visibly different from any number of other babies. That's because we all have the stone within us, and most people don't notice it. The alchemists tell us that the material of the stone is found everywhere. It is *eiectus in viam*, 'thrown in the street.'[2] This takes us back to our discussion in chapter two, where we saw that all magical experience begins with noticing magic. *The Gospel of Thomas* tells us that the New Jerusalem is already spread out on the earth and men do not see it.[3] When we pay proper attention, it's even more obvious than that triple-decker purple bus that Muggles never notice.

It's appropriate now to return to the beginning, the first book, and those important off-screen characters Nicholas and Perenella Flamel. The novel doesn't tell us what they did with the life and fortune the stone brought them. For that we can turn to Nicholas' own words in *Flamel's Heiroglyphics*, printed in London in 1624. He said that in Paris at the time of his writing in 1413, he and Perenella had founded and endowed 14 Hospitals, built three Chapels, and "enriched with great gifts and good rents, seven Churches, with many reparations in their Churchyards, besides that which we have done at Bologne, which is not much less than that which we have done here. I will not speak of the good which both of us have done to particular poor folks, principally to widows and poor orphans..."[4]

Attaining the stone involves sacrifice and transformation. Harry attained the stone through his sacrifice in the Forbidden Forest. He gained the power to fully use the stone, the *rubeus* stage of the alchemical process, by deciding to return at King's Cross, as opposed to taking that train for territories unknown. Tibetan Buddhist tradition calls such people Boddhisattvas, those who have attained illumination but vow to return and help until everyone attains it. Well before this stage, as seekers progress, they find increasing joy in working for others. It's completely natural. Once we've made our choice, we needn't drive the process. It carries us, as Rubeus carried Harry back to Hogwarts for the final battle. The 'rubeus,' the alchemical stage of reddening that produces the stone, carried him from the field of his mother's sacrifice, and carried him from his own. Ms. Rowling has given us another nice set of bookends.

Only he who wants the red philosopher's stone, but not for

SEEKER'S GUIDE TO HARRY POTTER

himself, can get it from the tricky Mirror of Erised. The sacrificial posture opens the mirror of desire to reveal its greatest treasure, the stone that Flamel used for others' good as well as his own. For us to transmit all its gifts they must pass through us, but they don't pass through us unless we intend to transmit them. A blocked pipe will soon be full of nothing but stagnant water.

Interestingly, Nicholas Flamel depicts the final stage of the process as a citrine (golden colored) and scarlet winged lion about to carry away the alchemist. This is enlightenment, an ultimate level of spiritual awareness. The Gryffindor seeker, Harry, attains it at last. Flamel also symbolizes enlightenment as an invincible and incorruptible king, the quintessence, the fifth element at the center of the alchemical wheel.[5]

The quintessence is the sovereign fifth element of spirit, uniting all others. As the lion is the king of beasts the illuminated alchemist or wizard becomes a king amongst men. Of course, it's only one step between the winged lion of Flamel's imagery and the griffin. Just pop on the head of the Ravenclaw eagle and you have it.

We can see the Griffin as the animal of a 5th symbolic 'house' at Hogwarts, the house of sovereignty, the house of the king who acts as the school's sacred center. It's significant that when Umbridge takes over the school, the headmaster's office seals itself against her. She's not the proper ruler and the griffin guards the door.[6]

We may have another example of JK Rowling's love of wordplay here. Here, Gryffindor becomes the 'griffin door,' the door the worthiest pass through to place of sovereignty in the headmaster's office. We've seen two Gryffindor headmasters, and know of two Slytherin ones, Phineas Nigellus, and of course, Severus Snape. One imagines that there must have been Ravenclaw and Hufflepuff headmasters in the past, but we only know of those from the two apparently dominant houses, primarily Gryffindor. (Snape gets there by improper means, though obviously, with the best of intentions.) We're also told that Dumbledore is Hogwarts' greatest headmaster.

Gryffindor may also be *Griffin D'or*, the 'golden griffin.' The griffin is a venerable symbolic beast. It appears guarding the tree of life in a Babylonian cylinder seal, and in King Minos' palace at Knossos in Crete, two huge griffins lie on either side of the throne amongst lilies, a Cretan royal emblem. According to the ancient Greek historian, Herodotus, the griffin is also the guardian of the ways of salvation. It's often depicted on tombs, or acting as a guide for the souls of the departed. Later it symbolized Christ's dual nature, St. Melitus said, *Aquila Christus...Leo Christus*. "The Eagle is Christ, the Lion is Christ." It became a symbol of the saints who are like eagles because of their lofty thoughts and like lions because of their moral courage.[7]

The griffin's dual nature made it a symbol of uniting opposites. Alchemists took the griffin as yet another symbol of the union between sulphur and mercury that produces the stone, along with the hermaphrodite, phoenix and king. The alchemical king in the picture that heads this chapter holds a phoenix.

GOOD KING HARRY

The king is the hub of the elemental wheel, the lynch pin who guarantees that the center will hold. Ms. Rowling gave Harry kingly associations from the start. From his kingly name to wielding Gryffindor's sword, pulled from the waters like King Arthur's Excalibur, he's as kingly as can be. King's Cross is also a way station at significant points on his journey. JK Rowling's parents met on a train to Scotland that departed from there. It was named for an unpopular statue of King George, now gone. A persistent legend associates it with an older monarch. It's said that Boadicca, a queen of the ancient Celtic Iceni tribe who led a rebellion against Rome, is buried under platform nine or ten.

The name 'King's Cross' also can't fail to evoke the cross of Christ as King, which we've already found in terms Ms. Rowling uses throughout the books, like the cruciatus curse and horcrux. In Mary GrandPré's American edition illustration for the moment before Harry opens his eyes in his near-death experience at King's Cross, the horcrux scar is gone. Here, there's no more pain for Harry. The only 'cross' remaining is the 'King's cross' — symbol of transcending the worst that evil can throw at anyone. It's like the cross through which Christ spoke to St. Francis of Assisi in visions. Christ isn't nailed to it, but stands before it with his arms outstretched, triumphant.

True sovereignty's triumph is hard won. As the sun rose over Hogwarts, "Harry was an indispensable part of the mingled outpourings of jubilation and mourning, of grief and celebration." He was the kingly, polarity uniting force, enabling them to bear their feelings. "They wanted him there with them, their leader and symbol, their savior and guide...He must speak to the bereaved, clasp their hands, witness their tears, receive their thanks, hear the news now creeping in from every quarter, as the morning drew on, that the Imperiused up and down the country had come back to themselves..."[8]

Many ancient cultures believed that the king holding his sovereign role enabled every one else to fill their proper roles. He was 'Lord of the Four Quarters' whose power and truth extended throughout the land. Harry breaks the imperius curse in all directions, and from each quarter the news returns that people have come back to themselves, to the truth of their own beings.

No one sits according to house after the final battle. Harry has amiably united all warring opposites, as Flamel says happens when the stone is made. Even the ill at ease Malfoys are there.

At the end of the last battle, the all-powerful wand flies from Voldemort's grasp to its true master, who catches it, like he has caught so many symbolic snitches, with "the unerring skill of the

Seeker." (You'll remember that the 'snitch' symbolism is also bound up with sovereignty, as I discussed in chapter four.)

At the end of this scene, Harry takes a few well-earned moments for himself, to resolve a few last important questions, to be with Ron and Hermione, and at last, to sleep. Yet Harry will never rest on his laurels. Like all seekers who attain the stone, he'll continue to be concerned with others.

Indeed, Harry, becomes both a supremely great wizard and a 'king.' In an interview after *Hallows*, JK Rowling said that at the time of the epilogue, Harry would be head of the Aurors Department at the Ministry of Magic. Auror means 'dawn,' and you could hardly have a grander sovereignty than to rule the dawn and those who bring light to the darkest places. She said that Harry and Ron revolutionizes the Auror Department, making it a great place to be, and that Hermione puts her intellect to work in the Department for Magical Law Enforcement. "So they're all at the ministry but this is a very new ministry. *They made a new world.*"[9]

I emphasize the last sentence because that's the point of the whole exercise. The seeker doesn't go through travails to 'fix' himself, or even to try and 'fix' the world, but to consciously recreate it. Shamans and wizards, like Harry, have often been accused of being mentally ill. Yet anthropologists have also said that their personalities are far different from the mentally ill in at least one important way—they are "remarkably resilient."[10] By his resilience, the shaman or wizard demonstrates what Dumbledore calls "the incomparable power of a soul that is untarnished and whole."[11] The power of the human soul to emerge, through the power of love, from helplessness in the face of life's chaotic reality as a co-creator with sacred powers.

Because we all feel helpless at times, we all experience loss and chaos, figures like Harry stand for all of us, not just the spiritually gifted. Part of what's required of us is the trust that

Dumbledore is always encouraging Harry to adopt. The cosmos responds to trust paired with right action.

SEALED ORDERS AND THE ROOM OF REQUIREMENT

More often than not, Harry trusts Dumbledore and does what he says. Though there's no personified God in *Harry Potter*, in some ways Dumbledore symbolizes Harry's 'higher power.' Now, I'm not saying that Dumbledore is just God, anymore than that he is *only* the *albus* in the alchemical process, but on one level, his relationship to Harry represents something of our relationship with God. Just as some of Ms. Rowling's characters embody alchemical processes and elements, as well as being characters, they also embody divine qualities and archetypes. Don't we all?

Like Harry, we also get 'instructions' from powers that know more than we do. We can think of this 'higher power' as God, spirit, higher self, gut instinct or true will. It's what Dumbledore might call 'the best in us.' We can learn to listen to its messages in many ways. However, all may not be clear to us at the moment when we receive those instructions, any more than it is for Harry. He's like a spy who receives orders sealed in an envelope, to be opened at a specific place and time. You know the sort of thing from films. "Go to the bench under the oak tree and ask the old lady if her roses are blooming." The spy doesn't necessarily have any clue what the question or the response means, they just do what they're told and trust that it's in the service of their cause they've committed to. Harry gets only what he needs to carry out the next step in Dumbledore's plan, nothing more.

Time and again, Dumbledore tells Harry to trust him. It's not easy. As I've noted, he's quite ruthless and puts Harry through hell — but it's hell with a point. Dumbledore takes Harry to a place that the unvarnished truth wouldn't have. At the end of *Phoenix*, Dumbledore asks when he should have told Harry about the prophecy that Harry took to mean that he and Voldemort would duel to the death. Most people wouldn't choose to tell an eleven-year-old this sort of thing.

Later, in *Hallows*, Harry reflects on how the way that Dumbledore withheld information actually showed how well he understood Harry and his friends—and enemies. He knew to give Ron the deluminator as a way back and knew that Wormtail felt some regret. He thinks of the Dumbledore the all (or at least mostly) knowing, in his head, who smiles at him and surveys him over the tips of his fingers, "pressed together as if in prayer." He wonders what Dumbledore knew about him. "Am I meant to know, but not to seek?" he wonders. "Did you know how hard I'd find that? Is that why you made it so difficult? So I'd have time to work that out?"[12] We don't always know why things can seem so difficult in the moment, but, upon reflection, it often becomes clear to us, as it does to Harry.

Of course, Harry still doesn't have the whole picture, even when he receives the penultimate truth from Snape's memories. Giving him the final piece of information would actually have made it impossible for him to do what was required for the best outcome.

First, if he'd been told that he'd ultimately have to sacrifice himself earlier it would have been very hard for him to conjure the reserves of hope, courage and happiness he needed to fulfil his mission. Even Harry sees the ruthless sense of it all.[13] But more than this, if he'd known the 'one fact beyond,' that if he offered himself completely he could survive, it would have made it infinitely harder to offer himself in the necessary way. Entering the sacrificial posture while thinking 'but actually, I'll get out of this' isn't actually entering it fully, and so, wouldn't bring through the power needed, as I discussed in the last chapter.

Was Dumbledore unethical? No. Harry had repeatedly agreed to do whatever it took to defeat Voldemort. He'd agreed to the mission, even if it meant his death. Dumbledore respected

Harry's free will, he didn't just use him. Harry had agreed to do whatever it took, and so, he'd also agreed to whatever Dumbledore had to do to get him where he needed to be. Like Harry, and the rest of Dumbledore's Army, we don't necessarily know what our commitment to good will bring us to, but there's also a facility to get us what we need when we get there.

The Room of Requirement first gets a mention in *Goblet* at the Yule Ball, when Dumbledore uses it as an example to Karkaroff of the fact that he doesn't know every mystery at Hogwarts. He describes finding a room full of chamber pots when he got up in the night to use the toilet. He says he's not sure how the room operates, if it's only there on a certain day or time, or if it's only there when the seeker has a full bladder.

The latter turns out to be the case. Harry and his friends find it in *Phoenix* with Dobby's aid. He tells them that the room can only be entered when a person has real need of it. It is "always equipped for the seeker's needs."[14]

Dobby uses it as a place to sober up Winky. Fred and George used it to hide from Filch. Harry finds it equipped to train Dumbledore's Army. He also finds it to be a place to hide Snape's potions book in *Prince* and even finds one of the final horcruxes in it in *Hallows*. (Of course, Draco also finds what he needs there for his wicked scheme in *Prince*. Sometimes it seems that fortune conspires to give bad guys what they need as well.) The Room of Requirement represents the idea that the cosmos aligns to support the person doing their true will. Joseph Campbell said that when you "follow your bliss," that role in life or activity which brings you delight in alignment with your true will, "doors open for you where you didn't think there'd be doors, and there wouldn't be for anyone else." St. Paul said that "all things work together for them that love God."[15]

Following our sealed orders brings us to a miraculous place, where we get just what we need to fulfill our purpose. This *doesn't* mean that everything always works out exactly as we might like. True will is not whim, and there's a world of importance in learning to tell the difference. However, getting what *we* need is only part of getting what we need. For most seekers, like Harry, the spiritual journey leads us to a place where we see that looking at the bigger picture and helping others is what we most need for ourselves. This isn't the most usual message that early 21st century Western culture gives us, however, which makes the vast popularity of Harry's story reassuring.

WEALTH, IMMORTALITY AND THE STONE

In *Stone*, Dumbledore describes the stone's gifts: "As much money and life as you could want! The two things most human beings would choose above all — the trouble is, humans do have a knack of choosing precisely those things that are worst for them."[16] To this end the *Harry Potter* novels seem to imply that you may be able to get your bare needs met magically, but not a lot more. You don't see witches and wizards starving and begging on the street until *Hallows*, when you see some desperate Muggle-borns deprived of wands. In *Prince*, Harry says that Voldemort's mother, Merope, could have gotten food and money by magic, but Dumbledore responds that she didn't want to use magic, or couldn't, after her heartbreak.

In one scene, cream sauce comes out of Mrs. Weasley's wand, but potatoes are grown in the garden and only peeled by magic. Ron is given a sprout-preparing chore one Christmas, no magic involved, much to his chagrin and Fred and George's amusement. Harry, Ron and Hermione certainly go hungry a lot in *Hallows*. Can only condiments be manifested straight from the ether? We may never know. However, it seems clear that the Weasleys can't just fill their bank vault with galleons by magic.

As the books tell us, all problems can't be solved by magic. We can't discuss magical operations to create wealth here, but there's one point I'd have you bear in mind. In my experience, when we begin to try to find our true will and align with the bigger picture, Spirit doesn't operate on surplus. What would be the point of giving a wizard a vast surplus of money that would just sit in a bank vault, when other beings need it? (Unless they distribute it, a point I'll return to.)

"What about the Malfoys?" you may ask. Well, they're not exactly aligned with their true wills, are they? It's a bit of a pain, isn't it? I'm not saying that worthy magicians are bound to be poor, the Weasleys have success in the end. It just seems that what a modern Westerner might call 'abundance' the cosmos calls 'excess.' If you reflect that according to some sources, if you have a roof over your head, food in a fridge and *any* money in the bank you're among the top 8% of the world's wealthy, you'll begin to see why.[17]

You don't get the impression that all the Hogwarts teachers are wealthy. Snape lives in what Bellatrix calls a "Muggle dunghill" outside of term time and Slughorn complains about his teachers' salary, but they still get to live in a castle most of the year. (Of course, Slughorn uses less than honest other means to find other nice places to live as well, though it doesn't seem he's doing any harm.) The magic of creativity and imagination can compensate for lack of funds. There's more than one way to skin a kneazle.

Though ingenuity is an important virtue, an even greater one is contentment. The Flamels had this quote inscribed above their door: "Let each be content with what he has, whoever has not this ease has nothing." Buddhist lama Matthieu Ricard says, "If you have contentment, it's like holding a precious jewel in your hands."[18] Benjamin Franklin even said that he who spends less than he earns has the philosopher's stone!

If we're content with what we have, then in many ways it's just the same as having great wealth. If we have all we need, then having a million 'extra' dollars or pounds in the bank only guards against fear, not privation. And if we're inclined to fear, no amount of currency will actually be enough to guard against it.

I particularly like something I once heard Yogi Bhajan say, "People buy things as though they were staying here!" Try sticking that quote on your credit card, or thinking about it before taking on an unaffordable mortgage. We're all *actually* renting, whether we 'own' our homes or not! The Dursleys wouldn't say so, of course. They *own* that company car, that house, those agapanthuses. They even accuse Harry of making up Voldemort's threat to them in *Hallows* to get their house.

Their possessions serve much the same purpose as Voldemort's horcruxes. They provide the illusion of safety from death. The motto of modern Western consumer culture might well be, "Buy! Buy! Buy in defiance of death! Buy as though you were staying here!" The Dursleys, just like Voldemort, and just like many modern Westerners, *place their souls in their stuff*. I think that this may be one of the biggest symbolic messages in Voldemort's horcruxes. Where your treasure is your heart is, to paraphrase the quote on Dumbledore's family's grave.

I've spoken before of JK Rowling's use of number symbolism and it pops up again here. The Dursleys live at number four Privet Drive. Four can represent the four directions and elements, in short, physical reality, *without* the governing 'fifth element' or quintessence of spirit. You'll remember that Voldemort starts out trying to divide his soul into seven parts, but ends up dividing it into eight, another number associated with natural cycles and materiality, double the Dursleys four. I think that JK Rowling may be telling us that Voldemort's and the Dursley's approaches are less different in kind than in *degree*.

Many people think their pleasure is more important than another person's is, as I mentioned in the last chapter in the discussion of evil. The psychotic, if we want to call Voldemort by a psychological term, thinks his own transitory pleasure is more important than another's suffering or death. Most of us wouldn't kill someone to own a particular coffee table or car if the person was standing right in front of us. However, modern Western culture insulates us from seeing how our actions create death and suffering for others. The Dursleys don't see a child dying in a flood caused by rising sea levels, global warming and deforestation. They don't choose to realize that their gas-guzzler and their coffee table are part of what created the situation. They may not realize that child slave labor manufactured some of Dudley's broken toys.

This is a state of 'unwitting psychosis.' It's the opposite of the good wizard's 'wit' that sees the big picture. Unlike Voldemort, the Dursleys don't specifically know how their pleasure is costing someone else their lives, health or happiness, but it is, just the same. Equally bad, they probably never reflect on what the money they spent on a toy that was broken the next day could have done for someone else. (For example, a five-pound or ten-dollar donation to the organization Feed the Children feeds an African child for a month.)

Harry, by contrast, transcends material desires throughout the books. To be fair, this hungry little boy gets a vault of gold and three square meals a day upon his entry into the wizarding world. As JK Rowling herself knows, when you've been deprived, sudden wealth *if approached correctly* can free you up to think of more important things.

At the start, of course, Harry wants a flashy broom and a golden cauldron and a few other frivolous items. Yet there is change. Remember how traumatized he was when his broom was broken in *Azkaban*? Remember when he lost his even more treasured Firebolt from Sirius in *Hallows*? I didn't think so. It barely even registers in the scene; we're so caught up in the action and the loss of Hedwig and Moody, as well as the possible losses of others before they arrive at the rendezvous place. We never read about him thinking of it again. His wand does register, but, for a wizard, the wand is more like an extension of the self than a material possession.

Kingly men are defined by generosity. Harry gives his Triwizard Tournament winnings to Fred and George to start up their business. Wealth is meant to remain in motion like the living quality of sovereignty itself. As the wealthy philanthropist Andrew Carnegie said, "He who dies wealthy dies disgraced." He went on to donate enormous funds to Scottish universities and numerous other causes. He felt that wealthy people had the obligation to ensure that their fortune was dispersed for the common good before their deaths. As a fringe benefit, of course, the wealthy would thereby get to enjoy the pleasures of giving. Seeing smiles on faces is a lot more fun than seeing numbers on paper. We don't have to sleepwalk through our lives 'consuming' everything in our path.

Neither the Dursleys, nor Voldemort, nor anyone else who behaves this way has been truly happy. The antidote to the world's ills and our own is one and the same. Harry chose it, JK Rowling chose it and it's also available to us.

HERMIONE AND THE ELVES: APPROACHING ACTION

The Hogwarts motto is *Draco dormiens nunquam titillandus*, "never tickle a sleeping dragon." We could think of a symbolic meaning, along the lines of "Let sleeping dogs lie." However, it's also a simple and practical injunction.

Spiritual perception, 'extra sense,' shouldn't override common sense. We must do more than pray or 'send light' in response to need. That doesn't mean we *shouldn't* do these things, just that we shouldn't only do these things. St. Ignatius of Loyola, founder of the Society of Jesus, suggested, "Use human means as though divine ones did not exist, and use divine means as though there were no human ones."[19]

Of course, the *Harry Potter* books don't use divine means overtly. No one prays. Though, as I've shown, the books are full of spiritual subtexts, the emphasis is always on the characters taking action. Inner change comes from outer challenges.

The books are, of course, jam-packed with action in the service of good. The most organized *activism* we see in the books is, however, Hermione's campaign to help the house elves. She founds the unfortunately named Society for the Promotion of Elvish Welfare, or S.P.E.W. As the name indicates, it provides comic relief, but it can still tell us something about how to take action. First — think through your acronyms!

Second, don't project your desires on to the 'afflicted' ones that you're seeking to help. The well-meaning outsider can be the best or the worst thing to happen to a cause. Certain kinds of activism tend to work better from within. Dobby and Kreacher end up changing things for the Elves more than Hermione

The broader issue to bear in mind in all life circumstances is the difference between empathy and sympathy. While people often use the term 'empathy' to mean understanding how others feel and showing kindness and concern, it's actually derived from the Greek *empatheia*, meaning to 'project' feeling onto something. In modern Greek, it signifies the 'evil eye.' By contrast 'sympathy' derives from *sympathiea*, meaning to feel *with*, to like or to be compassionate.[20]

Empathy is when a friend gets ill or gets dumped and we say, "Oh that must be terrible" while thinking how *we* would feel if we got that illness or if our partner dumped us. We then project those feelings back onto the person, so they get the weight of our fear and pain on top of their own.

Sympathy or compassion is when we try to feel *with* them, not feel how we'd feel under their circumstances. We might say. "Whew, that's challenging...do you want to talk about it?" Here, we don't project anything on to their situation. After all, even illnesses or break-ups can stimulate positive life-changes that make them into strokes of good luck.

Hermione is a bit empathetic with the elves. She comes from the perspective that their slavery is just wrong, and they must accept positive change. Hagrid, Ron and the House Elves themselves make it clear that they don't want change, but she continues to try and create the change for them. We never witness a scene where she simply sits down and talks to them with no agenda of her own projected. In the end, a kind of change comes from within, from one of their own, when Kreacher leads them into battle against the Death Eaters. You'll note that he doesn't act from a more human desire for personal freedom but from a house elf's devotion to his late master, Regulus.

Whatever the evil we're fighting, it's the goodness that keeps us going and that's what we need to focus on. Harry always says 'yes' to the process of life, not to everything that happens, not to every evil, but to the process as a whole. Harry sees the goodness in life even as he goes to his death. Of course, like many confronted with such a moment, he feels he should have valued it more. Sitting up after he learns that he must die from Snape's memories, he asks himself why he'd never appreciated what a miracle he was.

All the house qualities come into approaching action. Gryffindor bravery and moral courage support right action. There's an underlying idea that some defeats are worthier than other victories. In the final battle of Hogwarts, the Death Eater's children are allowed to leave, though they would have been valuable hostages in purely practical terms. Neville won't go to Voldemort's side despite his flattery and the fact that defeat seems certain.

Another very important virtue in altruistic work is Slytherin discernment. Excessive sentiment isn't a good idea, and it's a mistake a Slytherin wouldn't make. Look at Hagrid and his horrible creatures. He's sometimes right, about Grawp or Buckbeak, for example, but he's often wrong. Even empathetic Hermione wants to stamp on the blast ended screwts in *Goblet* and no one thinks Hagrid's right to defend the invading acromantulas in the final battle of *Hallows*.

Ravenclaw logic has its uses. We have to look at the biggest picture and apply ingenuity to solve as many problems as possible in one fell swoop. We have to be as efficient as possible. Finally, of course, there's no substitute for Hufflepuff hard work, simply *acting* in the face of all obstacles. There are many things we may see as obstacles to doing good work, from time to money to will. Our inner Ravenclaw can also work against us here, to reason us out of taking action.

BENEATH DEATH'S CLOAK

Of course, there's one obstacle to action that we may see as topping the list: death. It doesn't have to be. Death is one of JK Rowling's abiding concerns. Her own mother dying six months into Harry's genesis meant that, "Death became a central, if not the central, theme for the seven books." After *Hallows*, JK Rowling said that she was proud that many people believed that Harry would die. "Proud, not because that means that I've got people in tenterhooks, proud because it means that the books are imbued with a sense of genuine mortality. It was felt to be a possibility that the hero would die...because...that's how it would be...It could come to anyone."[21]

In fact, it *will* come to *everyone*, and sooner or later most of us give it some thought. Michael Bywater puts it well in *Lost Worlds*. "You Begin Immortal," he says. Later you realize that you aren't theoretically immortal but there may have been an administrative error. "And for a while, that's it. Then one night you wake at four in the morning, the suicide hour, and you *really* realize it. The distinguished thing. Hobbes Voyage, that great leap into the dark, is *real*, and you are going to go on it, and it is simultaneously imaginable and beyond comprehension. How can this thing happen? To *you*? God knows if *anyone* deserves to be let off it's you..."22

The world going on without us can be a very odd thought but on one level, it's salutary. Harry walks into the forest to face Voldemort in *Hallows* keenly appreciating each beat of his heart and each breath he draws. Minus the fear, it's a good state to consciously conjure up each day. The Japanese Samurai warriors spoke of 'freshening the mind' with the thought of death each morning. After all, it may come at any moment. We may not finish breakfast, let alone the report we're writing or the laundry. In the face of that truth, what actually matters?

As the Yaqui shaman, Don Juan, said to Carlos Castaneda, "In a world where death is the hunter, there are no big or small decisions, just those we make in the face of our own inevitable deaths." We can only hope or believe that death is as pleasant and full of promise as Harry's near death experience at King's Cross. I've always loved a rail trip. Joking (and hoping) aside, there are some ways that Harry's brave, magical and altruistic approach can help us transcend death.

Even though all seekers don't believe in God or an immortal soul, all seekers can still think in terms of continuities. Energy only changes, it's never destroyed. This is why Nicholas, Perenella and Dumbledore can go to their ends as their next great adventure or as a good rest after a long day. As Flamel said, he who attains the stone swells "in the imperial heaven." He has expanded himself into heaven, into his biggest self, connected with all being, even before his death. Security in this truth allows us to relax and be ourselves. Christ puts it economically in *The Gospel of Thomas*, "Become yourselves, passing away."23 This is the way of the world, the way of nature. Paracelsus, whose bust resides in a Hogwarts hallway, tells us "What then is happiness but compliance with the order of nature through knowledge of nature? What then is unhappiness but opposition to the order of nature?"[24]

Nature is continually giving away. Whatever we think may happen to our souls after death, they won't be housed in these particular bodies. Our bodies and everything else we 'own' will be given away. Embracing this fact and giving consciously aligns us with nature and happiness. Vainly attempting to hold back from the process brings unhappiness, as it does for Voldemort, whose name means one who 'flees death.' In *Stone* Flamel chooses to die at 665 — one year shy of the 'demonic' number 666. This implies that there are extremes of life extension that a good person wouldn't go beyond.

JK Rowling, in my mind quite rightly, sets fleeing death up as the source of the ultimate evil in her universe. It creates a lot of evil in ours as well, as noted in the horcrux discussion above. There are even more extreme examples, like people who pay vast sums to freeze their heads after death, buying an illusion of immortality, when the money could bring real life to hundreds of others. The political scientist Francis Fukuyama called 'transhumanism' the growing movement to attempt to make a human elite immortal through various technological means, the world's "most dangerous idea."[25]

The level of technology that makes such processes conceivable raises other issues. A few *Harry Potter* commentators, like Alan Jacobs, have drawn parallels between the moral issues magic raises and those raised by technology.

Perhaps the most important question I could ask my Christian friends who mistrust the *Harry Potter* books is this: is your concern about the portrayal of this imaginary magical technology matched by a concern for the effects of the technology that in our world displaced magic? The technocrats of this world hold in their hands powers almost infinitely greater than those of Albus Dumbledore and Voldemort: how worried are we about them, and their influence over our children? Not worried enough, I would say. As Ellul suggests, the task for us is "the measuring of technique by other criteria than those of technique itself," which measuring he also calls "the search for justice before God."[26]

Technology and magic are both difficult to regulate. For example, none of us voted for the internet, on which we can enjoy our favorite *Harry Potter* site and those so inclined can enjoy any amount of nasty fare. Even scientists who begin with the 'greater good' in mind, and careful parameters at an ivy league school or an Edinburgh lab have no control over some cowboy in a far off country who'll work for cash with no parameters. The *avada kedavra* might have originally been a humane method to kill livestock. It's significant that the magic word she draws it from, 'abracadabra,' is best known as the stage magician's innocuous pronouncement.

The bigger point is that human greed, whether for better technology, regardless of its consequences, or for longer life, always turns on itself. The self-same hunger for more life, sensation and pleasure is creating obesity and other health problems that will ensure that the generation that grew up with Harry, the Dudleys of the world, will be the first ever to live a shorter time than their parents. Greed really is the primary sin! Interestingly, it's the *only* thing ever actually called a sin in all of *Harry Potter*. Remember the inscription outside of Gringott's? "Enter, stranger, but take heed, of what awaits the sin of greed..."[27] Many cultures see greed as the 'root' vice that leads to all disharmony.

So how do we counteract this sin? Well, the alchemical antidote is to do the opposite. If Voldemort's greed is all about cheating death and hoarding all we can for ourselves, then the best thing we can do is the opposite, accepting death and putting all we can into what will continue, the next generation. This is obviously important to those who choose to have children, but it's also important to those who don't. In *Prince*, Dumbledore knows he's dying and resolves to die as usefully as he can. He died largely as he'd lived, for something beyond himself.

THE CROWNED AND CONQUERING CHILD

Harry's story is a tale for children about an abused child. Amongst the fantasy elements, the battle of good and evil and the epic scope of the narrative it's easy to lose sight of this simple fact. First, of course, Voldemort attempts to kill him and murders his parents. Then he's delivered to the Dursleys, who provide magical protection but inflict other kinds of damage. One also suspects that Dumbledore ruthlessly inflicts the Dursleys on Harry (and vice versa) as part of a calculated hero-making process.

This process, of course, brings him into further abusive situations. In some ways the creepiest was the graveyard scene in *Goblet*. Actor Ralph Feinnes mentioned this when he was interviewed after playing Voldemort in the film of *Goblet*. Speaking of the scene of Voldemort's rebirth, he noted, "It's a very disturbing scene. I mean, if you strip away the fairy tale, fantasy package, what you get is a little boy tied up while an older man humiliates him, and that, translated to the real world, is not children's fare *at all*."[28]

In the book, the blood forcibly taken from Harry helped generate new life for Voldemort. He became Voldemort's unwilling father. Voldemort also uses a bone from his first (also unwilling) father and the hand of his coerced servant. Voldemort triples the violation of free will of his first conception. The film of *Goblet* underscored the sexually abusive symbolism of the encounter when Barty Crouch Jr. revealed the dark mark tattooed on his forearm for comparison with the cut Pettigrew gave Harry. "I'll show you mine if you show me yours!" Poor Harry can only respond that he couldn't prevent what had happened. Of course, this low point of helpless torture and humiliation leads to Harry's ultimate triumph.

This is part of JK Rowling's repeated message that the darkest hour comes before the dawn. A lot of children's literature features this message because it helps us face the worst that can come to us in life. Fantasy in *Harry Potter*, as in fairy tales, allows children (and others) to enjoy and engage with a story that might otherwise be unacceptably horrific. I prefer to see the way adults are now turning to children's literature in their quest for meaning as a return to what's best and truest in us, rather than as an infantilization of culture, as some critics have said.[29] As we wrap up the various themes of this book, let's return for a moment to the books as that ancient form of story, the fairy tale.

THE TRUTH IN CHILDREN'S FANTASY

Literature is one of the best ways to convey wisdom and meaning to children and adults alike. Bruno Bettelheim, a therapist who worked with severely disturbed children, said that restoring meaning to their lives was the most important task he performed.

JK Rowling gives a clear nod to the importance of fairy tales in Dumbledore's final gift to Hermione. The volume of the fairy tales of Beedle the Bard includes the one about the very Deathly Hallows that feature in the final resolution of the seven volume series.

While Hermione is skeptical of the story's value in *Hallows*, years before, in *Chamber*, she asked Professor Binns, "Don't legends always have a basis in fact?"[30]

Myths and fairy tales can reveal facts, and more than facts. The German poet Schiller wrote, "Deeper meaning resides in the fairy tales told to me in my childhood than in the truth that is taught by life."[31] Meaning is one reason why adults are turning more frequently than ever to children's books, as readers and as writers.

The novelist Philip Pullman, (the Whitbread winning author of *The Amber Spyglass*, mentioned above) has said, "I have always been interested in questions that fall under the general heading of what we call religion, questions of reality and meaning and purpose and what are we here for and where do we come from and all that stuff."[32] Children's fiction is still dealing with the big questions of meaning that much adult fiction has moved away from.

GK Chesterton and CS Lewis said that fairy tales are "spiritual explorations" and hence, "the most life-like" since they reveal "human life as seen, or felt, or divined from the inside."[33] Fairy tales take place at a safe remove in time and space, allowing children (and others) to examine real issues like child abuse, poverty, evil and abandonment without being overwhelmed by them. By doing this, they help us engage more deeply with life.

Jack Zipes says that fantasy and fairy tales play "upon the imagination not to open it up to escape into a never-never land but to make greater contact with reality."[34] Fairy tales evolved over the ages to reach "the uneducated mind of the child as well as that of the sophisticated adult." They carry important messages "to the conscious, the preconscious and the unconscious mind, on whatever level each is functioning at the time."[35]

The way that authors like JRR Tolkien and JK Rowling create instinctively and get surprised by their own creation, points to the spiritual and subconscious origins of their work. It's not surprising that such stories would work on these levels for the reader as well.

This is one reason why ancient Irish tradition attributes healing and protective powers to certain stories. Traditional Hindu physicians may even prescribe meditation on a particular fairy tale to a troubled patient. The story may not have anything to do with the person's outer circumstances, which may seem insoluble, but it has a lot to do with their inner problems.[36] The stories are therapeutic, and meditation on them can get at the problem sideways rather than head on. In the case of *Harry Potter*, the fairy tale's therapeutic effects have returned to physical reality.

JK Rowling created another set of her neat 'bookends' by turning the proceeds of her fairy tale about a helpless orphan into help for orphans and other children. Her gifts to charity are well known, but in 2005 she founded the Children's High Level Group with Baroness Emma Nicholson of Winterbourne, a member of the European parliament. It's devoted to improving the welfare of vulnerable children in Europe. As just one example of what they do, in Romania they've enabled over 22,000 children to return to "family-based care in the past four years, with over half this number returning to their parents or relatives. A change in the law in Romania means it is now not possible to institutionalize children under two years old."[37]

She 'bookended' Harry's 17 year cycle (both Harry's age in the last book and the time it took her to write the series) by hand writing seven ornately bound copies of *The Tales of Beedle the Bard*. Six were given to people who helped bring Harry's story into being. The seventh was auctioned to raise money for the Children's High Level Group. It sold for just under two million pounds (about four million dollars) to the online bookstore Amazon. The first fairy tale in the book, *The Wizard and the Hopping Pot*, emphasized the importance of altruism.[38] Readers haven't been the only people to get a happy ending out of JK Rowling's work.

WHAT MAKES A GOOD ENDING, IN ART OR LIFE?
The fan debates about how the series would end raised the bigger

question of what makes a good ending in art or life. Are happy endings a literary 'easy out?' Is death a bad ending no matter what? Is dying for something noble a good or a bad ending?

We see Harry return to King's Cross one last time 19 years on in the Epilogue. (This is an astronomically significant period, the time it takes the moon to complete a full cycle of its movements through the heavens and rise and set in exactly the same place. Various ancient traditions ritually observed this cycle.) Everything has come full circle. The heroic children we first met have grown up and have their own children who are now boarding the Hogwarts Express. Old enmities have softened with maturity, as that little nod between Harry and Draco shows. The orphaned Teddy Lupin is kissing Bill and Fleur's daughter, and we learn that he often visits the Potter's house.

Softening the blow of his losses was evidently one of the main reasons that Ms. Rowling wanted to write the epilogue. Readers had mixed responses to it, but on measure, as she's said from the start that she always intended to write just seven novels, I'm glad she wrote it. If *Hallows* is truly the last we'll ever see of Harry, it's good to know he went on to live a happy and useful life.

There is, however, still loss for Harry, as there is for all of us. As the Hogwarts Express pulls away at the station "Harry walked alongside it, watching his son's thin face, already ablaze with excitement. Harry kept smiling, and waving, even though it was a little like a bereavement, watching his son glide away from him…"

Life will always present us with this sort of loss, whether we're parents or not; the loss of friends, family, times of life, even our own previous selves. One of the most poignant, beautiful bits of writing in all the books has to be the time Harry spends in the deserted Dursley house, before leaving it for the last time in *Hallows*.

The light was fading rapidly now, the hall half full of shadows in the evening light. It felt most strange to stand here in the silence and know that he was about to leave the house for the last time. Long ago, when he had been left alone when the Dursleys went out to enjoy themselves, the hours of solitude had been a rare treat: pausing only to sneak something tasty from the fridge he had rushed upstairs to play on Dudley's computer, or put on the television and flicked through the channels to his heart's content. It gave him an odd, empty feeling to remember those times; it was like remembering a younger brother whom he had lost.[39]

Stephen King singled out this example for praise in his review of *Hallows* and the series as a whole. He calls it "Honest; nostalgic; *not* sloppy."[40] We all have such moments of bittersweet reflection.

There's one way in which we're all sacrificed to a greater purpose, like Harry, whether we will or no: we'll all die. We'll all give way to the future, clear a place for our descendants or others to live. The question becomes not will we die for something, but what will we die for, and what will we consequently live for?

It's all about our choices — that other big theme in *Harry Potter*. Near the end of *Chamber*, Harry agonizes over his resemblance to the young Tom Riddle, and how the Sorting Hat nearly put him in Slytherin. Dumbledore prompts Harry to remember that he asked not to be put in Slytherin. This makes Harry very different from Voldemort. As he says, "It is our choices, Harry, that show what we truly are, far more than our abilities." Alan Jacobs wrote that Harry is stunned because he realizes for the first time that he's been confused about the wrong thing. He's been asking the question "Who am I at heart?" when he needed to be asking the question "What must I do in order to become what I should be?"[41]

It's a question we all have to answer, yet too much introspection gets in the way of becoming the person we always wanted to be, whether or not we think we have it in us. Harry often doesn't think he has it in him to become what destiny seems to ordain, but he acts in spite of fear, insecurity and helplessness. Action is the ultimate alchemical antidote.

I'm going to ask you directly to do something here. It's safe to assume, if you've read this far, that you like JK Rowling's writing, so I'm going to ask you to do something for her other work, do something for a child. Stop reading right now...no wait a minute, get ready to stop reading at the end of this paragraph. I haven't said what you'll be doing yet.

Go and make a donation to a children's charity. It doesn't matter if it's small. Make it as small as it needs to be for you to do it instantly, without thought. You can write a check for a single unit of whatever currency you use. You can go online and donate to JK Rowling's charity or to another. You can even go to sites where clicking on a button or playing a game donates food, protects rainforests, buys children books, pays for children's healthcare and helps in other ways with no cost to you at all. (Some details are in the *Further Resources* appendix.)

If you don't have a computer, go get an item of clothing or piece of bric-a-brac to which you're unattached and give it to a charity shop. If you have absolutely nothing do something else. Pick up some rubbish in your neighborhood and recycle or throw it away. That way, children don't have to play near broken glass or walk through rubbish. That way, the beaches they build sandcastles on have a few less plastic bags and a few more living birds. Everyone is a former child and all today's children will inherit the world we create, so don't be put off doing something if for some reason you can't do it for children in an obvious way. Pick an option and do it now.

There—isn't that better? A doctor in the Nobel Prize winning relief organization, Médicins Sans Frontières said, "It's easier to be in the field, getting your hands dirty, feeling involved, than it is to be sitting at home watching the world's crises unfold on TV."[42] These doctors risk their lives and endure all kinds of hardships to bring help, and still say it's easier than sitting by. That's because action is always easier. It's our natural state, not sitting passively watching things. The *Harry Potter* books encourage action. JK Rowling's writing comforts us, but doesn't encourage us to become *comfortable*.

I once heard the Aramaic scholar and spiritual teacher, Neil Douglas-Klotz, speak of the way that Jesus and his contemporaries saw time as a caravan. They didn't see the bit of time in which we live as being all that exists. This time, and those in it, are just a few people and camels in the middle of the caravan. The ancestors have gone up ahead, and the descendants follow along behind.[43] Similarly, the bit of track that the Hogwarts express occupies at any given moment isn't the only bit of track that exists. The journey's start and the journey's end and every point in between all exist as well, and make the journey possible.

In the same kind of way, our ancestors and descendants are all on our journey with us, we're all in it together, as magic and science both teach us. We fulfill and complete our ancestors and they fulfill and complete us, as do our children. Exchange and making meaning goes in all directions. When Harry looks in the Mirror of Erised for the first time, he sees vast numbers of ancestors, sees his hair, his eyes, even his knobbly knees on other people, and gets a sense of the continuum he's part of. We bear our ancestors qualities, and their visions of life, into the future.

Of course, we aren't just in the caravan with families of blood, but also with families of affinity, like the Hogwarts houses. Harry's children aren't only named for his family, but for two men who, each in their own way, were part of Harry's family of affinity. Though they left no blood descendants, this naming symbolizes their legacies of wisdom and courage continuing.

There are deep sorrows and abiding joys in every instant of the process if we dare to feel them. Our interactions with ancestors and descendants, with their dreams and visions, and with our own, are full of sorrowful joy and joyful sorrow. Harry shows us something of how we can participate joyfully in the world's sorrows.[44]

Few know loss as well as Harry. He unites the Hallows, the Holy things. He brings together union and loss, joy and sorrow in spiritual awareness beneath death's cloak, where we can bear each of them, and bear the transitions between them, with the resilience of the child who laughs with tears on his cheeks.

Harry is able to retain his capacity for joy even in the face of terrible loss because of what he's been given. The child psychologist and authority on fairy tales, Bruno Bettelheim, ended his book *The Uses of Enchantment* on the positive note of a fairy tale that focussed on parental love, which, as a parent, he preferred to the grimmer parental interactions that sometimes appear in fairy tales.

He spoke of how the love between parent and child goes on to help form the love we feel for a spouse, as Harry loves Ginny and Ron loves Hermione. Of course, other relationships are also important to us. Harry has friends and mentors whose love and support get him through life. His family of affinity includes Ron, Hermione, Sirius, Lupin, Dumbledore, the Weasleys and many others. Bettelheim goes on to say something that could have been written about Harry.

Whatever may be true in reality, the child who listens to fairy tales comes to imagine and believe that out of love for him his parent is willing to risk his life to bring him the present he most desires. In turn, such a child believes that he is worthy of such devotion, because he would be willing to sacrifice his life out of love for his parent. Thus the child will grow up to bring peace and happiness even to those who are so grievously afflicted that they seem like beasts. In doing so, a person will gain happiness for himself, and his life's partner and, with it, happiness also for his parents. He will be at peace with himself and the world. This is one of the manifold truths revealed by fairy tales, which can guide our lives; it is a truth as valid today as it was once upon a time.[45]

There are fairy tales and myths to help guide us at all stages of our lives. There are also myths that appear to guide us through specific points in history, messages that come at just the right time to set us on the right course. As I said at the beginning of this book, the *Harry Potter* phenomenon tells a lot about what Western culture lacks at the front end of the 21st century, and the books tell us a lot about how we fill those voids.

I've shown some of the ways that Harry's story resonates magically, morally and symbolically with ancient wisdom. I hope I've also shown the value of this wisdom today. *Harry Potter* gives us insights into the magic and meaning of our lives, and we can use his example as an alchemical antidote to the culture of complacency.

We fully attain the stone by giving to others, as Harry does. We multiply our wealth by focussing it where it will do the most good, where the cost of a cup of coffee saves a life. By doing so, we extend our lives' impact in time and show that love is stronger than death.

Harry's greatest message is love's generosity in the face of loss. We can be as generous to the future as he is, experiencing ourselves as part of that caravan in time. We can follow our ancestors up ahead as he follows his parents' positive examples. We can love and support the children who glide away from us into a magical future. We can experience our world as inspiring and in-spirited along the way. Doing so, we can meet even the

most apparently insurmountable challenges, and for us, as for Harry and his loved ones, all will be well.

# ENDNOTES

References are given in the Harvard author / year format. To find the source referred to, look under the author's last name and the date in the bibliography. As this isn't an academic book I've tried to keep references and endnotes to a minimum.

INTRODUCTION
1. Stevenson, 1879
2. McHardy, 2003, pp. 45-8

I. Beginning: A Letter in Green Ink
JK Rowling quote from *Hallows*, Chapter 24, UK p. 391, US p. 483 Antoine de Saint Exupéry quote from *The Wisdom of the Sands*, on the opening page of Barker, 1988
1. Bettelheim, 1991, p. 4
2. Bettelheim, 1991, p. 5
3. Anatol, 2003a, p. xiv
4. For example, see Kronzek, 2001, Colbert, 2005
5. A primarily pro-Harry Christian book I've read is Bridger, 2001. An internet or online bookstore search will turn up a wealth of other options.
6. http://en.wikipedia.org/wiki/Harry_Potter, accessed 17th April 2007
7. http://en.wikipedia.org/wiki/Harry_Potter%28statistics%29, accessed 17th April 2007 and Vieira interview with Rowling, 2007.
8. Nel, 2001, p 27

9. Blake, 2002, p. 4. (The last book came out within a month of Tony Blair leaving office.)

10. Gupta, 2003, p. 8 quoting Lynch, 2001, p. 26

11. Anelli and Spartz interview with Rowling, 16th July 2005

12. Levine and Carvajal, 1999

13. Shapiro, 2003, pp. 93-94

14. Schoefer, 2000, quoted in Anatol, 2003, pp. x-xi

15. Nel, 2001, p. 27

16. Nel, 2001, p 63, Quoting from Scott and Shulman, 1999, 2000

17. In her interview along with Steve Kloves on the *Chamber of Secrets* DVD

18. Jung, 1976, p. 60

19. Nel, 2001, p. 62, quoting from Acocella, 2000

20. Nel, 2001, pp. 31-2, 84, note 7. He adds, "I am indebted to Gloria Hardman for alerting me to Rowling's use of primes in this chapter."

21. See Murray, 1988, pp. 38-39

22. See Chetan and Brueton, pp. 23-82 if you're particularly interested in yews and their symbolism.

23. The calendar she refers to has been widely reproduced but originates in *The White Goddess* by Robert Graves. See Graves, 1992, pp. 207-8. Graves assigned trees to parts of the year, as in astrology, based on his interpretation of an ancient Welsh poem. There's lots of ancient Celtic tree symbolism, but no clear evidence for a tree calendar any older than Graves' creative interpretation.

24. JK Rowling's web site, at: http://www.jkrowling.com/textonly/en/extrastuffview.cfm?id=18 accessed 15 July 2007

25. Nel, 2001, pp. 13-14

26. Nel, 2001, p. 83, note 3, quoting Woolf, 1966, pp. 144-154

27. Simpson interview with Rowling, 1998

28. Coad interview with Rowling, 2005

II. BETWIXT AND BETWEEN AT PLATFORM 9 ¾

Dumbledore quote from Hallows, Chapter 35, UK p. 579, US. p. 723

Einstein quoted in Kalweit, 1988, p. 193

1. Hutton, 2006, p. 236
2. Fraser interview with Rowling, 2002
3. Here I follow David Abram and others. I think I first heard this use of alternate in preference to altered states in Roy Willis' *Anthropology of Consciousness* class at the University of Edinburgh, 1998
4. Matthews, Gareth, 2004, pp. 183-4
5. Dukes, 2005, p. 10
6. *Stone*, Chapter 6, UK p.70, US p. 93
7. Professor Ulf Leonhardt and Dr Thomas Philbin did the research. See Highfield, 2007
8. For the Emerald Tablet see Duquette, 1997, p. 54. Duquette's interpretation of the tablet also relates a bit to physics, p. 72. The physics part here comes from Davies, 1984, p. 101.
9. Chopra, 2005, p. 9
10. *Prince*, Chapter 26, UK p. 521, US p. 557
11. Davies, 1984, p. 114
12. Highfield, 2002, pp. 174-6
13. *Chamber*, Chapter 18, UK p. 242, US p. 417
14. *Goblet*, Chapter 12, UK p. 157, US p. 177
15. *Phoenix*, Chapter 24, UK pp. 468-9, US p. 530
16. See Lorimer, 1999, The Scientific and Medical Network Web site is www.scimednet.org
17. *Hallows*, Chapter 21, UK pp. 332-3, US pp. 406-409
18. *Stone*, Chapter 12, UK p. 151, US p. 205
19. *Goblet*, Chapter 20, UK p. 310, US p.354
20. *Stone*, Chapter 12, UK, p. 157, US p. 213
21. *Azkaban*, Chapter 3, UK p. 32, US p. 36
22. *Hallows*, Chapter 34, UK p. 559, US pp. 697-8

23. *Phoenix*, Chapter 35, UK p. 703, US p. 798
24. *Phoenix*, Chapter 38, UK p. 746, US p. 847
25. Dr. Bauer's web site is in the list at the end of this book.
26. *Hallows*, Chapter 33, UK p. 535, US p. 666
27. Ricard, 2006, p. 107
28. Ricard, 2006, pp. 192-7. Also see Macrae 2007 for the short-term meditation study.
29. Lackey, 2005b, p.3, quoting *Newsweek*, July 8, 2000
30. Whited, 2002b, p. 3
31. Rowling 2004, 15th August
32. Lipscomb and Stewart, 2004, p. 78
33. Hutton, 2006, see his chapter on "The Inklings and the Gods," pp. 215-238
34. Adler, 17th October 2007
35. *Hallows*, Chapter 16, UK pp. 266-8, US pp. 325-8
36. See Kondratiev, 2000.
37. Lévi-Strauss, 2001, pp. 245-246
38. Oakes, 2003, p. 121

III. FOUR HOUSES, FOUR ELEMENTS

The Professor Lupin quote is from an exchange between Professor Lupin and Harry from the Steve Kloves script for *Harry Potter and the Prisoner of Azkaban*. It distills a few different exchanges in the books, as a script must, and also nicely foreshadows Harry's actions in the final book. After *Azkaban* came out, JK Rowling said that there were elements in the film that she hadn't put there that people would think had been clues after the final book came out. I rather think that this was one of them.

Paracelsus quote from Paracelsus 1988, p.18

1. Paracelsus, 1988, p. 21
2. Anelli and Spartz interview with JK Rowling, July 16th 2005.
   Margaret Rustin, a child psychologist, and her sociologist husband, Michael, recently likened the sorting process to

therapy, where the therapist may tell you what 'type' you are! This was in a talk on the internal and external aspects of Harry Potter's family. (Rustin, 2007)

3. *Stone*, Chapter 7, UK p 85, US p. 114
4. Ashcroft-Nowicki, 1986, p. 50. Dolores Ashcroft-Nowicki has a very broad and practical approach to magic and heads *The Servants of Light*, a magical order begun by magician and novelist Dion Fortune, a prominent figure in the magical revival of the last century.
5. *Stone*, Chapter 3, UK p. 30, US p. 34
6. Excerpts are from the Hat's song in *Goblet*, Chapter 12, UK p.157, US p. 177
7. Charbonneau-Lassay, 1992, pp. 3-5, 239, 25-32
8. Carr-Gomm, 1994, pp. 84-5
9. *Stone*, Chapter 10, UK pp. 126-7, US p. 171
10. *Hallows*, Chapter 30, UK pp. 481-3, 499, US pp. 599-600, 620
11. *Stone*, Chapter 7, UK p. 95, US p. 128
12. *Goblet*, Chapter 14, UK p. 192, US p. 217
13. Old English gives us *witan*, to know, and the Old High German *wizzan*, the root of 'wisdom.' Hence Wizengamot, the wizard court, an assembly of the wise — ideally! See Harper, 2001, headword 'wisdom.'
14. Eriugena, 1990, p. 21, 25
15. *Hallows*, Chapter 24, UK p. 399, US p. 494
16. *Phoenix*, Chapter 21, UK pp. 405-6, US p. 459
17. *Stone*, Chapter 17, UK p. 221, US p.305
18. Charbonneau-Lassay, 1992, pp. 6-8
19. Lavoie, 2003, p. 40. The web site is at http://www.harrypotterfansonline.com/SortingCap.htm
20. Runcie, 2007
21. Rogers, 1984, pp. 119-121
22. Rolleston, 1910, pp. 181-5. Online at http://www.luminarium.org/mythology/ireland/cormacin

struct.htm, accessed 11th January 2008.

23. Jackson and Osborne, 2001. This exchange isn't in the books. It's one of many examples of how the writers of *The Lord of the Rings* films, Peter Jackson, Fran Walsh and Philippa Boyens, went for the spirit rather than the letter of the books. Doing so, I think they really got to the heart of the characters.

24. Patterson, 2004, p.122

25. Matthew 10.16

26. Jacobsen, 1976, pp. 193-215

27. Wilkinson, 1992, p. 109

28. The controversial magician Aleister Crowley, said "Do what thou wilt shall be the whole of the law." This is often quoted, but he also said, "Love is the Law, love under will." He's speaking of higher will not whim. His philosophy came to be called Thelemic, from the Greek *thelema*, meaning 'will.' (See Evans, 2007, pp. 26-27. Crowley, 1976, p. 9) He's sometimes seen as a 'dark' magician, though the quotes above show otherwise. He'd certainly have been sorted into Slytherin, however, and once said "Every man and woman is a star." It's tempting to see the Slytherin Blacks, with their celestial names and dark arts, as a Crowley reference. Only Ms. Rowling knows for sure!

29. Kaplan, 1997, p. 19

30. *Hallows*, Chapter 33, UK p. 535, US p. 666

31. The interview with Jason Isaacs is on the *Harry Potter and the Chamber of Secrets* DVD extras disk, in the interviews with *Professors and More.*

32. *Hallows*, Chapter 33, UK p. 549, US p. 684

33. *Stone*, Chapter 7, UK p. 88, US p. 118

34. Ashcroft-Nowicki, 1986, p. 79

35. *Phoenix*, Chapter 25, p. 488, US p. 553

IV. THROUGH THE MAZE: HEROIC JOURNEYS

Joseph Campbell quote from Campbell 1993, p. 391

Harry Potter quote from *Prince*, Chapter 23, UK p. 479, US p. 512

1. Buxton, 2004, p. 154

2. Many scholars have looked at the hero's journey and its stages, the first probably being Lord Raglan in *The Hero: A Study in Tradition, Myth and Dreams*. Alfred Nutt also looked at the heroic process. The Celtic scholar, Tómas Ó Cathasaigh created a synthesis of versions in his book, *The Heroic Biography of Cormac Mac Airt*, which I draw from.

3. Campbell, 1993, p. 30

4. Minerva McGonagall is named for the Roman goddess of wisdom (Athena in Greek tradition) often shown with an owl.

5. *Stone*, Chapter 2, UK p. 27, US p. 30

6. *Stone*, Chapter 5, UK p. 61, US p. 79, Chapter 4, UK p. 42, US p. 51

7. Ostry, 2003, pp. 93, 97

8. Kipling, 1899. For a comparison with Harry, see Cockrell, 2002, pp. 18-19

9. For the kundalini see Rawson, 1978, particularly pp. 168 to 170 and the twin serpents picture on page 96. The kundalini is often depicted as twin serpents twining up the column of the spine, an image echoed in Mercury's caduceus and in the image of the smoky twin serpents, "in essence divided" that emerge from one of Dumbledore's instruments in *Phoenix*, Chapter 22, UK p. 416, US p. 470.

10. McLean, 2002, p. 54

11. Millman, 2005, pp.43-44

12. Charbonneau-Lassay, 1992, pp. 320-1

13. Buxton, 2004, p. 93

14. *Goblet*, Chapter 35, UK p. 589-90, US p. 679

15. Campbell and Moyers, 1988, p. 102

16. Zettel, 2005, pg. 90
17. *Hallows*, Chapter 30, UK p. 483, US p. 600
18. Anelli and Spartz interview with Rowling 2005, 16th July
19. Rowling writing as Whisp, 2001
20. You can read the full story a http://www.sacred-texts.com/egy/leg/leg07.htm. The number 142 figures prominently in it, as the number of enemies that Horus slays in lion form, for example. You'll remember that Hogwarts has 142 stairways. In December of 2007 Harry became the 42nd wizard featured as 'wizard of the month' on JK Rowling's site. I wonder if she's quoting Douglas Adam's *Hitchhiker's Guide to the Galaxy*, where a supercomputer takes about a zillion years to determine that the meaning of "life, the universe and everything" is the number 42? No explanation, just 42, which shows how important it is to frame your questions well.
21. See also Greppin, 1973
22. *Hallows*, Chapter 36, UK p. 585, US p. 731
23. From: http://www.booksfromscotland.com/Books/Jim-Hewitsons-Scottish-Miscellany-9781902927848/Extract#bagame, accessed 14th October 2007. Also see Robertson, 2004. A Trevarthen actually died playing the Cornish game, the 'scrum' can get quite rough. For the symbolism of the Mayan ball game, discussed below, see Gillette or Tokovinine, 2007.
24. Interestingly, the Latin translation of the classic book, *The Little Prince*, by Antoine de Saint Exupéry, translates the title as *Regulus*. I wonder if Ms. Rowling intended a link?
25. *Hallows*, Chapter 36, UK p. 596, US p. 744

V. THE ART

The Nicholas Flamel quote is from his *Summary of Philosophy*.
The Clive Barker quote is from Barker, 1989, p. 5

1. Rowling and Fry, 2003
2. See Winnicott, 1994, pp. 10-12
3. Colwyn Trevarthen, 1987, quoted in Bjørkvold, 1992, p. 12. He's also my father-in-law, in case you were wondering about the last names.
4. *Stone*, Chapter 17, UK p. 216, US p. 299
5. *Goblet*, Chapter 20, UK p. 303, US p. 347. The exchanges about, and experience of, the felix felices 'lucky potion' are in Chapters 14 and 22 of *Prince*. The Beedle the Bard stories are reviewed by Daphne Durham of Amazon at www.amazon.co.uk/beedlebard, accessed 11th January 2008.
6. Paracelsus, 1988, p. 137
7. I've read the snail example somewhere but haven't been able to find the reference. Enlightenment via email would be welcome, if you happen to know it!
8. *Prince*, Chapter 10, UK p. 185, US p. 195
9. *Stone*, Chapter 15, UK p. 188, US p. 257
10. Campbell, John Gregorson, 2002, p. 250
11. Quoted in Bridger, 2001, p. 29
12. Bridger, 2001, p. 26
13. *Stone*, Chapter 16, UK p. 208, US p. 287
14. Byatt, 2003
15. Le Guin, 1976, p. 56
16. *Goblet*, Chapter 14, UK p. 192, US p. 219
17. Crowley, 1973, p. 131
18. It's the first point he makes on his web site: http://www.lonmiloduquette.com
19. *Prince*, Chapter 1, UK p. 24, US p.18
20. Shinn, 1989, p. 95
21. Moore in Vylenz, 2006
22. *Stone*, Chapter 10, UK p. 127, US p. 171
23. LeGuin, 1976, p. 28-29
24. *Azkaban*, Chapter 4, UK p. 55, US p. 68. See Morris, 2004

25. Highfield, 2002, p. 303
26. Moore in Vylenz, 2006
27. Crowley, 1973, pp. 137-8
28. Hall, 2003, p. 155
29. You can read details on this and all other spells used in the books at http://www.mugglenet.com/info/other/spells.shtml
30. *Goblet*, Chapter 37, UK p. 633, US p. 730
31. McLean, 1979
32. McLean, 1979
33. *Stone*, Chapter 17, UK p. 215, US p. 297. Shortly before Joseph Campbell died, he spoke of death as going "on to the next adventure" in his series with Bill Moyers, *The Power of Myth*.
34. Jung, 1995, p. 162
35. Charbonneau-Lassay, 1992, p. 442
36. Granger, 2007, pp. 61-2, Gilchrist, 1991, p. 43
37. Jung, 1993, p. 445
38. Gilchrist, 1991, p. 45, JK Rowling quote from Richards, 2000
39. *Hallows*, Chapter 15, UK p.254, US p. 309
40. Jung, 1995, pp. 162-3
41. *Hallows*, Chapter 19, UK p. 308, US p. 379
42. Jung, 1995, pp. 163-4
43. Gilchrist, 1991, p. 28
44. McLean, 2002, pp. 98-100
45. Jung, 1991, p. 306
46. See www.harrypotterforseekers.com. I recommend you to Joscelyn Godwin's edition with Adam McLean's commentary, if you want to delve into its fascinating symbolism. I could have written a chapter on *The Chemical Wedding* myself here if I'd had the space!
47. *Hallows*, Chapter 8, UK p. 118, US p. 141. JK Rowling gave Evanna Lynch, the actress who plays Luna in the films, a necklace with a hare and a moon on it.

48. Jung, 1995, p. 161
49. JK Rowling's web site at http://www.jkrowling.com/textonly/en/extrastuffview.cfm?id=18
50. Granger, 2007, p. 101
51. See Gallardo-C. and Smith, 2003
52. Granger, 2007, p. 113
53. She said this to an audience at New York's Carnegie Hall, see Rowling, 22nd October 2007.
54. *Phoenix*, Chapter 37, UK p. 743, US p. 843

VI. THE TERRIBLE AND THE GREAT

Ollivander quote from *Stone*, Chapter 5, UK p. 65, US p. 85
Paracelsus quoted at the head of Davis, 1985

1. *Hallows*, Chapter 2, UK p. 24, US p. 20
2. Campbell and Moyers, 1991, p. 278
3. Zaehner, 1982, pp. 296-7
4. *Prince*, Chapter 20, UK p. 417, US p. 443. For a discussion of ambivalent morality in the *Mahabharata* see Fields, 1991, pp. 89-92.
5. Abram, 1997, p. 6. See also Abram and London 2006.
6. There's an excellent section on this in Duquette, 1997, Chapter 7
7. Jung, 1995, pp. 142, 154, note 3
8. *Hallows*, Chapter 24, UK p. 387, US p. 478
9. *Hallows*, Chapter 24, UK p. 391, US p. 483-4
10. This is one of various UK / US differences, some more substantive than replacing 'mum' with 'mom.' See Nel, 2002. Some are comical, for example, Sirius Black 'scarpers,' flees the scene in dissarray, after slashing Ron's bed curtains in the UK edition of *Azkaban*, and 'scampers,' Bambi-like, in the US. Some are just odd. In the US version of *Prince* Dumbledore doesn't just say he'll protect Draco's parents on the

astronomy tower, but that they'll fake his mother's murder by the Order of the Phoenix, because it's what Voldemort would expect and do himself under the circumstances. However, you'd think that this would be such an uncharacteristic move for Dumbledore's bunch that Voldemort wouldn't fall for it. I wonder why someone felt that the American edition needed this difference? *Prince*, Chapter 27, UK pp. 552-3, US pp. 591-2

11. Blake, 2002, p. 46
12. Lackey, 2005a, pp. 5-6
13. It's a common theme of myths and fairy tales that the legalism of magic causes the spell to work against the person who sets it up. It's important to be *very* specific what you ask for. A Voldemort type request for immortality is no good without the additional gift of eternal youth.
14. Granger, 2007, p. 38
15. One of the opening quotes of Rick Fields book, *The Code of the Warrior*.
16. *Prince*, Chapter 20, UK p. 417, US p. 445-6
17. *Goblet*, Chapter 32, UK p. 555, US p. 640
18. *Hallows*, Chapter 17, UK p. 282, US p. 345
19. Ingerman, 1991, p. 11
20. Vylenz, 2006
21. *Prince*, Chapter 23, UK p. 465, US pp. 497-8. "Against nature" is an interesting turn of phrase. Ms. Rowling could have referred to some sort of 'higher order' but chose not to. See Krause, 2005, p. 60
22. *Hallows*, Chapter 36, UK p. 591, US p. 738
23. Vieira interview with JK Rowling, 2007
24. Colbert, 2005, pp. 61-4. She spoke of the date of the final Hogwarts battle in Runcie 2007.
25. Fomoire is pronounced foe'-voy-reh
26. Kronzek, 2001, p. 24
27. *Phoenix*, Chapter 24, UK p. 475, US p. 538

28. Clarke, 2006, 7th March
29. Vieira interview with JK Rowling, 2007
30. Grof, 1989, pp· 2-7, 78
31. Hutton, 2006, p. 164
32. Hutton, 2006, p. 165
33. *Phoenix*, Chapter 24, UK p. 473, US p. 536
34. The Japanese Samurai warriors used to say, "The only way over the marshes is through."
35. Coad, 17th July 2005
36. Rose and Nelson, 18th October 2000
37. At http://www.mugglenet.com/info/other/spells.shtml, accessed 27th November 2007
38. *Azkaban*, Chapter 12, UK p. 176, US p. 237
39. *Phoenix*, Chapter 1, UK p. 22, US p. 18
40. Duquette, 1997, pp. 48-9. Interestingly, an early translator of this book, MacGregor Mathers, speculated that the Abraham the Jew who wrote it might have been descended from the Abraham the Jew who wrote the famous book that taught Nicholas Flamel how to make the philosopher's stone. (Mathers, 1975, p. xix) This is highly unlikely — after all, there have been many Jewish people named Abraham! But it's interesting that he, too, felt a link between the alchemical process of union that created the stone and the spiritual union cultivated between the wizard and the Holy Guardian Angel in Abramelin's ritual. For an excellent new translation, see Dehn and Guth's under 'Abraham' in the Bibliography.
41. *Hallows*, Chapter 36, UK p. 593, US p. 739
42. *Hallows*, Chapter 33, UK p. 545, US p. 679
43. He runs the Harry Potter Lexicon web site and was inter viewed on the DVD extras of *Phoenix*.
44. *Phoenix*, Chapter 8, UK p. 129, US p. 141
45. Quoted in Ram Dass, 1989, p. 185

VII. Using the Philosopher's Stone

Dumbledore quote from *Goblet*, Chapter 37, UK p. 628, US p. 724

Gandhi quoted from www.thehungersite.com

1. Ross, 1987, p. 65, saying 108
2. Jung, 1995, p. 150
3. Ross, 1987, p. 67, saying 113
4. Flamel, 1624
5. Flamel, 1624
6. In the novels, the knocker of the headmaster's office door is a Griffin and a gargoyle covers the entrance to the stairs. In the films, a griffin is at the entrance to the stairs to the headmaster's tower.
7. See Charbonneau-Lassay, 1992, pp. 397-409
8. *Hallows*, Chapter 36, UK p. 596, US pp. 744-5
9. Vieira, 2007
10. Silverman, 1967, p. 25
11. *Prince*, Chapter 23, UK p. 478, US p. 511
12. *Hallows*, Chapter 24, UK p. 391, US p. 483
13. *Hallows*, Chapter 34, UK p. 555, US p. 693
14. *Phoenix*, Chapter 18, UK p. 343, US pp. 386-7
15. Campbell and Moyers, 1988, p.150. The St. Paul quote is Romans 8:28.
16. *Stone*, Chapter 17, UK p. 215, US p. 297
17. Lon Milo Duquette's 1999 autobiography features some interesting thoughts on magic and finances. For more on the statistic, see my newsletter at: http://www.celticshamanism.com/dec04printable.html. I've recently found that the original source for this information is the systems analyst, farmer and environmentalist Donella Meadows. See Taub, 2001.
18. Flamel inscription quoted in Kern, 2003, p. 255, Ricard in Mansfield, 2007
19. St. Ignatius of Loyola, founder of the Jesuits, quoted in

Gracián, 1992, p. 141, aphorism 251
20. Trevarthen and Reddy, 2004, p. 10
21. Rowling in Vieira interview, 2007
22. Bywater, 2005, p. 264
23. Ross, 1987, p. 33, saying 42
24. Paracelsus, 1988, p. 203
25. Egan, 2007
26. Jacobs, 2000
27. *Stone*, Chapter 5, UK p. 56, US p. 72
28. Ralph Feinnes interviewed in the documentary *He Who Must Not Be Named* on *Harry Potter and The Goblet of Fire* DVD, Disk 2
29. See Byatt, 2003 or Bloom, 2000, for examples.
30. *Chamber*, Chapter 9, UK p. 113, US p. 190
31. Schiller, from *The Piccolomini*, III, 4, quoted in Bettelheim, 1991, p. 5
32. Mitchison, 2003
33. Bettelheim, 1991, p. 24, quoting from Chesterton, 1909 and C.S. Lewis, 1936.
34. Zipes, 1979, p. 141, quoted in Ostry, 2003, p. 89
35. Bettelheim, 1991, p. 6
36. Bettelheim, 1991, p. 25, Rees, 1990, p. 17
37. From www.chlg.org, accessed 15th December 2007.
38. Details and pictures were at www.amazon.co.uk/beedlebard at the time of writing.
39. *Hallows*, Chapter 4, UK p. 42, US pp. 43-4
40. King, 2007
41. Jacobs, 2000
42. See Bortolotti, 2004
43. Douglas-Klotz, 2002, p. 151
44. See Campbell, 1972, pp. 102-104
45. Bettelheim, 1991, p. 310

IBLIOGRAPHY

This Bibliography is in three sections. The first short section contains just the *Harry Potter* books in the editions I've used followed by the films under the primary producer's name.

The second contains all the interviews with, and talks by, JK Rowling. Interviews are alphabetized under the name of the interviewer, and referred to in the endnotes by the interviewer's name. Talks are under 'Rowling.' I've also put JK Rowling's non-Harry related writing that I've referred to, like her introduction to the *One City* book, here.

The third section is books and articles about JK Rowling and *Harry Potter*.

The fourth and final section contains everything else. See the *Further Resources* appendix for detailed recommendations.

1. HARRY POTTER NOVELS, RELATED BOOKS AND FILMS

Rowling, JK

1997, *Harry Potter and the Philosopher's Stone*, (London: Bloomsbury) trade paperback

1998, *Harry Potter and the Sorcerer's Stone*, (New York: Scholastic) trade paperback

1998, *Harry Potter and the Chamber of Secrets*, (London: Bloomsbury) trade paperback

1999, *Harry Potter and the Chamber of Secrets*, (New York: Scholastic) mass market paperback, 2002

1999, *Harry Potter and the Prisoner of Azkaban*, (London:

Bloomsbury) trade paperback

1999, *Harry Potter and the Prisoner of Azkaban*, (New York: Scholastic) trade paperback

2000, *Harry Potter and the Goblet of Fire*, (London: Bloomsbury) trade paperback

2000, *Harry Potter and the Goblet of Fire*, (New York: Scholastic) trade paperback

2001, as Kennilworthy Whisp, *Quidditch through the Ages*, (London: Bloomsbury)

2001a, as Newt Scamander, *Fantastic Beasts & Where to Find Them*, (London: Bloomsbury)

2003, *Harry Potter and the Order of the Phoenix*, (London: Bloomsbury) hardcover

2003, *Harry Potter and the Order of the Phoenix*, (New York: Scholastic) hardcover

2005, *Harry Potter and the Half-Blood Prince*, (London: Bloomsbury) hardcover

2005, *Harry Potter and the Half-Blood Prince*, (New York: Scholastic) hardcover

2007, *Harry Potter and the Deathly Hallows*, (London: Bloomsbury) hardcover

2007, *Harry Potter and the Deathly Hallows*, (New York: Scholastic) Deluxe Edition

Heyman, David

2001, producer, directed by Chris Columbus, *Harry Potter and the Philosopher's Stone*, (Warner Brothers) UK DVD double disk edition 2002

2002, producer, directed by Chris Columbus, *Harry Potter and the Chamber of Secrets*, (Warner Brothers) UK DVD double disk edition 2003

2004, producer, with Chris Columbus and Mark Radcliffe, directed by Alfonso Cuarón, *Harry Potter and the Prisoner of Azkaban*, (Warner Brothers) UK DVD double disk edition

2004

2005, producer, directed by Mike Newell, *Harry Potter and the Goblet of Fire*, (Warner Brothers) UK DVD double disk edition 2006

2007, producer, directed by David Yates, *Harry Potter and the Order of the Phoenix*, (Warner Brothers) UK DVD double disk edition 2007

2. JK ROWLING'S OTHER WRITINGS, TALKS, DOCUMENTARIES AND INTERVIEWS

Many of the interviews cited are available online at Accio Quote, http://www.accio-quote.org/, an invaluable resource. They've even transcribed public appearances and television interviews.

Adler, Shawn
> 2007, 17th October, "Harry Potter Author J.K. Rowling Opens Up About Books' Christian Imagery," at: http://www.mtv.com/news/articles/1572107/20071017/index.jhtml, accessed, 22nd October 2007

Coad, Emma
> 2005, 17th July, "One-on-one interview with J.K. Rowling," ITV, UK, transcript by Deborah Skinner at http://www.accio-quote.org/articles/2005/ 0705-itv-coad.htm, accessed 12th June 2007

Anelli, Melissa and Emerson Spartz
> 2005, 16th July, "The Leaky Cauldron and MuggleNet Interview," by Melissa Anelli, The Leaky Cauldron, and Emerson Spartz, MuggleNet, http://www.the-leaky-cauldron.org/#static:tlcinterviews/jkrhbp1, accessed 18th April 2007

Fraser, Lindsay
> 2002, November, "Harry Potter — Harry and me," in *The Scotsman*, at: http://www.accio-

quote.org/articles/2002/1102-fraser-scotsman.html,
accessed 15th July 2007

Richards, Linda
2000, October, "January Profile: JK Rowling," at in *January Magazine* at http://januarymagazine.com/profiles/jkrowling.html, accessed 11th January 2008

Rowling, J.K
2007, 22nd October, "JK Rowling Outs Dumbledore as Gay," on http://news.bbc.co.uk/1/hi/entertainment/7053982.stm
2006, "Introduction," to *One City*, by Alexander McCall Smith, Ian Rankin and Irvine Welsh, (Edinburgh: Polygon)
2004, 15th August, *Edinburgh Book Festival Talk*, online at http://www.jkrowling.com/textonly/en/newsview.cfm?id=80, accessed 11th January 2008

Rowling, J.K and Stephen Fry
2007, *J.K. Rowling and the Live Chat, with Stephen Fry on Bloomsbury.com*, July 30, 2007 (2.00-3.00pm BST), from http://www.accio-quote.org/articles/2007/0730-bloomsbury-chat.html, accessed 27th September 2007
2003, 26th June, *Conversation with Stephen Fry at the Royal Albert Hall*, online at http://www.accio-quote.org/articles/2003/0626-alberthall-fry.htm, accessed 11th January 2008

Runcie, James
2007, director, producer, *JK Rowling: a Year in the Life*, UK ITV Documentary, First broadcast 30th December, 5PM, ITV1

Simpson, Anne
1998, 7th December, "Face to Face with J K Rowling: Casting a spell over young minds," in *The Herald*, 7 December 1998, at http://www.accio-quote.org/articles/1998/1298-herald-simpson.html, accessed 11th January 2008

Vieira, Meredith

> 2007, 29th July, "Harry Potter: The Final Chapter," *Dateline*, NBC, transcript at http://www.accio-quote.org/articles/2007/0729-dateline-vieira.html, accessed 11th January 2008

5. BOOKS AND ARTICLES ABOUT HARRY POTTER AND JK ROWLING

Acocella, Joan

> 2000, 31st July, "Under the Spell," in *The New Yorker*, pp. 74-78

Anatol, Giselle Liza

> 2003, *Reading Harry Potter, Critical Essays, Contributions to the Study of Popular Culture*, number 78, (Westport, Connecticut, London: Praeger)
>
> 2003a, "Introduction," in Anatol, 2003, pp. ix-xxv
>
> 2003b, "The Fallen Empire: Exploring Ethnic Otherness in the World of Harry Potter," in Anatol, 2003, pp. 163-178

Baggett, David and Shawn E. Klein

> 2004, *Harry Potter and Philosophy, If Aristotle Ran Hogwarts*, (Chicago: Open Court) volume 9 of the Popular Culture and Philosophy series

Blake, Andrew

> 2002, *The Irresistible Rise of Harry Potter*, (London: Verso)

Bloom, Harold

> 2000, 11th July, "Can 35 Million Book Buyers Be Wrong? Yes." In the *Wall Street Journal*, online at http://wrt-brooke.syr.edu/courses/205.03/bloom.html, accessed 23rd April 2007

Bridger, Francis

> 2001, *A Charmed Life, the Spirituality of Potterworld*, (London: Image Books)

Byatt, A.S.

> 2003, 7th July, "Harry Potter and the Childish Adult," in *The*

New York Times, Section A, p. 13

Cockrell, Amanda

    2002, "Harry Potter and the Secret Password, Finding Our Way in the Magical Genre," in Whited, 2002, pp. 15-26

Colbert, David

    2005, *The Magical Worlds of Harry Potter, A Treasury of Myths, Legends and Fascinating Facts*, (London: Puffin, Penguin) 1st edition 2001

Cuarón, Alfonso

    2004, 28th May, (interview), "Alfonso Cuarón: the man behind the magic," *CBBC Newsround*. at: http://news.bbc.co.uk/cbbcnews/hi/tv_film/newsid_3758000/3758101.stm, accessed 17th July 2007

Gupta, Suman

    2003, *Re-Reading Harry Potter*, (Hampshire and New York: Palgrave Macmillan)

Gallardo-C., Ximena, and C. Jason Smith

    2003, "Cinderfella: J.K. Rowling's Wily Web of Gender," in Anatol, 2003, pp. 191-206

Granger, John

    2007, *Unlocking Harry Potter: Five Keys for the Serious Reader*, (Pennsylvania: Zossima)

Hall, Susan

    2003, "Harry Potter and the Rule of Law: The Central Weakness of Legal Concepts in the Wizard World," in Anatol, 2003, pp. 147-162

Highfield, Roger

    2002, *The Science of Harry Potter*, (London: Hodder Headline)

    2007 (8th August), "Physicists Have 'Solved' Problem of Levitation," in *The Telegraph*, at http://www.telegraph.co.uk/news/main.jhtml?xml=/news/2007/08/06/nlevitate106.xml&CMP=ILC-mostviewedbox, accessed 21st August 2007

Jacobs, Alan
  2000, January, "Harry Potter's Magic," in *First Things: A
  Monthly Journal of Religion and Public Life*, pp. 35-38
Keller, Julia
  2007, 21st July, "Review of 'Harry Potter and the Deathly
  Hallows': A dark and satisfying conclusion," in *The Chicago
  Tribune* online, at http://featuresblogs.chicagotribune.com/
  trib_books/ 2007/07/review-of-death.html, accessed 27th
  July 2007
Kern, Edmund M.
  2003, *The Wisdom of Harry Potter, What our Favorite Hero
  Teaches Us about Moral Choices*, (Amherst: Prometheus)
King, Stephen
  2007, August 20th, "J.K. Rowling's Ministry of Magic," from
  Entertainment Weekly, at
  http://www.ew.com/ew/article/0,,20044270_20044274_
  20050689,00.html, accessed 25th August 2007
Kronzek, Allan Zola and Elizabeth
  2001, *The Sorcerer's Companion*, (New York: Broadway Books)
Krause, Marguerite
  2005, "Harry Potter and the End of Religion," in Lackey, 2005
Lackey, Mercedes
  2005, editor, *Mapping the World of Harry Potter, Science Fiction
  and Fantasy Writers Explore the Bestselling Fantasy Series of All
  Time*, (Dallas, Texas: Benbella)
  2005a, "Introduction," in Lackey, 2005, pp. 1-6
  2005b, "Harry Potter and the Post-Traumatic Stress
  Disorder Counselor," in Lackey, 2005, pp. 157-162
Langford, David
  2006, *The End of Harry Potter?* (London: Gollancz)
Lavoie, Chantel
  2003, "Safe as Houses: Sorting and School Houses at
  Hogwarts," in Anatol, 2003, pp. 35-50

Levine, Arthur A., and Doreen Carvajal
    1999, 13th October, "Why I Paid So Much," in *The New York Times*, p. C14

Lynch, Dick
    2001, 12th October, "The Magic of Harry Potter," in *Advertising Age* no. 72, vol. 50, p. 26

Matthews, Gareth B.
    2004, "Finding Platform 9 ¾: The Idea of a Different Reality," in Baggett and Klein, 2004, pp. 175-185

Matthews, Susan R.
    2005, "Ich bin Ein Hufflepuff," in Lackey, 2005, pp. 133-144

Millman, Joyce
    2005, "To Sir, With Love: How Fan Fiction Transformed Professor Snape from a Greasy Git to a Byronic Hero... Who's Really, Really Into S & M," in Lackey, 2005, pp. 39-52

Mills, Alice
    2003, "Archetypes and the Unconscious in Harry Potter and Dianne Wynne Jones's Fire and Hemlock and Dogsbody," in Anatol, 2003, pp. 3-14

Morris, Tom
    2004, "The Courageous Harry Potter," in Baggett and Klein, 2004, pp. 9-21

Nel, Philip
    2001, *J.K. Rowling's Harry Potter Novels, a Reader's Guide*, (New York, London: Continuum)
    2002, "You say 'Jelly,' I Say 'Jell-O?' Harry Potter and the Transfiguration of Language," in Whited, 2002, pp. 261-284

Newman, Mimi
    2007, "Review of Harry Potter and the Deathly Hallows," from *Telegraph Reader Reviews*, at http://www.telegraph.co.uk/arts/main.jhtml?xml=/arts/exclusions/potter/nosplit/bo-harry-potter-

review.xml, accessed 26th July 2007

Oakes, Margaret J.

2003, "Flying Cars, Floo Powder, and Flaming Torches: The High-Tech, Low-Tech World of Wizardry," in Anatol, 2003, pp. 117-130

Ostry, Elaine

2003, "Accepting Mudbloods: The Ambivalent Social Vision of J.K. Rowling's Fairy Tales," in Anatol, 2003, pp. 89-102

Patterson, Steven W.

2004, "Is Ambition a Virtue? Why Slytherin Belongs at Hogwarts," in Baggett and Klein, 2004, pp. 121-131

Rose, Matthew, and Emily Nelson

2000, October 18th, "Potter Cognoscenti All Know a Muggle When They See One," in *The Wall Street Journal*, A1, A10, at http://www.cesnur.org/recens/potter_068.htm, accessed 11th January 2008

Schoefer, Christine

2000, 13th January, "Harry Potter's Girl Trouble," in *Salon*, online at http://archive.salon.com/books/feature/2000/01/13/potter/index.html?source=search&aim=/books/feature, accessed 11th January 2008

Scott, A. O. and Polly Shulman

1999, 23rd August, "Is Harry Potter the New Star Wars?" in *Slate*, online at http://www.slate.com/code/BookClub/BookClub.asp?Show=8/23/99&idMessage=3472&idBio=111 accessed 25th July 2007

Shapiro, Marc

2003, *J.K. Rowling, Princess of Dreams*, (London: John Blake)

Smith, Karen Manners

2003, "Harry Potters Schooldays: J.K. Rowling and the British Boarding School Novel," in Anatol, 2003, pp. 69-88

Taylor, Charles
    2003, 8th July, "Harry Potter and the Goblet of Bile," in *Salon*, online at http://dir.salon.com/story/books/feature/2003/07/08/byatt_rowling/index.html, accessed 18th April 2007

Watt-Evans, Lawrence
    2005, "Why Dumbledore had to Die," in Lackey 2005, pp. 111-118

Wells, Martha
    2005, "Neville Longbottom: The Hero with 1000 Faces," in Lackey 2005, pp. 101-110

Whited, Lana A.
    2002, editor, *The Ivory Tower and Harry Potter, Perspectives on a Literary Phenomenon*, (Columbia and London: University of Missouri Press)
    2002a, "Introduction," in Whited, 2002, pp. 1-14
    2002b, "What would Harry Do? J.K. Rowling and Lawrence Kohlberg's Theories of Moral Development," in Whited, 2002, pp. 182-210

Zettel, Sarah
    2005, Hermione Granger and the Charge of Sexism, in Lackey 2005, pp. 83-100

4. GENERAL

Please note that some items below are quite hard to find in recent primary sources. Various alchemical texts may only appear in old scholarly journals, for example. There just aren't any more recent or more accessible editions. Where possible, I've also referred to secondary sources that contain excerpts and web sites that contain texts and excerpts.

Abraham von Worms
    2006, *The Book of Abramelin*, compiled and edited by Georg

Dehn, translated by Steven Guth, foreword by Lon Milo Duquette, (Lake Worth, Florida: Ibis) Written between 1387 and 1427, existing manuscripts date from 1608, 1st printed edition 1725, (Cologne: Peter Hammer)

1974, *The Book of the Sacred Magic of Abra-Melin the Mage*, edited and translated by Samuel L. MacGregor Mathers, (New York: Dover) 1st edition 1900

Abram, David
1997, *The Spell of the Sensuous*, (New York: Vintage)

Abram, David and Scott London
2006, *The Ecology of Magic*, interview by Scott London, at http://www.scottlondon.com/interviews/abram.html, accessed 17th September 2007

Adams, Douglas
1986, *The Hitchhiker's Guide to the Galaxy: A Trilogy in Four Parts*, (London: Heinemann)

Andrews, Ted
1998, *Psychic Protection*, (Jackson, Tennessee: Dragonhawk)

Ashcroft-Nowicki, Dolores
1986, *The Ritual Magic Workbook*, (Northamptonshire: Aquarian)

Barker, Clive
1989, *The Great and Secret Show: The First Book of the Art*, (London: HarperCollins)
1988, *Weaveworld*, (London: Fontana)

Berman, Morris
1984, *The Reenchantment of the World*, (New York: Bantam)
Bettelheim, Bruno
1991, *The Uses of Enchantment*, (London: Penguin)
Bjørkvold, John Roar
1992, *The Muse Within: Creativity and Communication, Song and Play from Childhood Through Maturity*, (New York: Aaron Asher)

Black, Ronald
2005, "Preface" and "Introduction," in *Campbell, John Gregorson, 2002, pp. vii-lxxxii*

Bortolotti, Dan
2004, *Hope in Hell: Inside the World of Médicins Sans Frontières*, (Canada: Firefly)

Buxton, Simon
2004, *The Shamanic Way of the Bee, Ancient Wisdom and Healing Practices of the Bee Masters*, (Vermont: Destiny)

Bywater, Michael
2005, *Lost Worlds, What Have We Lost and Where Did It Go?* (London: Granta)

Campbell, John Gregorson
2005, *The Gaelic Otherworld: John Gregorson Campbell's Superstitions of the Highlands & Islands of Scotland and Witchcraft and the Second Sight in the Highlands and Islands*, edited and with commentary by Ronald Black, (Edinburgh: Birlinn)

Campbell, Joseph
1993, *The Hero With a Thousand Faces*, (Princeton: Bollingen)
1972, *Myths to Live By*, (New York: Viking)

Campbell, Joseph and Bill Moyers
1988, *The Power of Myth*, (New York, London: Anchor Books)

Carr-Gomm, Philip and Stephanie
1992, *The Druid Animal Oracle, Working with the Sacred Animals of the Druid Tradition*, (London: Fireside)

Castaneda, Carlos
1969, *The Teachings of Don Juan: a Yaqui way of Knowledge*, (New York: Simon and Schuster)

Cavalli, Thom F.
2002, *Alchemical Psychology: Old Recipes for Living in a New World*, (New York: Jeremy P. Tarcher)

Charbonneau-Lassay, Louis
  1992, *The Bestiary of Christ*, (New York: Arkana)
Chesterton, GK
  1909, *Orthodoxy*, (London: John Lane)
Chetan, Anand and Diana Brueton
  1994, *The Sacred Yew*, (London: Arkana)
Chopra, Deepak
  2005, "Flaws of Perception," in *Resurgence*, number 231, July /
    August, pp. 6-9
Clarke, Sarah
  2006, 7th March, "Earth in Grip of Mass Extinction," on *ABC*
    News Online, at http://www.abc.net.au/news/newsitems/
    200603/ s1586235.htm, accessed 21st November 2007
Clarke, Susannah
  2004, *Jonathan Strange and Mr. Norrell*, (London: Bloomsbury)
Crowley, Aleister
  1973, *Magick*, edited by John Symonds and Kenneth Grant,
    (London: Routledge & Kegan Paul)
  1976, *The Book of the Law*, (Maine: Weiser)
Davies, Paul
  1984, *God and the New Physics*, (New York: Simon & Schuster)
Davis, Wade
  1985, *The Serpent and the Rainbow*, (New York: Warner)
Denning, Melita and Osborne Phillips
  2000, The Foundations of High Magick, (New Jersey: Castle)
Douglas-Klotz, Neil
  2002, "Beginning Time: a New Look at the Early Jewish /
    Christian Ritual Time," in *Cosmos: the Journal of the*
    Traditional Cosmology Society, volume 18, pp. 143-158
Dukes, Ramsey
  2001, *Blast!*, e-book, (London: El-Cheapo/TMTS)
  2005, *Uncle Ramsey's Little Book of Demons, the Positive*
    Advantages of Personifying Life's Problems, (London: Aeon

Books)

Duquette, Lon Milo

1997, *Angels, Demons and Gods of the New Millennium: Musings on Modern Magick*, (New York: Weiser)

1999, *My Life With the Spirits: the Adventures of a Modern Magician*, (New York: Weiser)

Durham, Daphne

2007-8, *Amazon.com Review: The Tales of Beedle the Bard*, online at www.amazon.co.uk/beedlebard, accessed 11th January 2008

Dürkheim, Karlfried Graf Von

1985, *The Way of Transformation, Daily Life as a Spiritual Exercise*, (London: George Allen & Unwin)

Egan, Danielle

2007, 13th October, "Cheating Death: We're Going to Live Forever," in *New Scientist*, volume 196, number 2625, p. 46

Eliade, Mircea

1964, *Shamanism: Archaic Techniques of Ecstasy*, (Princeton: Bollingen)

Eriugena, John Scotus

1990, *The Voice of the Eagle, the Heart of Celtic Christianity, Homily on the Prologue to the Gospel of St. John*, translation, introduction and reflections by Christopher Bamford, (Hudson, New York: Lindisfarne)

Evans, Dave

2007, *Aleister Crowley and the 20th Century Synthesis of Magic, Strange Distant Gods that are not Dead Today*, (Oxford: Hidden)

2007a, *The History of British Magick After Crowley*, (Oxford: Hidden)

Fields, Rick

1991, *The Code of the Warrior in History, Myth and Everyday Life*, (New York: HarperPerennial)

Flamel, Nicholas
> 1624, *Flammel's Hieroglyphics: From His Exposition of the Hieroglyphicall Figures which he caused to bee painted upon an Arch in St. Innocents Church-yard, in Paris* (London) http://www.alchemywebsite.com/flamel.html, accessed 11th January 2008
> No date given, *Summary of Philosophy*, transcribed by Antonio Balestra, at http://www.alchemyweb site.com/flamsumm.html, accessed 11th January 2008

Gilchrist, Cherry
> 1991, *The Elements of Alchemy*, (Dorset: Element)

Gillette, Douglas
> 1997, *The Shaman's Secret, the Lost Resurrection Teachings of the Ancient Maya*, (New York: Bantam)

Gracián. Baltasar
> 1992, *The Art of Worldly Wisdom*, translated and introduced by Christopher Maurer, (London: Doubleday) 1st edition 1647

Graves, Robert
> 1992, *The White Goddess*, (New York: Noonday) 1st edition 1948

Greppin, John
> 1973, "Xvarenah," in *Journal of Indo-European Studies*, 1, pp. 232-242

Grof, Stanislav
> 1989, with Christina Grof, *Spiritual Emergency: When Personal Transformation Becomes a Crisis*, (New York: G.P. Puttnam's Sons)

Harner, Michael
> 1980, *The Way of the Shaman*, (New York: Bantam Books) first published 1972

Harper, Douglas
> 2001, *Online Etymology Dictionary* at http://www.etymonline.com/

Harvey, Graham
  1997, *Listening People, Speaking Earth, Contemporary Paganism,*
  (London: Hurst and Company)
Hepburn, Ronald W.
  1984, *'Wonder,' and Other Essays,* (Edinburgh: Edinburgh
  University Press)
Hillman, James
  1977, *Re-Visioning Psychology,* (New York: Harper Collophon)
  1st Edition 1975
Hutton, Ronald
  2006, *Witches, Druids and King Arthur,* (London: Hambledon
  Continuum) (1st edition 2003)
Ingerman, Sandra
  1991, *Soul Retrieval: Mending the Fragmented Self,* (New York:
  HarperCollins)
Jackson, Peter, Barrie M. Osborne
  2001, producers, *The Fellowship of the Ring,* written by Peter
  Jackson, Fran Walsh and Philippa Boyens, directed by Peter
  Jackson, extended DVD version
Jacobsen, Thorkild
  1976, *The Treasures of Darkness, a History of Mesopotamian
  Religion,* (New Haven and London: Yale University Press)
James, W.
  2002, *The Varieties of Religious Experience,* Centenary Edition,
  (London: Routledge)
Jamison, Kay Redfield
  1994, *Touched with Fire: Manic-Depressive Illness and the Artistic
  Temperament,* (Toronto: The Free Press)
Jokinen, Anniina
  1996-2007, "Irish Literature, Mythology, Folklore and
  Drama," section of *Luminarium* web site at
  http://www.luminarium.org/, accessed 11th January
  2008

Jung, Carl Gustav

1976, *The Portable Jung*, edited and introduced by Joseph Campbell, (London: Penguin) 1st edition 1971

1993, *Psychology and Alchemy*, (New Jersey: Princeton University Press)

1995, *Encountering Jung: Jung on Alchemy*, Selected and Introduced by Nathan Schwartz-Salant, (London: Routledge)

Kalweit, Holger

1988, *Dreamtime and Inner Space, The World of the Shaman*, (Boston: Shambhala)

Kaplan, Aryeh

1997, *Sefer Yetzirah, the Book of Creation, in Theory and Practice*, (Boston: Weiser)

Kipling, Rudyard

1899, *Stalky and Co.*, (London: Macmillan)

Kondratiev, Alexei

2000, "Thou Shalt Not Suffer a Witch to Live: an Enquiry into Biblical Mistranslation," originally published in *Enchante* 18 (1994) pp. 11-15, updated: July, 2000 at: www.draknet.com/proteus/Suffer.htm, accessed August 25, 2007

Le Guin, Ursula K.

1993, *The Earthsea Quartet*, (London: Puffin)

1976, *The Wizard of Earthsea*, (London: Puffin)

Lévi-Strauss, Claude

2001, excerpt from *La Penseé Sauvage*, (*The Savage Mind*) translated in Narby and Huxley 2001, pp. 245-7

Lewis, C.S.

1936, *The Allegory of Love*, (Oxford: Oxford University Press)

2001, *The Lion, the Witch and the Wardrobe*, (London: Collins)

Lipscomb, Benjamin J. Bruxvoort and W. Christopher Stewart

2004, "Magic, Science, and the Ethics of Technology," in

Baggett and Klein, pp. 77-91

Lorimer, David

1999, *Wider horizons: Explorations in Science, and Human Experience*, (London: Scientific and Medical Network)

Lukoff, David

1990-1991, "Divine Madness: Shamanistic Initiatory Crisis and Psychosis," in *Shaman's Drum* winter 1990-1991

Macrae, Fiona

2007, 10th October, "How to change your life with just five short meditation exercises," in *The Daily Mail*, online at: http://www.dailymail.co.uk/pages/live/articles/news/news.html?in _article_id=486707&in_page_id=1770, accessed 11th October 2007

Mansfield, Susan

2007, 14th April, "Are You Happy?" in Scotsman Magazine, pp. 7-8

McHardy, Stuart

2003, *The Quest for the Nine Maidens*, (Edinburgh: Luath)

McKee, Maggie

2006, (4th September), "Instant Expert: Quantum World," in *New Scientist* online at http://www.newscientist.com/channel/fundamentals/quantum-world/, accessed 27th August 2007

McLean, Adam

1995-2008, The Alchemy Web Site at http://www.alchemy website.com/index.html

2002, *The Alchemical Mandala: a Survey of the Mandala in the Western Esoteric Tradition*, (Grand Rapids, Michigan: Phanes)

1979, "The Birds in Alchemy," in *Hermetic Journal*, number 5, and online at http://www.alchemyweb site.com/index.html

McLean Adam and Joscelyn Godwin
  1991, *The Chemical Wedding of Christian Rosenkreutz*,
  (Michigan: Phanes Press) Magnum Opus Hermetic
  Sourceworks, volume 18
Mitchison, Amanda
  2003, 3rd November, "The Art of Darkness," interview with
  Philip Pullman, at
  http://www.telegraph.co.uk/arts/main.jhtml?xml=/
  arts/2003/11/04/bopull04.xml&page=1, accessed 11th
  January 2008
Moore, Alan
  2000-2005, *Promethea Collected Edition*, (La Jolla, California:
  America's Best Comics), 5 volumes
Murray, Liz and Colin
  1988, *The Celtic Tree Oracle*, (New York: St. Martin's Press)
Nagy, Joseph Falaky
  1985, *The Wisdom of the Outlaw: The Boyhood Deeds of Finn in
  Gaelic Narrative Tradition*, (Berkeley: University of California
  Press)
Narby, Jeremy and Frances Huxley
  2001, *Shamans Through Time, 500 Years on the Path to
  Knowledge*, (New York: Jeremy P. Tarcher / Puttnam)
Nutt, Alfred
  1881, "The Aryan Expulsion-and-Return Formula in the Folk
  and Hero Tales of the Celts," in *The Folk-lore Record*,
  volume 4
Ó Cathasaigh, Tomás
  1977, *The Heroic Biography of Cormac Mac Airt*, (Dublin: Dublin
  Institute for Advanced Studies)
Paracelsus
  1988, *Paracelsus: Selected Writings*, edited by Jolande Jacobi,
  (Princeton: Princeton University Press) 1st edition 1951

Pullman, Philip
    1995, *Northern Lights*, (London: Scholastic)
    1997, *The Subtle Knife*, (London: Scholastic)
    2000, *The Amber Spyglass*, (London: Scholastic)
Ram Dass
    1989, "Promises and Pitfalls of the Spiritual Path," in Grof,
    1989, pp. 171-190
Rawson, Philip
    1978 *The Art of Tantra*, (London: Thames & Hudson)
Rees, Alwyn and Brinley
    1990, *Celtic Heritage, Ancient Tradition in Ireland and Wales*,
    (London: Thames & Hudson)
Ricard, Matthieu
    2006, *Happiness: a Guide to Developing Life's Most Important
    Skill*, (London: Atlantic Books)
Richmond, M. Temple
    Year not given, *Sirius For Seekers: The Star Sirius in Astronomy,
    Myth, Religion, and History*, at http://www.harrypotter
    forseekers.com/articles/siriusforseekers.php, accessed 17th
    October 2007
Robertson, John
    2004, *The Kirkwall Ba', From The Water To The Wall*,
    (Edinburgh: Dunedin Academic)
Rogers, David J.
    1984, *Fighting to Win, Samurai Techniques for Your Work and
    Life*, (New York: Doubleday)
Rolleston, Thomas W
    1910, *The High Deeds of Finn and other Bardic Romances of
    Ancient Ireland*, (London: GG Harrap & Co.)
Ross, Hugh McGregor
    1987, *The Gospel of Thomas*, commentary and translation,
    (York: Ebor Press)

Rumi, Jalal al-Din

> 1998, *Rumi in a Nutshell*, edited and introduced by Robert Van de Weyer, (London: Hodder and Stoughton)

Rustin, Margaret and Michael

> 2007, "Harry Potter's Family: Internal and External Aspects," plenary talk at the EFTA/AFT Congress, 4th - 6th October, 2007

Saint Exupéry, Antoine de

> 1984, *The Wisdom of the Sands*, (Chicago: University of Chicago Press)

Shinn, Florence Scovel

> 1989, *The Wisdom of Florence Scovel Shinn*, (Simon & Schuster: New York)

Silverman, Julian

> 1967, "Shamans and Acute Schizophrenia," in *American Anthropologist* 69

Soudavar, Abolala

> 2003, *The Aura of Kings: Legitimacy and Divine Sanction in Iranian Kingship*, Bibliotheca Iranica. Intellectual Traditions Series, Number 11, (Costa Mesa, CA: Mazda)

Stevenson, Robert Louis

> 1879, *Edinburgh: Picturesque Notes*, available online at: http://www.undiscoveredscotland.co.uk/usebooks/steveson-edinburgh/index.html, accessed 27th September 2007

St. John of the Cross

> 2003, *The Dark Night of the Soul*, (New York: Dover)

Taub, David

> 2001, April, "The Originator and story behind 'The Global Village,'" at http://members.aol.com/UKpoet/global.htm accessed 11th January 2008

Tolkien, JRR

> 2001, *The Hobbit*, 70th Anniversary Edition, (London:

HarperCollins)

2004, *The Lord of the Rings*, Single Volume 50th Anniversary Edition, (London: HarperCollins)

Tokovinine, Alexandre

1997, "The Royal Ball Game of the Ancient Maya, an Epigrapher's View," online at http://www.mayavase.com/alex/alexballgame.html, accessed 14th October 2007

Trevarthen, Colwyn

1987, "Sharing Makes Sense: Intersubjectivity and the Making of an Infant's Meaning," in R. Steele and T. Threadgold, *Acquiring Culture: Cross Cultural Studies in Child Development*, (Kent)

Trevarthen, Colwyn and Vasudevi Reddy

2004, "What We Learn About Babies from Engaging with Their Emotions," in *Zero to Three*, Journal of Zero to Three: National Center for Infants, Toddlers and Families, January, volume 24, number 3, pp. 9-16, (Washington, DC) *www.zerotothree.org*

Trevarthen, Geo Athena

1997, *Spiritual Crisis in Early Irish Literature*, Masters Thesis, University of Edinburgh, available online at: http://www.celticshamanism.com/thesis.html

2003, *Brightness of Brightness: Seeing Celtic Shamanism*, unpublished Doctoral Thesis, University of Edinburgh

Underhill, Evelyn

1990, *Mysticism: A Study in the Nature and Development of Man's Spiritual Consciousness*, (New York: Image)

Vylenz, DeZ

2006, *The Mindscape of Alan Moore*, DVD, Shadowsnake Films, www.shadowsnake.com

Walker, Barbara G.

1988, *The Woman's Dictionary of Synbols and Sacred Objects*,

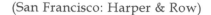

(San Francisco: Harper & Row)

Wilkinson, Richard H.

1992, *Reading Egyptian Art: A Hieroglyphic Guide to Ancient Egyptian Painting and Sculpture,* (London: Thames and Hudson)

Willis, Roy and Patrick Curry

2004, *Astrology, Science and Culture, Pulling Down the Moon,* (Oxford: Berg)

Winnicott, D.W.

1994, *Playing and Reality,* (London and New York: Routledge)

Woolf, Virginia

1966, "Jane Austen," in *Collected Essays,* volume 1, (London: Hogarth Press) pp. 144-154

Zaehner, R.C.

1982, editor and translator, *Hindu Scriptures,* (London: Dent), 1st edition 1966

Zipes, Jack

2001, *Sticks and Stones: The Troublesome Success of Children's Literature, From Slovenly Peter to Harry Potter,* (New York: Routledge)

1979, *Breaking the Magic Spell: Radical Theories of Folk and Fairy Tales,* (London: Heinemann Educational Books)

FURTHER RESOURCES

BOOKS ABOUT HARRY

I've read many books in the course of writing this one. These are a few on Harry I found particularly useful and I think would be most enjoyable for general readers. (See the Bibliography for full details under the author's last name and year)

Anatol, 2003, *Reading Harry Potter* — academic and wide-ranging articles

Baggett and Klein, 2004, *Harry Potter and Philosophy* — Enjoyable and meaningful articles

Blake, 2002, *The Irresistible Rise of Harry Potter* — UK based social and literary analysis

Bridger, 2001, *A Charmed Life, the Spirituality of Potterworld*, thoughtful pro-Harry Christian perspective

Colbert, 2005, *The Magical Worlds of Harry Potter* — a fun encyclopedia organized by questions about *Harry Potter*

Granger, 2007, *Unlocking Harry Potter* — An author who looks at alchemy and was also interviewed on the DVD of *Phoenix* — definitely one for deeper meanings.

Kronzek, 2001, *The Sorcerer's Companion* — a *Harry Potter* encyclopedia with a strong focus on magic and myth organized by topic

Lackey, 2005, editor, *Mapping the World of Harry Potter*, fun and insightful articles by science fiction and fantasy writers

Nel, 2001, *J.K. Rowling's Harry Potter Novels* — an excellent 'nutshell' guide

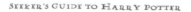
Shapiro, 2003, *J.K. Rowling, Princess of Dreams* — a biography
Whited, 2002, *The Ivory Tower and Harry Potter* — another good collection of academic articles

ABOUT SPIRITUALITY AND MAGIC

Obviously, look at my endnotes to find information on particular topics I refer to in the book. Here I'll simply recommend authors who provide good entry points. Some of their books are in the Bibliography, and some of their web sites appear below.

For the historical and contemporary academic study of magic and shamanism, look at Ronald Hutton and Dave Evans.

On the value and practice of meditation Matthieu Ricard's book, *Happiness*, is a good place to start. For magic as a practice in life, Lon Milo Duquette and Ramsey Dukes have a lot to say about applying magical philosophy and Dolores Ashcroft-Nowicki also has valuable insight to offer. Ted Andrews' *Psychic Protection* is a good collection of basic magical practices and principles.

Neil Douglas-Klotz is great on mystical, experiential Christianity. Mircea Eliade wrote lots of interesting works about shamanism and initiation. Holger Kalweit is also very good on shamanism and there are now loads of books on shamanic practices. Michael Harner's *Way of the Shaman* was the first major one. Adam McLean is a first stop for alchemy, both his books and his web site.

For me the best introduction to Joseph Campbell's thoughts on myth and life was his TV series *The Power of Myth* with Bill Moyers, and the book based on it.

FICTION YOU MAY ENJOY

Online bookstores and other web sites have lots of book-lists by Harry Potter fans with numerous additional suggestions!

Le Guin, Ursula K., 1993, *The Earthsea Quartet*, a young wizard's education, informed by anthropology and philosophy as well as a great read.

CS Lewis, the Narnia books, beginning with *The Lion, the Witch and the Wardrobe* — classics

JRR Tolkien, *The Hobbit* and *The Lord of the Rings* — more classics

Susanna Clarke, *Jonathan Strange and Mr. Norrell*, billed as "Harry Potter for grownups" when it came out, it's a meaty wizarding story set in an 'alternate' 19th century

Eoin Colfer, *Artemis Fowl* — a really enjoyable and humorous series about a boy criminal genius who's always running into supernatural trouble.

Philip Pullman, *His Dark Materials*, a trilogy beginning with *Northern Lights*, a great, philosophically stimulating read

Alan Moore — anything by him, really. He writes graphic novels informed by his own magical practice, for example, the *Promethea* series.

OFFICIAL WEB SITES

http://www.jkrowling.com

Her site has all sorts of secret bits and bobs.

See *http://www.hp-lexicon.org/about/sources/jkr.com/jkr-com.html* for a useful guide. You can see the sort of extras she does at *http://www.hp-lexicon.org/wizworld/wombat/wombat-results.html* which gives the no longer available WOMBAT tests

Be sure to look at her various 'good works' and other links by clicking the glasses.

http://harrypotter.warnerbros.co.uk/site/index.html
http://www.bloomsbury.com, UK Publisher
http://www2.scholastic.com/browse/index.jsp, US Publisher

FAN SITES

I can't be exhaustive here—there are loads! JK Rowling is known to visit the first three sites, below, and they've been particularly helpful to this book.

http://www.the-leaky-cauldron.org

JK Rowling gave an exclusive interview to Melissa Anelli, of The Leaky Cauldron, and Emerson Spartz, of MuggleNet, in 2005.

http://www.hp-lexicon.org/

Steve Vander Ark, who started this site, was interviewed on the DVD extras of *Phoenix*. It includes an interesting section with essays on magical theory, a guide to myriad other recommended sites and a timeline.

http://www.mugglenet.com/

This site has a list and description of all spells at and a *Harry Potter Encyclopedia*

http://www.accio-quote.org/

It would have been *much* harder to write this book if not for this site. It's a vast archive of articles about and interviews with JK Rowling. Invaluable.

http://www.veritaserum.com/

Another great site.

www.hogwartsprofessor.com

John Granger's web site. (See the Bibliography and references to his work in chapter 5)

http://www.harrypotterforseekers.com/

A great site by Hans Andréa and others that looks at spiritual and alchemical symbolism. It also has some articles based on papers given at various *Harry Potter* conferences.

http://www.harrypotterfanfiction.com/

What it says on the tin, nearly 41,000 stories.

http://en.wikipedia.org/wiki/Harry_Potter

An article on Harry Potter with loads of statistics.

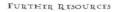
RELATED TOPICS

http://www.alchemyweb site.com/index.html is the site of Adam McLean, 'the man' on alchemy, offering original texts, alchemical images and courses.

www.scimednet.org

The Scientific and Medical Network, mentioned in chapter two, a group of academics, researchers and others devoted to exploring alternate views of reality, encouraging respect for the earth and community and challenging the adequacy of 'scientific materialism' as an exclusive basis for knowledge and values.

http://www.mythichero.com/, features some interesting essays on the hero's journey and Harry Potter as new-world mythology by Lynne Milum.

http://www.consciousnessandmeditation.com/, the website for the Washington Center for Consciousness Studies. I've quoted Dr. Rudy Bauer a few times in this book and owe him and his wife and co-teacher, Sharon, a lot of my understanding of awareness. This is their site.

http://www.lonmiloduquette.com

Lon Milo Duquette's website with details of books, talks and courses.

http://www.servantsofthelight.org/

Dolores Ashcroft-Nowicki's site, offering articles and classes in the Western mystery traditions.

GOOD WORKS WEB SITES

http://www.chlg.org

Children's High Level Group, founded in 2005 by JK Rowling and MEP Baroness Emma Nicholson of Winterbourne. Its aim is to improve the welfare of vulnerable children across Europe, operating politically and practically.

http://www.oneparentfamilies.org.uk/

A favorite charity of JK Rowling.

http://www.mssocietyscotland.org.uk/

Another favorite charity of JK Rowling's.

http://www.amnesty.org.uk/

An organization JK Rowling once worked for as a researcher, their "purpose is to protect individuals wherever justice, fairness, freedom and truth are denied."

http://www.thehungersite.com/

In the 'good works' line I thought I'd give you something you could easily do. A click here and on linked sites gives to a number of good causes for free.

http://www.freerice.com

A fun site where playing a vocabulary building game gives rice to the hungry.

AUTHOR'S SITE

My site, focussed on Celtic shamanism, but with a developing section on *Harry Potter*, is *www.celticshamanism.com*. It includes articles on specific topics I couldn't cover in detail in this book.

ILLUSTRATION NOTES

All images from alchemical and historical sources were re-drawn by the author. Other images are the author's original work, drawn or composed in Adobe Photoshop based on the author's photos or copyright free images as credited.

ILLUSTRATIONS AND ELEMENTS BEFORE THE INTRODUCTION

The title page Griffin is edited from *660 Typographic Ornaments*, p. 610, 2005, (Mineola, New York: Dover). The snitch and lightning border is by the author.

The dedication page image is edited from *Art Nouveau Motifs*, 2002, p. 29, (Dover)

The epigram page image of the Egyptian winged disk with two serpents, symbol of the deity, Horus is edited from *Historic Ornament and Designs*, 2003, p. 3, (Dover)

CHAPTER HEAD ILLUSTRATIONS

INTRODUCTION

Original image based on the author's photo of a statue of Queen and Saint Margaret, with Edinburgh castle in the background, seen from Princes Street Gardens. JK Rowling described walking here with her young daughter in her early days in Edinburgh. St. Margaret was an 11th century Hungarian-born queen of Scotland who's known for her charitable works and for promoting education.

I. BEGINNING: A LETTER IN GREEN INK
Collage incorporating an image from *Women: a Pictorial Archive from Nineteenth Century Sources,* selected by Jim Harter, p. 56, 1982, (Dover)

II. BETWIXT AND BETWEEN AT PLATFORM 9 ¾
Original image

III. FOUR HOUSES, FOUR ELEMENTS
The house diagram is (obviously!) an original image, with the central owl and border drawn after a Sunday chart by Jobst Cossman in 1490, on p. 167 of *Symbols, Signs and Signets* by Ernst Lehner, 1950 (New York: World Publishing)

IV. THROUGH THE MAZE: HEROIC JOURNEYS
An image drawn after a picture of the Assyrian deity Ashur in Lehner, 1950 p. 35.

V. THE ART
An image from Samual Norton's *Mercurius Redivivus* of 1650. Drawn after McLean, 2002, (in Bibliography) Mandala 19, pg. 99

VI. THE TERRIBLE AND THE GREAT
Alchemical image of Mercury as the *rebis* uniting all polarities from Milius' *Philosophia Reformata,* drawn after Jung, 1993, p. 233.

VII. USING THE PHILOSOPHER'S STONE
Original drawing based on elements from two alchemical images. The king with a phoenix is from an image about sublimation in Milius, drawn after Jung, 1993, p. 358. The winged disk and background elements are from the frontispiece to Christianus Adolphus Baldinus' 1675 *Aurum Hermeticum* drawn after McLean, 2002, Mandala 17, p. 93

ENDING ILLUSTRATION

Edited from *Art Nouveau Motifs*, p. 29, 2002, (Dover)

FANCY FIRST LETTERS

Based on the Able font with illustrations by the author.

ABOUT THE AUTHOR

Dr. Geo Athena Trevarthen combines academic skills with spiritual understanding and a sense of humor. Raised by a Hungarian father who was a cosmologist and NASA scientist, and a mother and grandmother who came from a Scottish and Irish shamanic tradition, she grew up in an in-spirited, inspiring reality akin to the wizarding world-view of the *Harry Potter* books.

She went on to degrees in the arts and Celtic studies, focussing on spiritual themes in early Irish literature. She trained in Gestalt and Transpersonal psychology under Dr. Rudolph Bauer, and went on to do a Ph.D. at the University of Edinburgh, examined in Celtic Studies and Anthropology, which became the first to academically demonstrate a full range of shamanic practices in early Celtic cultures. She is now a Post Doctoral fellow at Edinburgh and developed and taught a course on *Harry Potter* for their Office of Lifelong Learning.

She was the first person ever invited to speak on Irish shamanism to the Trinity College, Dublin, Theological Society. She's spoken at the invitation of many other academic institutions and has taught for 19 years at Holistic centers such as Omega

Institute (where she was visiting faculty on Celtic shamanism for a decade), Findhorn, Esalen and Naropa. She's a member of the Scientific and Medical Network, the Author's Guild, the Traditional Cosmology Society and is a Fellow of the Society of Antiquaries Scotland. Geo also enjoys exploring mythic and spiritual themes through art, music, film and television. She wrote *Sacred Ground*, a story for *Star Trek: Voyager* and received a Princess Grace Foundation Grant for her film work. Articles by and about Geo have appeared in various books, most recently in *Soul Companions* by Karen Sawyer (O Books).

She works with individuals as an *anama chara* or 'soul-friend,' (like a Holistic Life Coach) by Internet and phone from her home in the Borders near Edinburgh. She lives with her husband, David, a prehistoric archaeologist, and her children Téa, 4, (currently a singer) and Aurora, 18 months, (a percussionist!). Her web site is www.celticshamanism.com, and her email is tuath@celticshamanism.com.

BOOKS

O books
O is a symbol of the world, of oneness and unity. In different cultures it also means the "eye", symbolizing knowledge and insight, and in Old English it means "place of love or home". O books explores the many paths of understanding which different traditions have developed down the ages, particularly those today that express respect for the planet and all of life.

For more information on the full list of over 300 titles please visit our website
www.O-books.net

Daughters of the Earth
Cheryl Straffon

Combines legend, landscape and women's ceremonies to create a wonderful mixture of Goddess experience in the present day. A feast of information, ideas, facts and visions. **Kathy Jones,** co-founder of the Glastonbury Goddess Conference

1846940168 240pp £11.99 $21.95

The Gods Within
An interactive guide to archetypal therapy
Peter Lemesurier

Whether you enjoy analyzing your family and friends or looking for ways to explain or excuse your own strengths and weaknesses, this book provides a whole new slant. It can be read just for fun, but there is an uncanny ring of truth to it. Peter Lemesurier combines scholarship with wry humour, a compulsive mixture. **Anna Corser,** Physiotherapy Manager

1905047991 416pp £14.99 $29.95

Maiden, Mother, Crone
Voices of the Goddess
Claire Hamilton

This is a vividly written and evocative series of stories in which Celtic goddesses speak in the first person about their lives and experiences. It

enables the reader to reconnect with a neglected but resurgent tradition that is a part of the advent of the feminine in our time. **Scientific and Medical Network Review**

1905047398 240pp **£12.99 $24.95**

The Sacred Wheel of the Year
Tess Ward

A spiritual handbook full of wisdom, grace and creativity. It dips into the deep wells of Celtic tradition and beyond to gather the clear water of life. This is a book of prayer to be treasured. **Mike Riddell**, author of *The Sacred Journey*

1905047959 260pp **£11.99 $24.95**

Savage Breast
One man's search for the goddess
Tim Ward

An epic, elegant, scholarly search for the goddess, weaving together travel, Greek mythology, and personal autobiographic relationships into a remarkable exploration of the Western World's culture and sexual history. It is also entertainingly human, as we listen and learn from this accomplished person and the challenging mate he wooed. If you ever travel to Greece, take Savage Breast along with you. **Harold Schulman**, Professor of Gynaecology at Winthrop University Hospital, and author of *An Intimate History of the Vagina.*

1905047584 400pp colour section +100 b/w photos **£12.99 $19.95**